THE COMPLETE
Labrador Retriever

by HELEN WARWICK

Second Edition
ILLUSTRATED

1981—Seventeenth Printing

HOWELL BOOK HOUSE INC.

230 PARK AVENUE

NEW YORK, N.Y.   10169

To Dora and Joan,
With Love

BLUEPRINT OF THE BREED

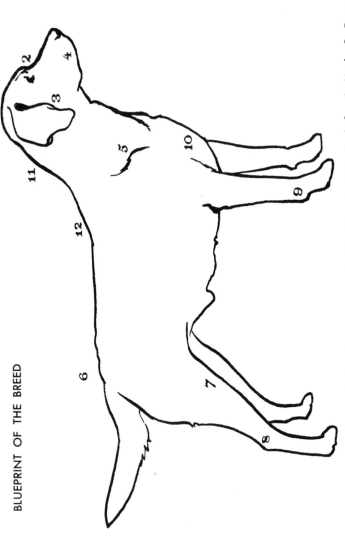

1. Skull. 2. Stop. 3. Cheek. 4. Muzzle or Jaws. 5. Shoulder. 6. Loin. 7. Stifle. 8. Hock. 9. Pastern. 10. Brisket. 11. Neck. 12. Withers.

Contents

TO AN OLD LABRADOR

A paw that's laid upon my knee,
And questing eyes that gaze at me,
And furrowed, slightly worried, brow
Twixt turn'd out ears; all ask—'What now?'
My hand goes out to smooth the coat
It sears *my* loving heart to note
The clear brown eyes now dimming blue,
And muzzle turned all grey in hue.
Full fourteen years, in canine age,
Will spell the turning of a page
Ere many moons shall pass. I know.
It is inevitably so.
Yet still her coat has shine and sheen,
And still her appetite is keen.
With greedy love, and hope, I pray,
That God may yet defer the day,
When shadow at my feet will be
Only the *ghost* that I shall see,
Soothing my mind with memory,
Of field and marsh and forest tree,
Where two hearts beat and were but one
In seeking what befell the gun.
My fingers fondle under ears,
I fight with sentimental fears.
I'm deeply troubled in my mind,
What best to do? . . . To leave behind
Will cause her misery and pain,
And if she comes, there's risk again.
The slope is steep on Forest Hill,
Even the very cleanest kill
May fall two hundred feet below,
To bramble, blanketed in snow
My own short breath and rheumy back
Confine me to the level track.

*   *   *

Although we brought home only two,
It did not seem, to us, too few.
We'd stolen yet another day
That no-one now could take away.
Contented, by the warm fireside,
Our love was not unmix'd with pride.

MAGPIE

Foreword

THE Labrador Retriever has long needed a complete, authoritative and thoroughly definitive work on its history, development and function as a sporting dog.

This handsome volume, replete with every facet on the breed, is that work. Helen Warwick has created herein an outstanding reference guide that is likely to stand for many years to come.

She has gone with rare dedication into its dim origins, and her research through the most reliable sources has been superbly documented with quotations from the best authorities.

In terms of dogs and kennels, THE COMPLETE LABRADOR RETRIEVER constitutes a very comprehensive study of the breed in America, Great Britain and other lands. The compilations of field and show winners, of outstanding producers, are extensive and as up to date as human effort can achieve. The information on colors, pedigrees, trials and every other aspect of the breed will be priceless to its followers.

From a standpoint of experience, she has given generously, in word and picture, an impartial evaluation of the Labrador Retriever which will benefit not only newcomers, but those already familiar with this unique and matchless Retriever.

THOMAS W. MERRITT, SR.
Director, The American Kennel Club
Past President of The Labrador Retriever Club
Past Vice President of the National Field Trial Club

Acknowledgments

IN writing this book I had no intention of compiling either a kennel directory, a stud book, or a treatise on training or genetics. Full justice can only be done such varied subjects by tackling them separately.

I have tried to give a picture of the breed in England and America, the two countries which have contributed so highly to its development in many fields.

In England the Labrador enjoys a long-established bench status, is one of the most popular gundogs, particularly on all upland game, and the breed's position in everyday life makes it almost a "national" dog. The breed in England is similar to that in America in its trial footing, which, although on a smaller scale, is equal to our own percentage-wise in its ascendancy over all other Retriever varieties.

Because of the Labrador's general popularity in England, one meets him constantly, in farm houses, at railway and gas stations, in tea-rooms, peering from under the table, accompanying nannies and their prams in city parks, dashing up the winding stair of the double decker London buses, sitting primly in subway trains on his way to shows, making the rounds with lamplighters on old town streets. Labradors are invaluable members of the London Police Brigade, mascots and enlistees for the Armed Forces, and first among chosen breeds for Guide Dog work.

Another reason for their popularity is that the English are given to taking long walks just for the pleasure of walking and observing the countryside in a leisurely fashion, and what better way than to share it with a Retriever, who will, for the most part, stick close to his sauntering master and not regard him wholly from the angle of sport. It is true that the still unspoiled quiet country lanes and rural byways are conducive to this pleasurable pastime, but one must not ignore the fact that the British have been for hundreds of years very close to nature and all her animal population, both wild and domestic, so that this heritage has influenced the people in general, thus developing a sportsman and sportswoman who has no counterpart in this country or any other.

Even though one may prefer the Labrador to other Retrievers, I feel one should learn to appreciate them all. This holds for novices and breeders alike. I do not share the view of some specialists who, in their narrow-minded and insular approach, feel that there is only *one*. The Retriever family is large and contains varieties to suit all tastes. The elegant Flat-Coat, the bright Golden, the rugged Chesapeake and Curly—all these have much to offer.

Sincere thanks for assistance regarding material for this book are tendered to the following in England: to the Hon. Lady Hill Wood, for her many instances of kindness through photographs and personal introductions; to Lord Dalkeith of the Buccleugh Labradors, for his kindness in giving me permission to quote from *The Labrador Dog, Its Home and History,* and to reprint pictures contained therein; to Col. and Mrs. M. Radclyffe, Mrs. Veronica Wormald, and Mrs. M. K. MacPherson for their help on my "yellow pages"; to Mr. Cliff Brown for the many times he went out of his way to assist me; to Miss Bourne, of *Fall,* for her unflagging patience in letting me go through her photographic files; and to all the breeders, the names of whom I cannot include in full because the list would be too long.

In America, my thanks to Messrs. Paul Bakewell III, Jasper Briggs, Lionel Bond, James Cowie, Mrs. S. H. DuPont, Mr. David Elliot, Mrs. Kathleen Starr Frederick, Mrs. Fletcher Garlock, The Hon. W. A. Harriman, Mr. Thomas Merritt, Dr. Samuel Milbank, Mrs. Curtis Read and Mr. Paul Svane. In Canada, to Mr. Ted Gundersen, registrar of the Canadian Kennel Club, for his painstaking letters relating to the early stock in that country, and to the many fine breeders, whose generosity in lending me photographs has enhanced the quality of this book.

1

Origins

THE name "Labrador" was originally given to Greenland. It was first spoken of and specified to Henry VII by a *lavrador* (the Portuguese word for yeoman or laborer) from an island in the Azores. This name was later transferred to the coast which is now so familiar to us.

The origin of the Newfoundland dog has over the years been extensively written about. Research through old papers, documents and letters has given rise to differing theories about its beginnings. One view is that it was a dog indigenous to North America; another is that it is of European extraction, with Eskimo alliances and heterogeneous matings with the dogs brought over from England and the continent by the earliest settlers.

Suffice to say that, from the nineteenth century on, the large Newfoundland was a breed of fashion in the British Isles, known everywhere as a dog of the greatest sagacity and bravery, and an inspiration to painters and writers. It is needless, therefore, to go into further detail about him and the qualities which inspired Robert Burns' immortal epitaph to Boatswain, as well as the following beautiful lines by Lord Byron upon the death of his Newfoundland dog:

"The poor dog! In life the firmest friend,
The first to welcome, foremost to defend,
Whose honest heart is still his master's own,
Who labors, fights, lives, breathes for him alone."

It is the purpose of this book to bring our contemporary Labrador out of the shadows and into focus. A summary of suggestions, some based on records and fact, others on conjecture and memories of personal experiences, is needed to establish him as a *distinct, separate* breed, apart from the Large or Great Newfoundland.

Before we start on our journey in search of the origin of our dogs, let us borrow a few excerpts from the book, *History of Retrievers* by Mr. Charles Eley. Mr. Eley lives at Bergholt in Suffolk, England and is the oldest living member of the Eastern Counties Retriever Society, whose first president he was in 1907.

He begins his chapter on the Labrador by saying, "The Labrador can in one respect challenge a favorable comparison with all breeds of Retrievers, perhaps with all canine breeds (except the Pekingese Spaniel) in that he is the hero of a romantic and mysterious history. Research has hitherto failed to elucidate satisfactorily the stories of his origin. . . . But after all, interesting as is the bare cold truth to those possessing a scientific mind, the discovery of the mystery would seem a poor recompense for the loss entailed by the possible shattering of a story at once so picturesque and so fruitful of engaging speculation.

"Where *did* the Labrador come from? The story which earliest reached the ears of the writer many years before his eyes lighted upon a specimen of the breed, was that the first Labrador to reach England swam ashore from vessels which brought cod from Newfoundland, and that the favoured spot was Poole in Dorset. It was claimed for them that their maritime existence, prolonged through countless ages, had resulted in webbed feet, a coat impervious to water like that of an otter, and a short, thick 'swordlike' tail, with which to steer safely their stoutly made frames amid the breakers of the ocean." A final and perhaps convincing touch was given to this account by the statement that Labradors were noticeably fond of a fish diet! . . . The name Labrador is sometimes recorded as a synonym for the small Newfoundland or St. John's dog. . . . Major Maurice Portal in *Guns at Home and Abroad* mentions that Blaine in his *Encyclopaedia of Rural Sports,* written in 1852, refers both to the Newfoundland *retriever* and the St. John's breed, which latter dog, Blaine says, is preferred by sportsmen on every account, being smaller, more easily managed, and sagacious in the extreme, his scenting powers being also very great. "Probably this latter," writes Major Portal, "is the ancestor of the Labrador as we know him today. How the breed was evolved it is hard to say, but the probabilities are that the fishermen of Newfoundland wanted a good strong water dog, since they are reported to have found them useful in cases of wrecks and wreckage on that coast, and crossed the heavy coated, strong black Newfoundland retriever with a black Pointer, and evolved in time a hard, short coated dog with great staying powers. That this is probably the origin is borne out by the fact that if Labradors are inbred, the result is often a light-made dog, long on the leg, light of bone, with a thin tail and Pointer-like ears."

Mr. Eley pursues the thought by asking why fishermen from Newfoundland would seek improvement of their breed by crossing it with a *Pointer* to achieve a water dog. "Surely," he maintains, "even if Labradors when inbred, revert to pointer type, it is no evidence that the *fishermen* were authors of the pointer cross. So those who wish to preserve this mystery must cast around and some other source whence possibly the pointer blood, so much insisted on, may have arrived."

Let us look at the earliest printed reference to the "Labrador Breed" in Col. Peter Hawker's classic, written in 1814, entitled, "Instructions to Young Sportsmen in All That Relates to the Guns and Shooting."

In the beguiling and enchanting chapter on shooting dogs in-general, which includes instructions on breaking a Pointer, a cure for the distemper, and the sketch of a mad dog, one comes upon his unaffected description of the Newfoundland dogs:

"Dogs have been such a universal subject for every sporting writer, that scarcely a word can be said about them, but that which we may find the counterpart in some publication or other. Every-one has his own caprice or fancy about Pointers, Setters, and Spaniels; and we meet almost every day, with some fresh man, *who has got the best dog in England.* (Italics Hawker's.) If you want game, take old dogs. Young ones, however fleet and well broken, know little more than the ABC of their business, while old ones are up to every kind of trick. I shall make one observation, which is, that a dog is far more likely to become a first rate one, by being made a companion of, and corrected by *rating* and *shaming* him, than being kept entirely away from the breaker, except to be taken into the field, and there *flogged* for every fault he commits. I had a friend—who was not only one of the best shots that ever lived, but who had, perhaps the very best dogs in Europe, and I know this was his plan."

'Newfoundland Dogs'

"Here we are a little in the dark. Every canine brute that is nearly as big as a jackass and hairy as a bear is denominated a fine Newfoundland dog.

"*Very different* however, are both the *proper Labrador and St. John's Breed* of these animals, at least many characteristic points are required in order to distinguish them.

"The one is very large; strong in the limbs; rough haired; small in the head and carries his tail very high. He is kept in that country for drawing sledges full of wood, from inland to the seashore, where he is also very useful by his immense strength and sagacity, among wrecks and other disasters in boisterous weather.

"The other, *by far the best for every kind of shooting,* is oftener *black* than of other colour, and scarcely bigger than a pointer. He is made rather long in the head and nose; pretty deep in the chest; very fine in the legs; has *short* or smooth hair; does not carry his tail so much curled as the other; and is extremely quick and active in running, swimming or fighting. . . .

"The St. John's Breed of these dogs is chiefly used on their native coast by fishermen. Their sense of smell is scarcely to be credited. Their discrimination of scent, in following a wounded pheasant through a whole covert full of game, or a pinioned wild fowl through a furzebrake, or warren of rabbits, appears almost impossible. The real Newfoundland may be broken in to any kind of shooting; and without additional instruction, is generally under such command that he may be safely kept, if required to be taken out with pointers. *For finding wounded game of every description, there is not his equal in the canine race;* and he is *sine qua non* in the general pursuit of wild fowl.

"Poole was, till of late years the best place to buy Newfoundland

14

COMMENCEMENT OF A CRIPPLE-CHASE, AFTER FIRING 2 LBS. OF SHOT INTO A SKEIN OF BRENT GEESE AND TWO WILD SWANS.

The Newfoundlander in the foreground was sketched from one of the artist's bitches imported from St. John's.

dogs; either just imported or broken in; but now they are becoming much more scarce owing to the (sailors observe) strictness of these 'd—— tax gatherers.' I should always recommend buying these dogs already broken; as by the cruel process of half starving them, the fowlers teach them almost everything; and, by the time they are well trained, the chances are that they have got over the distemper, with which this species, in particular, is carried beyond recovery.

"If you want to make a Newfoundland dog do what you wish, you must encourage him, and use gentle means, or he will turn sulky, but to *deter* him from any fault, you may rate him or beat him. I have tried poodles, but always found them inferior in strength, scent, and courage. They are also very apt to be seasick. The Portland dogs are superior to them.

"A water dog should not be allowed to jump out of a boat unless ordered, as it is not always required; and therefore needless that he should wet himself and everything about him without necessity. For a punt or canoe, always make the choice of the *smallest* Newfoundland dog that you can procure, as the smaller he is, the less water he brings into your boat after being sent out; the less cumbersome he is when afloat; and the quicker he can pursue the crippled birds upon the mud. A bitch is always to be preferred to a dog in frosty weather, from being by nature, *less obstructed in landing on the ice.*

"If, on the other hand you want a Newfoundland dog only as a retriever for covert shooting, then the case becomes different; as here you require a strong animal, that will easily trot through the young wood and high grasses with a large hare or pheasant in his mouth."

Further on, Hawker describes pheasant shooting in covert, alone with his dogs, and advises: "For one alone to get shots in a thick underwood, a brace or two of very well broke spaniels would of course be the best . . . but were I obliged to take a considerable bet, I should back, against the sportsman using them, one who took out a very high couraged old pointer, that would keep near him, and would, on being told, break his point to dash in and put the pheasants to flight before they could run out of shot. This office may also be performed by a Newfoundland dog. . . . The Newfoundland dog would always do best *kept close to your heels.* . . .

and particularly for *bringing the game;* as we rarely see a pointer, however expert in fetching his birds, that will *follow up* the scent of, *and find the wounded ones* half so well as the real St. John's Newfoundland dog."

The accompanying sketch by the talented Mr. Hawker shows very clearly that the type of dog he owned was very definitely the small Labrador, with a very adequate otter tail!

A Mr. Thomas Bell, for many years professor of history at London University, was a native of Poole, where he was born in 1792. He writes in his *History of British Quadrupeds:*

"There are several varieties of the Newfoundland dog which differ in size, character of fur, and marking. The old smooth breed, rather with a small head, white, with small black spots scattered over the body appears now to be extinct. The largest dogs now met with are of the breed which I have figured . . . but the most *common breed* at present is comparatively *dwarf,* not exceeding in height of a large Water Spaniel, almost wholly black. . . ."

So one can be assured that the then confusing name of "Labrador" included not only the very large, rough-haired breed, but the decidedly smaller or St. John's variety as well.

In 1847, Mr. H. D. Richardson described two varieties of Newfoundlands and two varieties of "Labradors":

"1. The Newfoundland, a dog of moderate stature, seldom exceeding twenty-six to twenty-seven inches, shaggy coated, pointed, wolfish muzzle, colour usually black, with a shade of brown through it, and occasionally some white.

"2. Another breed peculiar to Newfoundland is 'short-coated' and sharp nosed; is, by some, mistaken for the true Newfoundland breed . . . and often attains the height of thirty inches.

"3. The Labrador, a much larger animal, standing twenty-eight to thirty inches; it had a shorter muzzle and more truncated, the upper lip more pendulous, a coat coarser, and the dog exhibiting greater strength than the Newfoundland.

"4. The Labrador Spaniel, or lesser Labrador dog, which presents an appearance intermediate between the Newfoundland dog and the land spaniel."

Further reference to the smaller, smooth-coated dog of Newfoundland is found in W. E. Cormack's account of his journey on foot in 1822 from east to west coasts across Newfoundland. He was

17

a celebrated naturalist, a native of St. John's, and of the dogs he observed he wrote, ". . . the dogs are admirably trained as retrievers in fowling and are otherwise useful. The *smooth* or *short-haired dog* is preferred because in frosty weather the long haired kind becomes encumbered with the ice upon climbing out of the water."

In a letter to *The Field,* dated March 3, 1870, W. C. Halifax wrote that, "The Labrador dog is in my opinion *a distinct breed* . . . is an animal I know and have always been firmly impressed with the idea that formerly they were to be met with on that part of the coast of Labrador which is known to us as the South Shore of the Mainland in the Straits of Belle Isle. Certainly it is, that I never saw them to perfection . . . but there I have always thought that this *smooth breed of Labrador* dogs cannot be surpassed for sagacity by any of the canine race. I offered as high as ten sovereigns to the very poor men for their dogs, which has been refused, having been told several times that no money would tempt them to part with their chief support and ally."

In his book, *The Dog,* published in 1846, Youatt writes that the "true Newfoundland dogs have been used as retrievers. They are principally valuable for the fearless manner in which they will penetrate the thickest cover.

"They are comparatively *small,* but muscular, strong and generally black." Youatt continues by mentioning Blaine's reference to the "Labrador" and the St. John's breed, the latter being smaller and more docile, with the greatest of scenting powers. Youatt also quotes Blaine in remarking that, as a Retriever, "the Newfoundland dog is easily brought to do almost anything that is required of him . . . and he is so tractable likewise, that with the least possible trouble he may be safely taken with pointers to the field, with whose province he will not interfere, but will be overjoyed to look up the wounded game, which he will do with a perseverance that not speed or no distance can slacken, nor any hedgerow baulk. In cover he is very useful; some indeed shoot woodcock to a 'Newfoundland' and he never shines more than when he is returning with a woodcock, pheasant, or hare in his mouth, which he yields up, or even puts in your hand unmutilated. . . ." From these accounts, we can see that the dogs of those early days possessed courage in cover, gifted noses, and tender delivery.

18

General Hutchinson, in his classic work, *Dog Breaking,* published in 1847, considered that the best retrievers were bred from a cross between the Setter and the Newfoundland, adding, "I do not mean the heavy Labrador, whose weight and bulk is valued because it adds to his power of draught . . . but the *far slighter dog* reared by the settlers on the coast."

Jukes, in his *Excursion in and about Newfoundland,* written in 1839, mentions that "a thin, *shorthaired,* black dog . . . came off to us today. This animal was of a breed different from what we understand by the term 'Newfoundland Dog' in England."

Another keen observer of the St. John's breed of Newfoundland was J. H. Walsh, whose pseudonym, "Stonhenge," is more familiar to readers. In his book, *Retrievers* (fourth edition, 1887), which brings them further along into the nineteenth century, he remarks on the breed's uses and popular demand:

"In Great Britain the *small* variety of the Newfoundland is seldom kept as a mere companion, being chiefly used as a retriever. . . . Many of these Retrievers are imported direct from Newfoundland to Hull and other ports trading with that island; others are bred in this country from imported parents. . . . This fashionable breed, now considered a necessary adjunct to every shooter, even if he only attends a battue or drive, is often pure St. John's or Labrador; at other times he is more or less crossed with a Setter. The colour is always black without white, and Mr. Bond Moore who is considered to be the highest authority on the breed, would disqualify a dog for a white toe or white spot of the smallest kind on the breast or forehead. This is very absurd for a dog intended for use. Fancy dogs may be measured by any rule however artificial, but a shooting dog should only be judged by points which are relevant to his work."

Herewith follows a Standard, probably the first ever to be drawn up for Labradors. One hundred points are given for perfection. Our present-day Standard of course has no tabulation—to my mind, a most dubious way of judging an animal—but let us look to see what were considered the most important qualifications for the "black water dogs" of that period.

Accompanying this Standard is a charming drawing of a St. John's dog. In build and expression, it is quite orthodox for our contemporary tastes, except for the coat quality, which even today crops up in various lines upon occasion. Note that the highest point ratings went to general structure, soundness and strength, including the head (skull), gradual improvements having been made in coat texture, tails and feet.

THE POINTS OF THE ST. JOHN'S LABRADOR DOG

Skull	15	Quarters and Stifles	10
Nose and Jaws	5	Legs, Knees and Hocks ..	10
Ears and Eyes	5	Feet	5
Neck	5	Tail	5
Shoulders and Chest	10	Coat	5
Loins and Back	10	Colour	5
Symmetry	5	Temperament	5

Specific mention of the individual parts of the anatomy are worth noting here. From this description the present modern Standard was no doubt patterned; the same faults that appeared then still appear today, but in lesser forms, due to selective breeding.

The Skull:	is wide, but not so much as in the larger variety; flat at top; moderately long.
Nose and Jaws:	These must be long enough to carry a hare and wide enough for development of the nasal organs of scent; with open nostrils. Teeth level.
Ears and Eyes:	The ears are small and pendant, close to the head; the hair short with a very slight fringe at edge. Eyes of medium size, intelligent and soft.
Neck:	Moderately long, that is to say, *as long as can be got,* imported and pure Labradors being often too short to stoop for a scent without difficulty.
Shoulders and Chest:	The chest is apt to be barrel-like, but it is better somewhat narrow and deep, for lodging more *oblique shoulders,* and rendering the dog *better able to stoop.* The back and loins should be strong and *well coupled,* with deep back ribs.

20

Quarters and Stifles:	Bent stifles are seldom met with in this breed, but they should not be confined in width. The quarters are generally straight, but a slight slope is by no means a disadvantage.
Legs, Knees and Hocks:	These ought always to be straight, muscular and strong in bone. The feet are large, and should be specially attended to, as they are apt to be flat and thin-soled.
Tail:	The tail is bushy without Setter feather. It is carried high during excitement but should not be curled over the back.
Coat:	is moderately short, but wavy, from its length, too great for absolute smoothness. It is glossy and close, admitting wet with difficulty to the skin, owing to its oiliness, but possessing no undercoat.
Colour:	a rich jet black without rustiness. No quantity of white is admissible, but the best-bred puppies often have a white star.
Symmetry:	is of some importance, as indicating adaptation to the work this dog has to do. It is often considerable.
Temperament:	Without a good disposition and temper, no dog can be made into a good Retriever, and therefore this point should be carefully examined in it.

In this factual and authentic manner, we are dealing with a very substantial and realistic breed, which can easily be appreciated and assessed, and whose beginnings are comparatively pure and well founded.

2

Early Development

In order to have as much tangible evidence as possible for an accurate perspective on the Labrador's evolvement, it is essential that we be at least superficially familiar with other Retriever varieties, water dogs, and their standards, which are bound up inevitably in the past and in some instances indistinguishable from each other during their individual developments.

It has been proved beyond doubt, from excerpts of early breed annals, that our Labrador sprang from a smaller variety of the recognized Large Newfoundland. The name "St. John's breed" may well have been kept on, but he was permanently christened "Labrador" shortly after his integration in England in the latter part of the nineteenth century.

It is comparative child's play to trace forebears of the "setting family," or the Hounds and Spaniels, for they have long graced history in statues, paintings, tapestries and scrolls, and detailed mention of them is to be found in the earliest dog books. But the Retriever is a very recent breed, as we count by time, and has gone through many transitional periods in a short space of years.

The basic purity of the St. John's breed did much to simplify the development of a type and form of animal required by early breeders to satisfy their sporting needs and esthetic tastes.

In searching through any of the earliest dog books, including Dr. Caius' famous treatise, *Of Engglishe Dogges,* published in 1567, there is no mention of a Retriever breed as such. Dr. Caius classifies his gundogs as those "which findeth game on land, and those which findeth game on water." Gervase Markham's book, *Hunger's Prevention and the Whole Art of Fowling by Land and Water,* published in 1621, is much on the same lines, although his quaint and colorful account of the "Water Dogge" bears retelling, for interest's sake, as it has in its background some traits and qualities of our Retrievers-to-be. His Water Dogge may well be a link, if somewhat conjectural, in our theoretical chain, long before "black water dogs" appeared on the shores of England. Although he may be drawn upon more advertently for a history of Water Spaniels, Curly Coats, and certain types of Poodles, these were all very much a part of early Retriever development and point, besides, to future characteristics, such as his propensities in the water, and physical qualities, such as coat color—black or liver, repeating itself without fail in all the Retriever varieties. There is even the observation that blacks were known then to be of harder mettle, as many people believe them to be today.

There is no other mention in print of the Water Dogge until the late eighteenth or early nineteenth century. Around 1700, water dogs in England were divided into the "Great Rough Water Dog" (Canis Acquatisus), the "Large Water Spaniel" (Canis Inquisitor), and the "Small Water Spaniel or Poodle" (Canis Acquatisusminor). Anybody up on their Latin will be sure to understand these terms.

The most common usage of water dogs was to drive ducks and geese into man-made decoys in the fenny areas of the country. Decoys were large ponds, dug in the fens, with several creeks running from them, in various lengths, growing gradually narrower until they came to a point. The banks were well planted with undergrowth. Wildfowl were enticed into these ponds by tame ducks bred for the purpose. Large nets were spread near the tops of the trees lining the banks and fastened to hoops which reached from side to side, making the passage wide and high enough so that the fowl would not notice them.

In the meantime, a decoy man threw corn into the water, which the tame ducks did not hesitate to devour, thus encouraging the wild visitors until they were all collected under the sweep of the

A St. John's Labrador.

The Water Dog.

net. At this point, the decoy man called up his dog, perfectly trained in the art of perfidy, who rushed from behind the undergrowth into the water, swimming directly after the trapped fowl.

In trying to take wing, the fowl were brushed down by the net, then swam forward to avoid the dog, which followed them until they were caught in the narrowest point at the end of the creek.

Markham's description of the Water Dogge is as follows:

"The Water Dogge is a creature of such general use and so frequently in use amongst us here in England that it is needlesse to make any large description of him. This is a Water Dogge, bred for the water. I will heere describe as neere as I can, the best proportion of the Perfect Water Dogge. First, for the Colours of the best Water Dogge; albeit some will describe more excellence to one Colour than another; as the Blackes to be the best and the hardest, the Lyverhued swiftest in swimming, and the pyed or spotted Dogges quickest of scent. Yet in truth, it is nothing so, for all Colours are alike, and so a Dogge of any of the former Colours may be excellent good Dogges according to their first Ordering and Trayning; for Instruction is the Liquor wherewith they are seasoned and if they be well handled at the first, they will ever smell of that discretion, and if they be ill handled they will ever stink of that Folly. To proceed then.

"Your Dogge may be of any Colour yet excellent, and his hair in generall would be long and curled, not loose and shagged; for the first shews hardiness and ability to endure Water, the other much tenderness and weakness, making sport grievous; his Head would be round and curled, his Ears broad and hanging, his Eyes full lively and quick, his Nose very short, his Lippe houndlike, his Chappes with a full set of strong Teeth, and the general features of his whole countenance be united together, as a Lyon might be, for that shews Fierceness and Goodeness; his Necke should be thicke and short, his Brest like the Brest of a Shippe; sharp and compass; his shoulders broad, his forelegs straight, his Chine square, his Buttocks round, his Ribbes compass, his belly gaunt, his thyes brawny, his Cambrels [hocks] crooked, his posterns strong and Dewclawde, and all his Foure Feete spacious, full and rounded, and Closed together to the cley like a Water Duck, for they being his Oares to row him in the Water, having that Shape, will carry his body away the Faster."

When one goes over the points in this ancient "standard" and realizes that this was written in 1621, it is quite clear that certain inherent characteristics, such as coat texture and shape of feet and pads, as well as favored coat colors, were already under consideration even then, thus possibly laying the groundwork in shaping certain physical features for the future of our modern water dog.

As the years progressed, many breeds of gundogs came into being and slowly took form along the lines of their potentialities. Bloodlines were set in primitive fashion; rough but conclusive records were kept by early gamekeepers and private kennels, with individual breeds often known by the names of the castles at which they were kennelled.

We shall have to start at a strategic (albeit hazy) point in the 1800's to pinpoint the gradual rise and recognition of the St. John's breed of Retriever. This was brought about through a combination of regular importation, judicious experimentation, and, finally, the fixing of type and purity by a few far-seeing breeders following their personal tastes. Finally the breed emerged, firmly on its own, with authenticity, distinction, and a future that could not be denied.

It is true that Labradors were destined to be bred primarily for work, but at the same time they also had to be established outwardly in purity of line, conformation, and singular type. Not until years later were these to be held concretely in breed Standards. They had to be bred consistently true from generation to generation, while simultaneously keeping pace with the rare working qualities that were the first attraction of the breed.

It is fortunate indeed for the Labrador that its small beginnings were given impetus by the most capable hands in the British Isles. It was further to their advantage there, and later in America, that their start was developed in circles other than commercial—which may be the main reason why they are still fundamentally unspoiled, unharmed by passing trends and plebeian tastes.

Labradors arrived at their highest potential as dual purpose dogs just prior to World War II. Appreciation is due these Retriever pioneers, whose canny dog knowledge and perseverance evolved the product we take so blithely for granted today. It is impossible now to realize the pitfalls and disappointments that must have beset their paths in the early days before success crowned their efforts.

WAVY-COATED RETRIEVERS, PARIS AND MELODY.

L. WELLS.

Retriever (crossed with Setter).

Before proceeding further into the ancestry of our dogs, it is well to be aware of the prime force that has made dog breeding the powerful thing it is today all over the world. Whatever crossing and interbreeding took place among gamekeepers, with their black retrieving Setters and black Border Pointers; whatever attempts were made at individualizing the breeds with available "water dogs" from Newfoundland—all this was done before the formation of the Kennel Club.

The Kennel Club of England was organized in 1878, under the auspices of a remarkable Retriever man, Mr. S. E. Shirley, whose Flatcoat Kennels at Ettington were the byword for many years in a constructive breeding program for the furtherance of purebred Retrievers.

Through the firm principles of the Kennel Club, rules, regulations and Standards were drawn up for the promotion of all pure-bred dogs, for the advancement of ethical participation in shows and field trials, and to compile correct records of dog genealogy for Stud books. Charles Eley, in his *History of Retrievers,* pays Mr. Shirley a handsome and justified tribute. "It is difficult," he begins, "at this distance of time for people who have grown up to find the Kennel Club and its Stud Book the established factor in all matters of control, to realize the greatness of the task which had been accomplished by Mr. Shirley and his supporters and the far reaching effects that this movement had upon Retrievers and indeed upon all gundogs. So dominant was Mr. Shirley's kennel in the 80's of the last century that it was quite usual to hear the Wavy Coated Retriever spoken of as the Shirley Retriever. But this was not allowed to continue because the popularity of the breed increased by leaps and bounds and soon there were several kennels which were serious rivals to that at Ettington. The Setter and Pointer being not uncommonly used for retrieving in Scotland in the 60's and 70's, everything points to the retrieving Setter as being a fore-runner to the Flatcoated Retriever, and in order to improve his powers as a Water Dog, thus bringing him to a reasonable equality with his then great rival, the Curley coated Retriever, there is little doubt that sportsmen crossed their retrieving Setters with the small St. John's Newfoundland, which species, curiously enough in view of modern development, is called the Labrador, by several of the early writers. The result was to produce a heavy, wavy coated dog—

Flat was not used until much later, with a broad, shortish skull, very heavily stopped; an animal big in bone, and frequently showing weak quarters and a rolling gait.

"There is now no means of knowing how these early dogs compared with their Curley coated rivals for work, but it is probable that they met the requirements of many shooters whose particular countries they could negotiate and to whom the somewhat untameable character of the old Curley coated dog was somewhat distasteful. But the subject of this article was not long allowed to remain in this stage of development and a new type of gundog that unquestionably filled a vacant space among the requirements of shooters soon found many supporters and enthusiastic breeders. The early specimens had frequently shown tan and brindle—this glaring evidence of their forebears was at once made a point of attack, and pure black was ordained as practically the *sine qua non* for any self respecting dog who was destined to take his place among leaders of his society.

"No more remarkable man than Mr. Shirley has appeared in connection with Retrievers or indeed dogs in general. He was inspired by a great love for the new breed, whose improvement he sought regardless of time and expense. He was anxious to maintain and improve its capacity in the field as well as to fix type which would satisfy his ideals of canine beauty. Above all he was gifted with imagination to foresee an immense future of the breeding and exhibition of dogs in this country and possessed the energy and determination to undertake and nurse to success the specialization of dogs in England."

Firmly entrenched at that period, then, on British soil and in British hearts, were two Retriever breeds whose fortunes were to change with the advent of the Labrador's meteoric rise. As the late Croxton Smith aptly stated in his *Dogs Since 1900*, "It is better to write of them alphabetically, for if one did not, the last would be first from the start."

Gordon Stable's colorful book, *Our Friend the Dog*, lists the four well-known Retrievers indigenous to Britain at that time:

1. The Curly Coat
2. The Flat-Coat
3. The livercoloured Retriever
4. The Norfolk Retriever

On the Curly Coat he maintains that good specimens were exceedingly taking, and was of the opinion that this breed was a mixture of Newfoundland with the old Curly Water Spaniel. The Curly is taller and heavier as a rule than his Flat-Coated brother. The coat is distinctive and completely different. The muzzle and whole face and brow are covered with soft, close hair, but all other parts of the body, tail and all, should be clothed with short, crisp curls. Mr. Stable writes, "I do not like to see the curls coming down too far on the brow and of course there should be no vestige of a topknot! Sometimes in bad specimens you see a flat coated patch on the top of the shoulders; this is called a saddle and shows too much of the Newfoundland. The tail or stern is carried pretty straight or stiff; it is a longish, tapering tail, very strong and thick where it joins the body. I specially direct the reader's attention to the fact that the tail should be like the other parts of the body, covered with short, crisp curls, no flag. Not many years ago, before dog shows were so common in bonnie Scotland as they are now, some English exhibitors crossed the Border with a team of Curley Retrievers that had already gained many honours in England. They had entered them at a certain show which shall be nameless, and in due time appeared in the ring before certain judges.

"Very much to the surprise of the Saxons, the prizes fell to 'mongrels' with wavy, flagged tails, while their grand specimens were not looked at. When one Englishman ventured to appeal to Judex, he replied in the following strain: —'What—I didna look at your dogs? Is that what yer sayin'? Losh, mon, I couldna look for lauchin! Sic a tail I never saw in my born days before. Gae awa hame, mon, and shut the puir brutes up till the hair grows. I wonder your no ashamed to gang aboot wi' him!' "

The Curly Coat is probably the oldest of the Retriever varieties. Other possible crosses used to intensify the curl in his coat may have been with the large Continental Poodle; colors of the Curly ranged from the traditional black to the rarer liver and red hues. From various reports and histories concerning the Curlies which corroborate each other, his lack of favor with the majority of the public was due to several causes: some put it to hard mouth, others to surly disposition. Whatever the cause, there was a swift decline in his position, and he was neatly edged out by the oncoming Flat-Coat, even before large field trials were inaugurated.

For show fanciers, according to Croxton Smith and others, his primrose-colored eye was certainly no point in his favor; this plus a coat most unsatisfactory to maintain in show condition without curling irons, razors and sundry paraphernalia—no inducement for a breed wanting to be taken up by popular amateur fancy. However, for many years he was known as a "keeper's dog," and without a doubt still has many faithful adherents among sportsmen in shooting circles.

Greatly different then (and today) was the Flat-Coated Retriever. At his best he is an eye-taking dog of symmetry, elegance and grace, and coat colors of either shining black or liver, with rare occurrences of yellow. He has indisputable eye appeal, and is by nature affectionate and charming. Gordon Stable's experience with them is personal and warm.

He describes ". . . some of Mr. Shirley's grand and lovely specimens before my mind's eye as I write. . . . In general character and style, the black Flat-Coated Retriever is not unlike a small Newfoundland, only with far finer points. He is, you might say, a Newfoundland very much refined, but has a longer head and not so much breadth of skull. The coat is not so massive but more glossy than the water dogs.

"I do not remember ever hearing of any great authority on dogs saying anything about the size of a Retriever of this variety, but all other things being equal, I have always, when judging them, given prizes to the medium size animal. When too large they are apt to be coarse, and a dog of this stamp does not do well in the field. On the other hand a very small dog would be useless as a Retriever."

A Flat-Coat Standard was published in 1885 in a pamphlet entitled, "Points for Judging the Different Varieties of Dogs." It was compiled from Stonehenge by Mr. William Tileston, the first President of the Westminster Kennel Club, in 1877. I reprint it here because it has several references to physical features, pointing to characteristics that made themselves apparent in early Labrador breeding and also tended to confuse the "Wavy Coat" with the new breed emerging. Here Stonehenge adapts his description from his earlier Standard of the St. John's breed on selected points:

"*Ears:* Must be small *to suit the Labrador fancier.* . . . With the Setter cross they are considerably larger. In any case they should lie close to the head and be set on low. With regard to the hair on them, it must be *short in the Labrador,* but in the Setter cross it is nearly as long as the Setter itself.

Tail: In the 'Bond Moore type' it should be bushy and not feathered, which is a sign of the Setter cross. [By bushy, we take it to mean that it is a thick, short-haired contour, as a true otter tail. H.W.]

Colour: A rich black, free from rustiness. In many *good imported dogs* there is a white star on the breast and a white toe or two, but the fashionable breeders now go in for a total absence of white . . . as long as Dr. Bond Moore maintains his position. That the public does not agree with him is plain, from the fact that in answer to an advertisement offering to give away several puppies bred by him with white on their toes, etc., he received 150 applications. It also showed that even his own breed cannot be depended upon for absence of white and that it is purely an arbitrary sign, altogether independent of race. Hence, in my opinion it is absurd to disqualify a dog absolutely because it shows a small white star or white toe. However, it is quite within the powers of the judges to penalize him to the extent of the allowance for Colour in the scale of points.

Symmetry and Temperament: The symmetry of this dog is often considerable, although there is no grandeur as in the Large Newfoundland. The evidence of good temper should be regarded with great care, since the utility of this dog depends upon it."

One can surmise that due to sources that finally started crossing and mingling varieties, the principal problem confronting the early Labrador breeders was the elimination of what they considered was not typical.

Many Retrievers of that day were classified by their coats. In individual litters it was common to find both wavy and short coated puppies (as was demonstrated continually among the Fox-terriers), so they were separated into varieties according to this point. In some instances, one member of a litter would be winning in a show ring under the Labrador banner while another was winning as a Flat-Coat; this led to the formation of the Labrador Club of England, and the drawing up of a Standard. In 1905 Labradors were separately classified as a sub-variety of Retriever.

From these references from the past, we now have a uniform picture of the small "black water dogs," with their unparalleled scenting powers, love of water, courage, speed, and a natural gift for retrieving tenderly. Coming into focus are the consistent references to size, coat texture, and tail.

It was for the breeders who followed to carry on and develop these attributes, which finally resolved themselves into the dog we know today.

3

Earliest Breeders and Bloodlines

ALTHOUGH Labradors were unknown to the general public until the end of the nineteenth century—they were kept in comparative obscurity in private shooting kennels—they were nonetheless well scattered throughout the western counties of England, and known thereabouts as the St. John's breed.

Mr. Thomas Bell, aforementioned as having been a native of Poole, probably saw them in Devon, Dorset, Somerset or Cornwall; he mentions that "they were exceedingly common in those parts, intimately connected with the Isle of Newfoundland." In noting the regular arrivals of dogs to Poole harbor, the same activity could also have applied to the south of Scotland, where Greenock was also a thriving port of entry for fishing fleets coming in constantly from Newfoundland. According to Robert Burns, there is a record of a large Newfoundland being known in Ayreshire as early as 1786, and Lord John Scott surmises, in his *History Of The Labrador,* that if the larger dog was there at that time, it may be reckoned that the "smaller more useful animals" were there also.

The earliest records in print were disclosed by the Fifth Duke of

Buccleugh (1806–1884), his brother Lord John Scott (1809–1860), and the Tenth Earl of Home (1769–1841). The Scott-Middleton book notes "that old records show that in 1839 the Fifth Earl of Buccleugh took his Labrador Moss on his yacht to Naples, and the Tenth Earl of Home who was with him, took his Labrador Drake and both these dogs were small black dogs." Other Labradors owned by him were Brandy, Moss, Drake (1840), and Nell (1848). Brandy earned his name on board the small craft in which he crossed the Atlantic. Having gone overboard into a rough sea after the cap of one of the crew, he was in the water for two hours before he could be picked up again, and was so exhausted he had to be revived with brandy.

The kennel from which the greatest number of contemporary dogs is descended is that of the Third Earl of Malmesbury (1807–1889) at Hurn Court, which was only a few miles from Poole. In describing his dogs in a letter to the Sixth Duke of Buccleugh, he writes, "we always call mine Labrador dogs and I have kept the breed as pure as I could from the first I had from Poole. . . . The breed may be known by having a *close coat* which turns off water like oil and above all *a tail like an otter.*"

No mention of otter tails is made by Col. Peter Hawker in his early treatise, but those in the western and southern counties who were familiar with the Malmesbury dogs and others paid particular heed to breed characteristics such as otter tails and water-resistant coats. These early dogs were kept as pure as possible, breeding going on primarily among the imports and their close progeny; as a matter of fact, they were almost in isolation in their respective private kennels, certainly never sold, but the best given as highly prized gifts. It was not until very much later at the dog auctions at Aldridge's that Retrievers finally came "on the market." Fortunately for them, this was not a "common" market, and such financial transactions that took place guaranteed them the right circumstances in which to develop and grow.

One can observe the type of dog bred by the Eleventh Earl of Home, as shown in the old photograph of Nell (c. 1865) taken when she was nearing twelve years of age; also one of Avon at the age of eleven, and an earlier one of him in 1876. These specimens were typical of the sort of Labrador used for shooting in Scotland and England at that time. They had strong, broad heads and the

35

THE ELEVENTH EARL OF HOME'S "NELL"
(Probably born 1856, photographed 1867.)

Alex: Craw's "Nell:

Stellshaw Nell (Buccleugh Jock ex The Earl of Home's Juno), bred to Netherby Tar in 1896, was the dam of Brayton Sir Richard.

correct tails. Occasional white markings on toes and elsewhere appeared then more habitually and in greater areas than they do today, but in the case of these old dogs pictured, one cannot be certain whether the white is mis-marking or the result of old age. A few years ago we saw a contemporary import, Ch. Toots of Dunecht, brought over as a young dog in the 1950's by the late Mrs. Madeleine Austin, and bred by Viscountess Cowdray. He was solid black but in his old age, bordering on eleven, he had white feet, a snow white muzzle and was "cotton-tail" white under his quarters.

Dogs from Newfoundland were also used for shooting as early as 1809 at Hurn Court by the Third Earl of Malmesbury. In his colorful "Shooting Journals," he made reference in that year to his "Newfoundland dog that caught a woodcock in a brake at Avon cottage. . . ." In another reference, he "made a double shot at a snipe and a partridge both of which were winged and yet, though they ran off, my Newfoundland dog Caesar brought them both to us one after the other. . . ."

Among the pioneer breeders and importers of the nineteenth century one finds, besides the Dukes of Buccleugh and Lord Malmesbury, the names of Lords Grimston, Saltoun, Ruthven and Wimborne; Capt. Radclyffe of Wareham; Sir Frederick Graham of Netherby; and the Hon. Holland Hibbert, later Lord Knutsford. As a result of the efforts of these men, the original foundations of the modern Labrador Retriever consist of the following dogs:

Bred by Lord Malmesbury (Third Earl) and given to the Sixth Duke of Buccleugh

		SIRE	DAM
Ned	1882	Lord Malmesbury's Sweep (1877)	His Juno (1878)
Avon	1885	Tramp	His Juno (1882)
Nell	1886	Lord Wimborne's dog (1882)	Juno

Given to Lord Home

Dinah	1885		
Juno		Lord Malmesbury's Nelson	His Nell
Smut			

37

Brayton Sir Richard (Netherby Tar ex Craw's Nell) was bred by A. Craw, keeper to Sir Richard Graham. He was the sire of Ch. Brayton Swift and Munden Sovereign.

Buccleugh Avon (Lord Malmesbury's Tramp ex His Juno) is the ancestor of all modern Labradors. Note the dense coat and thick "otter" tail.

Bred by the Duke of Hamilton

| Sam | 1884 | Preston Hall Diver | His Fan |
| Diver | | Lord Malmesbury's dog | |

Bred by Sir Frederick Graham (Netherby)

| Keilder | 1872 | Boatswain | Nell |

Bred by Mr. Montagu Guest

| Sanjey | | Lord Malmesbury's Sweep | Lord Wimborne's bitch |

An anecdote from Lord Scott's book bears retelling here. It concerns Ned and Avon, mentioned above. "Ned was taken out shooting in August 1883, being in the hands of an incompetent man. The dog had not been taught to carry. The man who had taught him nothing said he was useless. At that time most of the dogs at Langholm Lodge belonged to the keepers, and it is possible that had Ned belonged to him he would have taken more trouble. Ned was transferred to the care of a good breaker and in 1885 he stood out as a paragon.

"Where is Ned?" was the general cry of everybody with birds to pick up. Ned was in fact, a revelation of keen excellence and when Avon arrived as a puppy at Hurn Court he was handed over to a first class man. Avon even outshone Ned but there was not much to choose between them. Ned was a compact little dog of perfect shape, about nineteen inches; Avon was slightly larger, perhaps nearer twenty inches and a lovely little dog in his prime." The shoulder measurements of these early dogs seem to bear out the conclusion that the Labrador's source was indeed from that of the "small water dogs" from Newfoundland.

Imports started to dwindle after the inauguration, in 1885, of the Newfoundland Sheep Protection Act, which provided that a majority of electors in any district could decide whether the keeping of dogs should or should not be prohibited in their own districts. Dog licenses were much higher for bitches than for males, so most of the bitch puppies were destroyed.

Another stumbling block was the Quarantine Act, which provided that any livestock brought into Great Britain had to go through a strict six-month quarantine on veterinary premises.

An authority of the times considered that these Acts were not entirely responsible for the lack of importations, pointing out that the fishing trade, which had flourished for centuries by taking out supplies from Poole and returning with fish, had gradually lost its importance and almost completely died out by the end of the nineteenth century.

Two imports mentioned in the Scott-Middleton book are Hero and Stranger, bought by the Hon. D. H. Cairns in 1900 from the family of a fishing captain who had died. Hero was considered to be a "real water dog" but was quite untrained as a retriever. His coat was dense and he looked coarser than the dogs of Lord Malmesbury.

In August, 1908, Mr. Stuart Menzie of Culdares, visiting Norway, thought he had seen a Labrador on the quay at Trondheim. Upon inquiring, he was told that the dam had been brought over in whelp from North America. He bought the dog (which had to be quarantined) and called him Stranger. Stranger was described as rough in coat, with a grand nose. He did not retrieve for he had not been broken, but stood over a bird until it was picked up.

In spite of the obstacles, as late as 1932 a few breeders (through the good offices of Sir John Middleton, then Governor of New-foundland) made strenuous efforts to obtain black water dogs from their original shores. Between 1932 and 1933, two were found and brought over. One was a bitch called Fanny, the other a dog called Buccleugh Cabot, which was given to the Seventh Duke of Buccleugh. According to all reports, Cabot was good-looking and became sire of several litters that seemed to have all the desirable qualities of Retrievers in outward appearance and working ability. A letter about these dogs from the Islands said, "The owners of the dogs are fishermen. . . . The dogs are said to live in the water, and are used for shooting in winter and for hauling wood."

One of the earliest breeders to guide the fortunes of the Labra-dor into the channels that brought it to its enviable peak in the Retriever world was the Hon. Holland A. Hibbert, later third Viscount Knutsford. The year 1884 marked the rise of his Munden kennel through Sybil, his first Labrador, from Lord Grimston.

Lord Knutsford worked uninterruptedly for the advancement of the new breed during its most perilous, formative period, and to him goes the supreme mark of recognition for the classic and orthodox results. It was Lord Knutsford who, in 1903, was a guiding force in getting Labradors recognized and accepted in the Kennel Club Stud Book, shortly after which classes for them were inaugurated for the first time at Cruft's Dog Show, held in those days in the old Crystal Palace. The first Labradors to gain entry into the Stud Book were Munden dogs—Sentry, Single, and Sovereign—and the first bench champion in the breed's history was Broome Park Bob, owned and bred by Lord Knutsford in 1906.

Much of the Munden kennel success was based (as are all fortunate breeding endeavors) on top-caliber bitches. Lord Knutsford had a lion's share in Single, Sarah, Scottie, Saba, and many more of equal merit.

Three generations removed from Malmesbury's Tramp, Munden Sixty (Buccleugh Nith ex Munden Sarah) sired the famous litter of the three S's—Single, Sentry and Spratt—which in their turns were to make such effective inroads in early breeding impressions.

To *Munden Single* goes the unique honor of having been the first Labrador to place at field trials.

Sherfield Spratt produced Waterdale Gamester, which sired the first Labrador Field Trial champion, Peter of Faskally, under whose aegis one finds in later generations, Scandal of Glynn, whose son, Dual Ch. Banchory Bolo, was to become standard bearer for the matchless prefix Banchory of Lorna, Countess Howe, after World War I.

Munden Sentry sired Satrap, out of Lord Knutsford's original bitch, Sybil, in 1903; thus Satrap, owned by Mr. Owen Mansell, subsequently produced a black dog called Landsdowne Benjamin, whose daughter, Nawton Brownie, was to play a vital part in Yellow Labrador development under the auspices of Mrs. Veronica Wormald's Scottish kennel of Knaith.

The founding of the Gun Dog League in 1895 was the turning point towards serious field trials in England. It was first named the International Shooting Dog Club and its activities were confined to autumn trials for Pointers and Setters. About 1899 it joined forces with the Sporting Spaniel Club and inaugurated the third and last branch of the League in 1900, calling it the Retriever Society, after which all three branches associated themselves under the title of International Gun Dog League. Curiously enough, many old supporters of early gundog trials had scant faith in the future of Retriever tests, feeling that they would be of little benefit or

Munden Sentry, whelped in 1900 (Munden Sixty ex Munden Scottie), bred and owned by Lord Knutsford.

practical use to prove the merits of a Retriever at work; nevertheless, due to the perseverance of a Mr. S. Smale, the winter of 1899 witnessed a small private meeting of Retriever sponsors on the estate of Mr. B. J. Warwick near Havant, where victory resulted for a Wavy Coated Retriever called "Painter," owned by Mr. Warwick. If Painter's win went more or less unnoticed at the time, it was of all importance to the breed to which he belonged, for the meeting was an unqualified success and put at rest the doubts in many minds of the possibility of future Retriever gatherings.

The Retriever Society's first venture in trials was in 1900, on October 12th and 13th, on the same grounds. The judges were Mr. W. Arkwright of Pointer renown, and the host, Mr. Warwick. There were ten entries and the winner was a brown Wavy Coated Retriever bitch called Rust, owned by J. Abbot, gamekeeper to Mr. A. Williams.

The year 1904 marked the auspicious date when the first Labrador appeared and placed at a trial. This was the black bitch, Munden Single, then five years old, who also placed at the I.G.L. trials held at Sherburne. Single placed again the following year at Sutton Scarsdale, as did Mr. Mansell's black Labrador, Satrap. In 1907, at the inauguration of the Kennel Club's first stakes for Retrievers, Single placed fourth.

It was her last time out. When she died, her body was mounted and presented to the British Museum for all to see what a Labrador should look like. In many opinions, justice was scarcely done "this beautiful and intelligent creature. Her gentle and sagacious countenance was a joy to behold and her methods at work usually interesting." In 1959 we visited the British Museum in search of Single, only to be told by the curator, himself a Labrador lover and owner of a Ballyduff yellow, that since World War II she had been removed to a small private museum at Tring. We were unable to get to Tring at the time, but I recall vividly the twinkle in Lady Howe's eye when we told her about it; she understood and appreciated our disappointment.

The I.G.L. trials in 1906 heralded the arrival of Major Maurice Portal's Flapper, whose phenomenal success was to place the Labrador breed to the forefront, in serious competition with the hitherto unsurpassed Flat-Coated Retrievers, thus assuring the breed the place as first favorite among the increasing supporters of Retriever trials.

In his report to The Field on December 5th, Walter Baxendale describes Flapper's triumph as pointing the way for the Labrador's greatest use and value in the field: "it is interesting to watch him looking up at his owner while Mr. Portal is shooting and one of his most pleasing characteristics is his intense keenness, and those who saw his fine performance at Horstead are not likely to forget it. A pheasant which neither Mr. Portal nor his dog saw, fell well over the river some 120 yards from the bank and Flapper was set the task of swimming the stretch, getting away from where the other birds had fallen and working out further and further by hand, until he got the line and found the bird. No performance of any past or present dog is so well remembered as that one of Flapper at Horstead."

Flapper ran four times and Horstead was his last trial, as his pace was slowing down and he was beginning to show his age. His appearance was, through contemporary eyes, that of a model Labrador; big but not over-size, very active and powerful, and showing brains. He had an astounding stud career, siring no fewer than 700-odd puppies in Major Portal's ownership. All were great winners in their day, including many well known Dungavel dogs and bitches from the kennel of the Duchess of Hamilton.

Flapper also had an indirect bearing upon future Yellow Labradors through his black son, Lift, owned by Major A. Browne and descending from early bloodlines of Major Radclyffe's imports besides those of Knaith ancestry. Whelped in 1902, Flapper died in 1914, one of the early greats that will not be forgotten.

Regarding trial handling methods in those days one may mention Mr. Peter Clutterbuck, whose dog, Sarratt (Flapper ex Munden Single), was a successful contender from 1908 through 1913, winning a 1st, 2nd, 3rd, 4th, a reserve, and numerous CMs. Mr. Clutterbuck was of the school of thought that it is best to leave one's dog to the business of retrieving its game with little or no interference from the handler. Charles Eley writes, "It was indeed a treat to see the free and independent way in which Sarratt went about his work. He was very fast but seldom over-ran his nose and the longest day's work failed to get to the bottom of him. This invaluable quality of *tirelessness* cannot of necessity be given full credit at field trials. The impossibility of really completely testing *stamina* at a trial is very unfortunate from two points of view; it sometimes permits a dog of *indifferent stamina* to achieve high honors and also prevents a dog of *exceptional stamina* from exhibiting fully this great quality. A resultant injury to the breed may well ensue from this, owing to the use for breeding of animals deficient in stamina, due to this serious defect being unknown to breeders."

The next step in Retriever recognition was the offering in 1909 by the Kennel Club of the first Retriever Championship stake, which became a competition for the National Championship and is open to selected winners of all chief meetings held during the year. Also in 1909, at the Kennel Club meeting, a new star arose in Mr. Archibald Butter's Peter of Faskally. By a Munden dog, Sherfield Spratt, Peter's career was brilliant and his mark as a producer was equally so in the dazzling roster of his get, which include Field Champions Patron of Faskally and Peter of Whitmore; Dual Ch. Banchory Bolo's sire, Scandal of Glynn; stake winner and Bench champion Withington Dorando; and countless good bitches from the early prefix of Mr. Heaton, Northaw. When Peter won the stake in 1911, his daughter, Gwendoline, owned by Capt. Glen-Kidston, was second to him. It was supposedly a fixed tradition in those days to breed successful Flapper bitches to Peter of Faskally, and Gwendoline's dam was one of these.

Apart from the dog's individual brilliance, it was greatly due to the new method of handling, in direct opposition to that of Mr. Clutterbuck, that first brought Peter into the public eye. Mr. Butter's system was based on the old hand-signaling and whistling of sheep dog work and trials, hitherto never applied to gundogs; it was a revelation in its novelty when displayed by this dog-man team. "The soundness of this method of breaking was considered rational enough," observes Mr. Eley, "when it was exercised by Mr. Butter with Peter and other future inmates of the Faskally kennel; however critics of the day were quick to discover that the success due to the novel methods employed was responsible in great measure to the superlative 'dog sense' and patience of Mr. Butter himself." He had countless imitators, "whose efforts," laments Mr. Eley, "in some cases bordered almost on the ludicrous, and produced sardonic inquiry as to whether the vendor of such canine treasures might be relied upon to include in the price of the bargain the necessary set of Pan's pipes!"

Societies continued to be formed all over England and Scotland. One of the most important was the Scottish Gamekeeper's Association, of which Mr. Mackay Sanderson was secretary until his death a few years ago. Two stakes were decided upon, one for keepers and one for ordinary members, and at the first meeting one noted the emergence of the sound Scottish kennel of Mr. McCall and his St. Mary's prefix. At the same period the Eastern Counties Retriever Society was brought out for the counties of Essex, Norfolk, and Sussex. Mr. Eley became its first president in 1907, and its first trials were held on his estate at Bergholt. Today, Mr. Eley is the only original member still on the club list, which includes many of the greatest names in Labrador breeding history, both in England and through importations to this country. Dr. Stanton was an honorary member until he died in the fall of 1962. The prefixes of Ballyduff, Greatford, Galleywood, Uffington Hockham, Hiwood, and others grace the membership array, as well as the 1960–61 award list of stakes won by member's dogs, many of which are in America now.

The apex of quality at work was reached by the early dogs in 1913, just prior to World War I. One of the last and most important meetings saw the addition of the Irish Retriever Society, whose first trial was held at Lord Dunraven's estate at Adare, County Limerick. Competing at this first trial there were no fewer than thirteen Labradors claiming Peter of Faskally as sire, with future Field Trial Champion Peter of Whitmore as the Open stake winner, and the Non-Winners stake going to another Whitmore hopeful—Type, bred and owned by Mr. Twyford and handled by Mr. John Cady.

The last few trials before the war were to aid the Prince of Wales Relief Fund. All entry fees were donated to the Fund and trophies were privately subscribed.

So time was marked until 1918, when sport and breeding could be resumed and some of the most powerful breeding forces in Labrador annals could emerge, to rise to their greatest magnitude between the two wars.

4

The Golden Age

DESPITE the disruption of civilized pursuits during 1914–1918, the twenty years that followed brought an unparalleled program of constructive breeding—with a dozen kennels contributing their share of bloodlines, types and records—and reached a height of quality probably never to be equaled again.

It was truly the golden age of the breed. How disheartening to concede that, brought to such a peak of perfection, it should have had to suffer partial oblivion during World War II and its aftermath.

To succeed, any endeavor requires extraordinary impetus—a unique force to set it on its heights—and one need look no further for dedication of purpose than the Banchory Kennel of Lorna, Countess Howe.

"There is no need," as the late MacKay Sanderson put it, "to detract from the credit due others to increase the fame of this kennel, as its achievements were big enough to place it beyond the reach of comparison with any other of the time. During a period filled with great events in Labrador history it played a part the effect of which may appear even more fully to posterity than to the present generation."

The name Banchory will alway remain a hallmark. Its stamp

Banchory Jack (Ch. Kinpurnie Kam ex Dunkeld Duchess), bred by Mrs. M. MacPherson and owned by Lorna, Countess Howe.

Field Ch. Banchory Ben (Banchory Corbie ex Beningbrough Tansey), bred by Lord Chesterfield and owned by Lorna, Countess Howe.

pervaded all the dogs that Lady Howe either bred or acquired, because she had a genius for bringing together animals of divergent bloodlines from all corners of the kingdom while consistently maintaining the uniformity of type she was looking for and determined to establish. She was indefatigable in pursuing the very best, and she recognized the importance of *buying* right as well as breeding right.

The names of her dogs ring proudly down the years, from her great Bolo to the post World War II Ch. British Justice, to the time when she gave up her Labrador kennel and active participation in trials. Her close association over these years with Mr. Tom Gaunt, her gifted trainer, established an unbeatable team, and between the two of them there was not a good dog anywhere that escaped their consideration. It is without a doubt that many of the great dogs in our contemporary backgrounds today would have been relegated to oblivion had Lady Howe not had the discernment to unearth them and give them the opportunities that only she in her position was able to offer.

Over these years her kennel held four dual champions, twenty-nine bench champions, seven field champions and innumerable stake and CC winners. At least thirty champions were sired by Banchory inmates and, in like proportion, sixteen field champions were produced by these.

One of the greatest services rendered the breed was Lady Howe's encouragement of the gamekeepers; she inaugurated classes for them annually at Crufts Dog Show and special stakes for them at trials. Gamekeepers are valuable members of trial clubs and often act on committees. Following is a list of great gamekeeper prefixes:

Beeding	Mr. Ling	Towyriver	Mr. Jones
Brayton	Mr. Nichols	Tripwire	Mr. Carter
Cheverell	Mr. Leach	Wemyss	Mr. Campbell
Glenhead	Mr. Annand	Orchardton	Mr. Carruthers
Angerton	Mr. Dawson	Adee	Mr. Bell
Lochar	Mr. Dinwoodie	Suddern Warren	Mr. Alexander
Westwater	Mr. Foster	St. Marys	Mr. McCall
Siddington	Mr. Goodall	Kirkmahoe	Mr. Coleman
Alby	Mr. Grant	Rockstead	Mr. M'Donald
Mallardhurn	N. Robinson	Reanacre	J. Johnson
	Courtcolman	M. A. Wood	

Field Ch. Kirkmahoe Rover, by Dual Ch. Banchory Bolo, was, in

1925, the first gamekeeper-owned Labrador to win the National Championship stake. He later joined the Banchory kennel and, as producer, challenged the best by siring Bramshaw Brimble (dam of Dual Ch. Bramshaw Bob) and Chs. Banchory Blackberry and Lady of Airlour, litter sisters to Bob and by Ch. Ingleston Ben.

Lady Howe's first Labrador was a dog called Scandal of Glynn, a son of Field Ch. Peter of Faskally. Scandal died at the age of five after having sired, in 1915, a litter of thirteen puppies, only one of which was a dog. This was to become Banchory Bolo. Bolo entered competition at the age of five in 1920, became a field champion that year and a dual champion in 1922. His was a most singular career. He was given to Lady Howe when already two years old, after a rough spin with various trainers who gave him up as a thoroughly bad one with a surly disposition, his former owner admonishing Lady Howe that the dog be destroyed if he did not please her. Lady Howe worked hard with him, pulled him through two near-death illnesses, gained his confidence and affection and transformed him gradually into a unique and matchless dog. Mr. Sanderson's tribute to Bolo in the British Stud Book bears quoting, for it could not have been more appropriately written:

"In order to assess the imprint of the descent from Malmesbury's Tramp in its wholeness and right proportion, a separate feature has to be accorded in the line from Field Ch. Peter of Faskally through Scandal of Glynn which gained its fullest expression with the emergence of Dual Ch. Banchory Bolo. Between the period which had given birth to Tramp and the advent of Bolo some forty years later, no single figure had arisen which had exercised such a great and moulding influence on progress.

"Bolo's coming may be said to have breathed a spirit of new life for the breed, the prestige enjoyed by this dog as a competitive and stud force giving lasting impetus to Labrador fortunes, and subsequently his name runs like a golden thread through all the vital streams of progress. Bolo was undoubtedly triumphant and predominant during his period, his dominance being referable to qualities other than are actually wrapt up in his prestige as a stud force.

"He came at a time when prestige both in a competitive and breeding sense was being put to rigorous tests. Behind the full story of remarkable expansion during the last period, lies the priceless contribution made by Bolo and his descendants. In the interval since Bolo caught the imagination of the public, one can discern certain events of change and significance, and the feats of this remarkable dog and his progeny give joy to the memory as one contemplates the advance which followed. The name and fame of Bolo will always be indissolubly bound up with the Banchory kennel of Lorna, Countess Howe, of which he was such a distinguished inmate."

Although Bolo never sired any yellows, several of his sons contributed to the color, one of the most outstanding being Ch. Banchory Danilo, bred by Lord Knutsford. Danilo had thirty odd CC's to his credit and in 1926 won the CC at Crufts, at the Kennel Club, at the Scottish Kennel Club, at Birmingham and at Manchester, a feat never equaled by any other Labrador.

Danilo sired Ch. Badgery Richard, destined to be an outstanding force for yellows in the next decade. Another son, Ch. Brocklehirst Donner, sired yellow Field Ch. Burnfoot Slider and others. Banchory Bluff produced Cock Robin, which in turn was to sire the yellow Ming, the first English and American field trial champion in 1940.

Other dogs of the highest caliber at Banchory were Dual Ch. Bramshaw Bob; his remarkable sire, Ch. Ingleston Ben; Field Chs. Balmuto Jock and Hewildo; Dual Ch. Peter The Painter; Ch. Ilderton Ben, and others. It is to Lady Howe, more than to any other single person, that the Labrador owes its high position in the gundog world today.

One of the most influential kennels of these early times, dating from 1910, was the Whitmore prefix of Mr. Twyford. Until 1931 it produced some of the most prominent dogs of the day. Whitmore dogs are at their best under the sire heading of Netherby Boatswain and include Dual Ch. Titus of Whitmore, whose imprint was felt to an immeasurable degree on stock at that time emerging from various new kennels. Whitmore was skillfully directed throughout its greatest period by the able Mr. John Cady; the excellent working blood brought forward through its high quality bitches, many of which were champions on the bench, infinitely enriched the breed's future.

For working brilliance, no kennel of the period could surpass

Field Ch. Tag of Whitmore (Field Ch. Patron of Faskally ex Tactful of Whitmore) was the great-grandsire of Peggy of Shipton. He was bred and owned by Mr. T. Twyford.

Field Ch. Balmuto Hewildo (Balmuto Tanco ex Balmuto Kate), bred by Mr. David Black and owned by Lorna, Countess Howe.

that of Mr. Reginald Corbett's Adderley. It is staunchly behind many lines today. Mr. Corbett won his first trial in 1925 with Field Ch. Vidi of Adderley, bred by the Earl of Bradford, and from that time on until just prior to World War II, he won thirty-five stakes, eighteen seconds and thirteen thirds, with the added distinction that almost every one of his dogs was owner-bred, trained and handled. The most brilliant Adderley inmate was Field Ch. Adderley Trim, by Field Ch. Beningbrough Tanco, a grandson of Bolo through Banchory Corbie. Trim won her first stake in 1927, when under nine months of age, and her last in 1935, in her ninth year. In over seven seasons this remarkable bitch won thirteen stakes.

Trim descends from Malmesbury's Tramp and ranks next to Field Ch. Balmuto Jock's record in stake wins; she was handled throughout her entire career by Mr. Corbett. The kennel produced five field trial champions, four of which were bitches: Vidi, Trim, Tax and Bee; Adderly Tyke was the dog. Tyke was a grandson of Vidi out of Trim and was an international champion, qualifying for the honor in India.

Old prefixes and kennel names that are no longer in existence but have a strong bearing on our present lines are: Balmuto, owned by Mr. David Black, who will forever be remembered through his distinguished dogs, Field Chs. Jock and Hewildo, property of Lady Howe; the late Lord Joicey's Scottish affix of Flodden; Withington of Mr. Hulme; Kinpurnie of Sir C. Cayzer; Hawlmark of Mr. Anderton; Hamyax of Mr. Whitworth; Colwill of Mr. Collins; Treesholme of Mr. Smith; and Pettistree of Mr. Kennard. One cannot overemphasize the importance of Pettistree, which figures in so many backgrounds of our dogs through Dan, Poppet and Shadow, and through Colwill Diamond, Dan's son, in Britain and the United States. The Drinkstone prefix of Dr. Monro Home and the Orchardton dogs of Mr. Carruthers furthered the breed immensely in the early days in America. They were beautiful in type and gentle and biddable in nature.

Many of us have dreamed of an ideal pedigree on paper, and have tried to visualize the results in the flesh. Even if perfection exists in the mind alone, the following illustration, imagined by the late eminent Mr. Richard Anderton is worth studying:

53

My Ideal Pedigree

"My ideal pedigree would start with a direct male line back to Bolo; preferably through Danilo; and therefore, I select for the paternal grandsire, Ch. Drinkstone Dan (no more, alas, in this country) but being out of Ch. Pride of Somersby, he fills all my requirements to perfection on paper, and came close to doing so in the flesh.

"For the maternal granddam, I must have a bitch of exceptional feminine qualities, springing from a long line of good bitches, and cannot therefore do better than insert the name of the aforesaid Pride of Somersby, out of Dungavel Juniper. Incidentally, this brings in Ch. Ilderton Ben, and goes right back to Flapper.

"Seeking the ideal, I can think of no better female line to choose for paternal granddam than that which lies behind Brocklehirst Nell, with good Munden support, while the remaining quarter, that of maternal grandsire needs little selection. I cannot get beyond the claims of Ch. Ingleston Ben, not only on the score of modern achievement but also because his direct male inheritance is to Ch. Withington Dorando and Peter of Faskally. It included Ch. Manor House Belle, and moreover a very useful reinforcement to Bolo blood to offer.

"Please do not write to shatter my dream by telling that its fulfillment is not possible; I know that well. If we have to make do with some slightly less promising material, we may be able to get bricks from some of the same kilns and achieve much of the same results in the end, and if my ideal pedigree does not contain a lot of champion names, that is more by accident than by design.

"For ideal sires I seek *intense masculine character:* real he-dogs that stamp their image on their produce, and live again in the deeds of their sons.

For ideal matrons, give me typical, compact bitches from prolific strains, as perfect in conformation as possible, free from any absurd exaggerations, and they must have personality and unshakeable temperaments.

"Avoid all strains which are deficient in actual 'leverage' (which is power in hindquarters), or in driving power (which is partly will power). The shy, timid creature may have to be coaxed.

"Please do not think that I attach an undue importance to a

mere collection of dogs with a magic prefix, but it does mean something. On the other hand, I could, I believe, point to a few pedigrees which rank very high in the estimation of many breeders and which contain very few champion titles, but they are composed of close relations of champions, or have actually bred champions—which latter is the greatest of all." (The foregoing was kindly contributed by Mrs. S. Hallock DuPont of Squirrel Run Kennels.)

The following kennels were being established in the late 1920's and most of them are active, progressive pillars of the breed today. Their feeling of responsibility towards the Labrador Retriever in the field and on the bench is reflected in uncompromising standards and enviable breeding achievements during the difficult fifteen years that followed World War II.

HIWOOD: Owned by the Hon. Lady Hill Wood. She founded her kennel in 1925 with a bitch puppy by Dual Ch. Titus of Whitmore, and from this blood came the winner of the 1932 Yellow Labrador Club Trial, Hiwood Lux. In 1927 Lady Hill Wood acquired another bitch puppy by Dual Ch. Beningbrough Tanco; this bitch puppy, as Field Ch. Hiwood Chance, took her place with Adderley Trim as one of the greatest working bitches in England. Hiwood has always had innumerable first-class, good-looking workers. One of the most colorful, and perhaps easily the greatest force of good for America, was Eng. and Am. Field Ch. Hiwood Mike, bred by C. Kennard, sired by Pettistree Dan ex Poppet. Lady Hill Wood breeds both blacks and yellows and the quality of her bitches runs high; included are superlative ones such as Field Ch. Hiwood Gypsey, a Greatford Teal daughter, and yellow Hiwood Peggy, daughter of Staindrop Saighdear and dam of four field champions. The 1960 National Championship was won by Field Ch. Hiwood Dipper, a Greatford Teal son. This kennel can claim a breeding record for having bred three winners of the Retriever Championship in the past six years.

Lady Hill Wood is a most admirable and forthright person and there are few that know their dogs better than she. When not at trials or training, she often exhibits at shows; as a judge, both for the bench and field, she is very much in demand.

GLENHEAD: Owned by Mr. J. Annand of Perthshire, Scotland. The influence of Glenhead dogs is legendary, if not unique throughout most authoritative dual purpose channels. The Glenhead

Ch. Abbess of Harpotts (Monk of Winscales ex Judy of Woodlea), bred and owned by Mrs. Harvey, showed substance, good rear angulation and a head of real feminine quality.

Field Ch. Hiwood Chance (Field Ch. Beningbrough Tanco ex Rockstead Swift) was bred by Mr. Culling and owned by Lady Hill Wood.

bitches, Bess, Nan, Biddy and Bee, were a fount of excellence through which there appeared Field Ch. Glenhead Sweep, whelped in 1936 and later exported to the United States, and Glenhead Jimmy, whelped in 1939, whose eleven field champion progeny and countless grand get include two of the greatest of each color: black Field Ch. Glenhead Zuider and yellow Dual Ch. Staindrop Saighdear. Glenhead, although not as active in recent years, is still close behind every well-known contemporary field kennel today; there is an extraordinary amount of good looks and class, bred consistently along with the natural style and innate game-finding ability.

BALLYDUFF: This kennel needs little introduction to current American fanciers. Dr. Acheson owned his first Labrador in 1929, a bitch called Stately Girl (Ch. Stainton Stately ex Ch. Election Girl). She was an excellent worker and was largely responsible for the doctor's forsaking another grand breed, the Irish Water Spaniels, with which he had had much experience. Bloodlines, although not strictly followed at Ballyduff, have always been successful in producing animals of good type that work well, and only studs with good looks and proven working ability are used. Both colors find favor at Ballyduff and many first-class dogs have resulted from interesting breeding programs. A few of the better-known ones have been the bitch, Field Ch. Ballyduff Jassie; Field Ch. Ballyduff Jester, exported to America; Yellow Ch. Ballyduff Orangeman, a half brother to Am. Ch. Ballyduff Candy; and the late Ch. Whatstandwell Ballyduff Rowena, considered by many to have been the best black bitch to be seen at shows during the last decade. Ballyduff's principle of using only working blood, even for their bench winners, adds lustre to a very sound kennel. Both the doctor and Mrs. Acheson are championship show judges.

HOLTON: Owned by Mr. M. C. W. Gilliat and his daughter, Miss Daphne Gilliat. This kennel is situated in one of the loveliest parts of East Sussex. Founded in the 1920's on a bitch, Liddly Peregrine, by Ch. Tatler of Whitmore ex Toddy of Whitmore, it is essentially a dual-purpose kennel and has consistently produced dogs of classic type. All are blacks, with superb coats, balance of frame and biddable temperaments. There have been many good bitches here, including the litter sisters Dusk and Diver, grand get of Liddly Bulfinch, both having placed at trials and won at shows. Diver had, in 1938, the distinction of winning the Banchory Bolo

Ch. Ballyduff Orangeman (Ballyduff Major ex Ballyduff Venus) was bred by Dr. T. S. Acheson and owned by Mrs. L. Browning.

```
                                                    Triumph of Treesholme
                                    Ch. Treesholme Thunder
                                                    Treesholme Tune
                    Forbes of Blaircourt
                                                    Darky of Elmbank
                                    Craigluscar Dusk of Blaircourt
                                                    Craigluscar Black Gem
        Ch. Ruler of Blaircourt
                                                    Treesholme Trigger
                                    Lawrie of Blaircourt
                                                    Fiona of Blaircourt
                    Olivia of Blaircourt
                                                    Darky of Elmbank
                                    Craigluscar Dusk of Blaircourt
                                                    Craigluscar Black Gem
Ch. Sandylands Tweed of Blaircourt
                                                    Int. Ch. Donnybrook Thunder
                                    Treesholme Trigger
                                                    Treesholme Twilight
                    Ch. Laird of Lochaber
                                                    Ch. Gold Rand of Glengour
                                    Thrill of Treesholme
                                                    Ch. Treat of Treesholme
        Tessa of Blaircourt
                                                    Darky of Elmbank
                                    Int. Ch. Emperor of Blaircourt
                                                    Craigluscar Black Gem
                    Ch. Imp of Blaircourt
                                                    Lochar Gold Flake,
                                    Sandra of Blaircourt
                                                    Tauna of Treesholme
```

Pedigree of Ch. Sandylands Tweed of Blaircourt.

Cup for best Retriever. Holton has had two exceptionally fine bench champions in Holton Joyful and the late Holton Baron, which besides his twenty-five Challenge Certificates, had many Certificates of Merit at trials. Mr. Gilliat's dogs are gunned over regularly and have an air of class and quality about them. He is a championship show and trial judge and, upon the death of Lady Howe in 1961, became chairman of the Labrador Retriever Club of England.

TIBSHELF: Owned by Mr. J. G. Severn. It is familiar to earlier American and Canadian breeders and known in many parts of the world. He bred some excellent dogs in Chs. Marksman and Louvil of Tibshelf, and exported, in prewar times, Handsworth Beau, a very good dog that became a dual champion in Australia. Mr. Severn has always been interested in the future of the chocolates, and most partial in advancing the color.

LIDDLY: Owned by Mr. and Mrs. James Saunders. It was started in 1922, based largely on Whitmore lines through their first bitch, Toddy of Whitmore. Much of their good stock stems from her and Mr. Whitworth's Ch. Tar of Hamyax, whom they purchased. Liddly strains figure strongly in early American and Canadian pedigrees and both colors are adhered to. Mr. and Mrs. Saunders are truly sporting people, and their belief that a Labrador should be first and foremost an intelligent worker with the essential characteristics of the breed has been amply sustained over the years through their own successes and their popular exports to many parts of the world. Both are trial and show judges, with some forty years' experience in these fields.

WHATSTANDWELL: Owned by Mr. and Mrs. Horace Taylor. Until recently this was a small and choice kennel of blacks and yellows. Dogs of distinction have been kennelled here; among them are Field Ch. Whatstandwell Hiwood Brand; Ch. Whatstandwell Ballyduff Robin, a first-class worker of grand type, who but for a devastating illness in his prime would easily have become a worthy dual champion (offers in four figures were made for him by America many times, but the Taylors were too fond of him to let him go); the aforementioned Ch. Rowena, owned by the Achesons and bred here, by Ballyduff Robin ex Ch. Lady Juliet of Hamdere; and Mrs. J. Salisbury's Ch. Whatstandwell Coronet, by Field Ch. Hiwood Brand ex Ch. Honey of Whatstandwell, one of the

59

Field Ch. Whatstandwell Hiwood Brand (Dual Ch. Stain-drop Saighdear ex Staindrop Carnation) was owned by Mr. and Mrs. Horace Taylor.

Dual Ch. Staindrop Saighdear (center) with son, Field Ch. Staindrop Ray (left) and daughter, Field Ch. Hiwood Peggy.

really top yellow stud dogs of the post World War II period. Both Mr. and Mrs. Taylor are also championship show judges.

STAINDROP: A household word in the States for Labrador and Springer Spaniels. The kennel, owned by the late Mr. Edgar Winter, was most capably taken over by his talented daughter, Mrs. Joan Hayes, and her mother, Mrs. Winters. Staindrop has had a roster of prominent dogs since the 1930's, some bred there and some acquired, as happens consistently with breeders of acumen and good judgment, so that this prefix may be taken with confidence as a hallmark of quality in the field. With us it will be forever associated with one animal that probably contributed more to the ascension (or perhaps the first full-hearted acceptance) of the yellows than any other. This was Dual Ch. Staindrop Saighdear. He was Scottish bred, as are so many of the best, by Sgt. J. Murray Dewar, of the Murrayville prefix, in 1944. Saighdear (the Welsh word for "soldier") came to Staindrop at nine months of age, a rank but talented puppy. Through Mr. Winter's adroit and uncanny tutelage he won his dual title in 1947, when just over three years of age. He was the first yellow to become a dual champion. Under the powerful black aegis of Malmesbury's Tramp, he carried the black blood of Ch. Ingleston Ben through Dual Ch. Bramshaw Bob and yellow Ch. Kinpurnie Kam through Glenhead Jimmy. He won his first stake in 1946 at the All Age Yellow Labrador Club trial in Yorkshire, and placed third in the National Championship stake the same year. His record as a producer is unassailable. All through the 1950's statistics indicated that he continued as a dominant sire and grandsire, with only black Field Ch. Treveilyr Swift and his young black half brother, Field Ch. Glenhead Zuider, close seconds.

Saighdear, descending from a long line of blacks, was a handsome animal with the air of true breeding and "raffinement." His progeny are brainy, appealing in nature and blessed with extremely rugged physical fitness, as he was himself. Saighdear was actively at stud until he was fourteen years of age. He died recently, in 1959, a rare and invaluable contributor to the notable generations that have succeeded him. Staindrop bitches are of high calibre, and those like Winkie, Carnation, Cindy and others, although never shown on the bench, reflect the pride taken at Staindrop in accredited good looks and solid working credentials.

61

Ch. Holton Baron (Sandylands Bob ex Holton Whimbrel), bred and owned by Mr. M. C. V. Gilliat.

Dual Ch. Staindrop Saighdear (Glenhead Jimmy ex Our Lil), bred by Sgt. M. Dewar and owned by Mr. E. Winter.

GREATFORD: Owned by Major Hugh Peacock, this is a kennel of assured quality in working lines. Its record in National Retriever Championship competition includes the winnings of the bitches, Field Ch. Greatford Uffington Brandysnap, in 1950, and Field Ch. Greatford Churchfield Jet, in 1951 (prior to her exportation to Canada). Further credit to the kennel came from the winnings of Oxendon Dan in 1953, Field Ch. Greatford Teal in 1955, Lady Hill Wood's Hiwood Dipper in 1960 (by Teal, ex her Glenhead Zuider bitch Field Ch. Hiwood Gypsey), and Mrs. Harcourt Wood's remarkable successes with Teal through her unique little Field Ch. Norham Blackie, a Zuider daughter.

SANDYLANDS: This kennel has been active since the 1930's. It is owned by Mrs. Gwen Broadley, who was fortunate in securing as her first Labrador, Ch. Wilworth Rip, by Ch. Withington Banter ex Brocklehirst Daisy (a daughter of Lady Howe's Bolo), and Scottish bred by the late Mr. Dinwoodie. The lines quickly became assured as to real substance and quality. Primarily a black kennel, in which purity of type has always been consistent, her recent interest in yellows is proving she has the Midas touch. Her prefix appears in many pedigrees of other kennels devoted to the improvement in type generally, and one can say without contradiction that no breeding aims have come closer to the standard than hers. At their best, Sandylands dogs are compact, clean cut, and classically headed, with extra good coats, tails and outgoing temperaments. Mrs. Broadley is a recognized judge of all gundog breeds and her encouragement and kindness in helping novices has long been proverbial.

BLAIRCOURT: Owned by Mr. and Mrs. Grant Cairns of Glasgow, Scotland. A comparatively recent kennel, Blaircourt has had singular success, based at first on Mr. and Mrs. Reid's prefix Craigluscar, which unfortunately is no longer in existence. Three champions from their first litter, Chs. Emperor, Empress, and Echo of Lisnamallard, owned by Mrs. Audrey Mayes, were quite well known.

One of Blaircourt's biggest winners has been Ch. Ruler of Blaircourt, whose untimely death in 1962 at the age of five was a tragic loss to the breed. As a sire he was very prepotent, and one of his greatest virtues, for which reason he was in such demand, was his reliability of temperament. The kindly, sensible, easily trainable

Ch. Ruler of Blaircourt (Forbes of Blaircourt ex Olivia of Blaircourt).

Ch. June of Sandylands (Ch. Jerry of Sandylands ex Ch. Janice of Sandylands), bred and owned by Mrs. Gwen Broadley.

Labrador character had in many postwar strains been at a low ebb, manifesting itself in such nontypical demonstrations as snap biting, gunshyness, and surly over-aggressive natures between dog and dog. Mr. Cairns is to be warmly commended for the modest stud fees on this great dog, and his generous preoccupation with his breed as a whole. He has made it possible for others to benefit who might otherwise have not been able to afford it.

In 1959 Ruler was winner of best in show at Crufts; he has won over twenty CCs in all. Through his Craigluscar background he carries the best of tried-and-true lines of Treesholme and Glenhead Jimmy. As one of the few important postwar blacks, his sterling qualities are being carried on with vigor through his son, Ch. Sandylands Tweed of Blaircourt, bred by Mr. Cairns and now owned by Mrs. Broadley. Although Blaircourt dogs have not competed at trials, they are intelligent, useful gundogs. Mr. Cairns is an able and popular championship show judge.

Prefixes and names of dogs less familiar to Americans were:

KINPURNIE: owned by Sir Charles Cayzer, breeder of Field Ch. Tullymurdoch Spanker (Field Ch. Banchory Donald ex Field Ch. Kinpurnie Kate) and the highlight of his kennel, yellow Ch. Kinpurnie Kam, litter brother to Spanker. But for the war, Kam would no doubt have become a dual champion, so brilliant was his work in the field.

CLAVA: owned by the late Col. Sharp. This kennel housed an outstanding worker and producer in Field Ch. Tag of Clava, bred by Dr. Monro Home of Drinkstone by Dual Ch. Titus of Whitmore ex Ch. Drinkstone Gyp. Tag sired two field champions in Glenravel Jock and Glenravel Nimrod, the latter deserving prominence as the sire of Our Lil, dam to Staindrop Saighdear. A third brother, Punch of Clava, also a strong competitor at prewar trials, sired the first postwar field champion in Blackhambleton Skell, a black bitch later owned by Sir Gordon Richards, renowned jockey in the 1940's. The Glenravel dogs founded the Irish kennel of Capt. Hodges at Ballymena, County Antrim.

Here we must mention the prefix of Murrayville, owned by Police Sgt. J. Murray Dewar. It seems ironic that it was never attached to the many grand dogs he bred, which were later owned and developed by others. He has a record to be envied, having bred one of the greatest dual champions, in Saighdear; two field cham-

Ch. Kinpurnie Kam (Ch. Orchardton Donald ex Field Ch. Kinpurnie Kate), bred and owned by Sir C. Cayzer.

Ch. Sandylands Tweed of Blaircourt (Ch. Ruler of Blaircourt ex Sh. Ch. Tessa of Blaircourt), bred by Grant Cairns, owned by Mrs. Broadley; outstanding contemporary sire.

pions, in Glenravel Jock and Nimrod; and Punch of Clava, mentioned above.

At the outbreak of the War in 1939, these flourishing accomplishments were completely curtailed. With the sad dispersal of kennels, there followed understandable but unwarranted panic among some breeders and the wholesale destruction of priceless and irreplaceable stock. This was the starting point for bad breeding with disastrous although temporary results at the end of the War. As there were no Championship shows for guidance in the right direction until the last two years of the War when restrictions were slightly relaxed, what was called the radius show made its appearance. Such shows were held within a radius of twenty-five miles of where one happened to live, prohibiting from competition those exhibitors from kennels further away.

These minor shows certainly did much to keep the dauntless British sporting spirit alive, and this type of show became the only form of competition for *comparison*. The result, however, was the scattering of these shows into a number of disconnected areas with the winning representative from one small section never meeting his counterpart from another. This produced disastrous effects on many breeds besides Labradors in actually corrupting *type,* for in each isolated show area the Best of Breed winner was regarded as something extraordinary when more than frequently it was a very mediocre example of the breed, differing greatly from the Standard and therefore not typical.

The situation reached such unreasonable proportions that in some quarters owners claimed that the Standard was wrong and ought to be altered to fit the type of winning dog—their own! One can forgive their point of view, but it is important to realize the untold damage that could result from taking such a stand. Fortunately, the War came to an end, and these detrimental forces were stamped out although the corruption lived on in subsequent generations.

At shows a whole new generation of a new type of exhibitor— the "one dog owner" and "town" resident—appeared, eliminating many of the large country estate sporting kennels of the past. Their greatest godsend was in having the prewar kennels (that are still in existence) to lean upon for assistance and experience, which is paying off in dividends of a dual purpose character in the newly formed Working Test Clubs. These clubs are sweeping the country much as "obedience trials" did at the beginning, many years ago, and encompass real outdoor retrieving work for bench Retrievers. They are based to a great extent on simple American "fun trial" tests. These are exercises in set-up tests—the kindergarten of American licensed trial stakes—with unfamiliar doubles and triples and blinds, which are called "unseens." Dummies covered with rabbit fur are used as a rule, but game is employed occasionally.

The traditional British insistence upon rock steadiness and polished manners in their dogs is displayed in various tests of diversions thrown and shots fired in front of rows of sitting dogs. It is a most interesting hobby and pursuit. Some of the bench dogs thus trained can easily get their "qualifiers" for their bench titles, and can even go further—into Nonwinners and Novice stakes at the regular British field trials. Lady Hill Wood and many trainers and gamekeepers have been of invaluable aid in fostering these Working Tests, which indeed fill a void in what has always been a well-balanced dual purpose ideal for Retrievers in England.

Working kennels of note are: The Lord Rank's SCOTNEY; Mr. Vincent Routledge's HALLINGBURY, winner of the 1962 Retriever Championship; Mr. Cock's ROFFEY; Mrs. Heywood Lonsdale's SHAVINGTON; Mrs. Harcourt Wood's GLENFARGE; Mrs. W. A. Fellowes' POLEBROOK; Mr. Lawrence Taylor's GALLEYWOOD; Mr. C. V. Watney's CORNBURY; Mr. R. G. Baldwin's WHINCOVERT; Mrs. D. Purbrick's STRATTONLEY; Col. H. C. Kingsford-Lethbridge's CREEDY PARK; Mrs. R. Crawshay's NAZEING; Mr. R. N. Burton's BRACKENBANK; Mr. R. S. Wilkins' SENDHURST; Mrs. G. Roslin-Williams' MANSERCH; Capt. F. Stephens BLACKHAMBLETON; and others.

British Dual Champions

Banchory Bolo (Scandal of Glynn ex Caerwell Nettle), Wh. 1915; breeder Maj. Banner; owner, Lorna, Countess Howe

Banchory Sunspeck (Ch. Ilderton Ben ex Dungavel Juniper), Wh. 1917; breeder, J. Alexander; owner, Lorna, Countess Howe

Titus of Whitmore (Twist of Whitmore ex Teazle of Whitmore), Wh. 1919; breeder and owner, Mr. Twyford

* Flute of Flodden (Dual Ch. Titus of Whitmore ex Wemyss Rachel), Wh. 1922; breeder, Mr. A. Campbell; owner, Lord Joicey

Bramshaw Bob (Ch. Ingleston Ben ex Bramshaw Brimble), Wh. 1929; breeder, Sir J. Thursby; owner, Lorna, Countess Howe

* Banchory Painter (late L'Ile Buster Bill) (Peter the Painter ex Glenhead Bess), Wh. 1930; breeder, John Annand; owner, Lorna, Countess Howe

* Lochar Nessie (Lochar Peter ex Lochar Biddy), Wh. 1933; breeder, J. Dinwoodie; owner, Mrs. Morris

* Staindrop Saighdear (Glenhead Jimmy ex Our Lil), Wh. 1944; breeder, J. Dewar; owner, Mr. Edgar Winter

* Knaith Banjo (Poppleton Golden Russett ex Knaith Brilliantine), Wh. 1946; breeder and owner, Mrs. Veronica Wormald

* It is interesting to note that five out of these nine were Scottish bred. Lochar Nessie was the only dual champion Labrador bitch in England. Knaith Banjo died in 1961, and, as of 1962, there were no dual champions added to the ranks.

British Bred Duals Abroad

U.S.A. Treveilyr Swift (Penlan Don ex Treveleir Starlight), Wh. 1946; breeder, Mrs. L. William Owens; owner Ed. Spaulding

INDIA Toilet of Whitmore (Field Ch. Beningbrough Tanco ex Ch. Tulip of Whitmore), Wh. 1927; breeder, Mr. Twyford; owner, Maharajah of Jind

Jaffa (Golden Mystery ex Juno of Calcady), Wh. 1929; breeder, Mr. Watts; owner, Mr. David Elliot; later, Maharajah of Jind (yellow)

Labrador Bloodlines, Tabulated Under Six Approved Headings,

from the English Stud Book; Compiled by Mackay Sanderson, and Listed in Order of Their Dominance.

1. Malmesbury's Tramp
2. Netherby Boatswain
3. Malmesbury's Sweep
4. Ch. Ilderton Ben
5. Bright
6. Buccleugh Bachelor

The following is a list of contemporary producing sires and dams apart from field records since World War II. Due to lack of space it is impossible to include more than four representative pedigrees, which will illustrate the prominent bloodlines.

DOGS

Y *Ch. Kinpurnie Kam* (Ch. Orchardton Donald x Field Ch. Kinpurnie Kate)

B *Glenhead Jimmy* (Ch. Kinpurnie Kam x Knappies Lass) (11 field ch. get)

Y *Dual Ch. Staindrop Saighdear* (Glenhead Jimmy x Our Lil)

B *Field Ch. Glenhead Zuider* (Glenhead Jimmy x Ariston Jet)

B *Field Ch. Hiwood Don* (Field Ch. Glenhead Zuider x Hiwood Peggy)

B *Field Ch. Greatford Teal* (Greatford Pettistree Shadow x Mackland Honeysuckle)

B *Dual Ch. Treveilyr Swift* (Penlan Don x Treveilyr Starlight)

B *Field Ch. Galleyood Shot* (Field Ch. Staindrop M. Marksman x Hiwood Peggy)

B *Field Ch. Brackenbank Jasper* (Sudborough Ben x Banchory Murton Mystic)

B *Field Ch. Roffey Dunlop* (Field Ch. Glenhead Zuider x Roffey Sally)

B *Field Ch. Greatford Pettistree Shadow* (Pettistree Dan x Scotney Doushka)

Y *Field Ch. Whatstandwell Hiwood Brand* (Dual Ch. Staindrop Saighdear x Staindrop Carnation)

B *Field Ch. Grousadee* (Field Ch. Scotney Kinsman x Westhelm Black Princess)

B *Field Ch. Hiwood Dipper* (Field Ch. Greatford Teal x Field Ch. Hiwood Gypsey)

B *Dullingham Danger* (Field Ch. Treveilyr Swift x Lordship Dinah)

Hiwood Reeve (Field Ch. Greatford Teal x Field Ch. Hiwood Gypsey)

Banchory Jack (Ch. Kinpurnie Kam x Dunkeld Duchess)

BITCHES

B   *Adderley Thought* (Adderley Ted x Field Ch. Adderley Bee)

B   *Brackenbank Jessie* (Field Ch. Brackenbank Jasper x Brackenbank Belle of Auburn)

B   *Glenhead Bess* (Field Ch. Ledsham Peter x L'Ile Bouncing Girl)

B   *Banchory Murton Mystic* (Glenhead Jimmy x Staindrop Hycup Dusk)

B   *Staindrop Glenhead Wren* (Glenhead Jimmy x Ariston Jet)

B   *Field Ch. Hiwood Gypsey* (Glenhead Zuider x Hiwood Peggy)

Y   *Hiwood Peggy* (Dual Ch. Staindrop Saighdear x Cheverells Sally)'

B   *Field Ch. Norham Blackie* (Field Ch. Glenhead Zuider x Venney Queen)

Y   *Field Ch. Zelstone Darter* (Durley Bracken x Glenmorag Parella of Podington)

Y   *Field Ch. Zelstone Moss* (Bench x Ch. Zelstone Leapear Lass)

B   *Field Ch. Nazeing Soot* (Nazeing Butch x Nazeing Nigger)

B   *Staindrop Cindy* (Hiwood Reeve x Staindrop Nipsy)

B   *Staindrop Nipsy* (Field Ch. Staindrop Murton Marksman x Staindrop Glenhead Wren)

B   *Staindrop Winkie* (Glenhead Jimmy x Glenhead Nan)

Black and Yellow Sires and Dams Sustaining and Influencing Postwar Type at Bench Shows:

YD   *Field Ch. Whatstandwell Hiwood Brand* (Dual Ch. Staindrop Saighdear x Staindrop Carnation)

YD   *Ch. Whatstandwell Coronet* (Field Ch. W. Hiwood Brand x Ch. Honey of Whatstandwell)

YD   *Ch. Diant Swandyke Creamcracker* (Ch. Poppleton Golden Flight x Lassie of Freiston)

YD   *Ch. Landyke Lancer* (Nokeener Novelcracker x Ch. Landyke Poppy)

YD   *Dual Ch. Knaith Banjo* (Poppleton Golden Russett x Knaith Brilliantine)

YD   *Ch. Poppleton Golden Flight* (Poppleton Golden Russett x Modney Crocus)

71

YD   *Ch. Poppleton Lieutenant* (Poppleton Beech Flight x Poppleton Golden Sunray)

BD   *Sandylands Bob* (Sandylands Ben x Ch. Sandylands Harley Superb)

BD   *Ch. Sandylands Justice* (Ch. British Justice x Ch. S. Belle of Helenspring)

BD   *Banchory Jack* (Ch. Kinpurnie Kam x Dunkeld Duchess)

BD   *Ch. Whatstandwell Ballyduff Robin* (Sudborough Ben x Ch. Lady Juliet of Hamdere)

BD   *Ch. Ruler of Blaircourt* (Forbes of Blaircourt x Olivia of Blaircourt)

BD   *Ch. Sandylands Tweed of Blaircourt* (Ch. Ruler of Blaircourt x Tessa of Blaircourt)

BB   *Craiglsucar Dusk of Blaircourt* (Darkie of Elmbank x Craiglsucar Black Gem)

BB   *Craiglsucar Black Gem* (Black Eagle of Glengour x Black Arrogance of Glengour)

BB   *Ch. Lady Juliet of Hamdere* (Rockstead Footprint x Trixie of Keewatin)

BB   *Sandylands Shadow* (Ch. Sam of Blaircourt x Diant Pride)

YB   *Mandy of Breakneck Farm* (Cambark Sam x Jane of Highleigh)

Dual Ch. Banchory Painter (Peter the Painter ex Glenhead Bess), bred by Mr. J. Annand and owned by Lorna, Countess Howe.

F.C. Peter of Faskally, 1908
(under the heading of
Malmesbury's Tramp)

Sherfield Spratt

Hon. A. Hibbert's Munden Sixty

Munden Sixty — Buccleugh Nith — Buccleugh Avon, 1885
— Buccleugh Gip, 1880
Munden Sarah — Lord Grimston's Scipio II
— Munden Saucy

Munden Scottie

Buccleugh Drake — Buccleugh Avon
— Buccleugh Gip
Buccleugh Belle, 1892 — Buccleugh Ned
— Buccleugh Trick

Waterdale Gamester

Munden Sentry

Munden Sixty — Buccleugh Nith
— Munden Sarah

Munden Scottie — Buccleugh Drake
— Buccleugh Belle

Waterdale Twinkle

Ward's Venus

Ward's Bramble — Buccleugh Jock, 1892
— Ward's Rose

Schoolbred's Solo — Graham's Netherby Otter
— Menzies Rock

Munden Sovereign

A. Nicholl's Brayton Sir Richard,
1899

Sir R. Graham's Netherby Tar — Lord Verulam's Sweep, 1889
— Graham's Netherby Esk, 1892

A. Craw's Nell — Buccleugh Jock
— Earl of Home's Juno

Munden Single

Munden Sixty — Buccleugh Nith
— Munden Sarah

Munden Scottie — Buccleugh Drake
— Buccleugh Belle

Birkhill Juliet

Buccleugh Bruce

Buccleugh Sailor — Lord Grimston's Scipio II
— Lord Grimston's Sappho II

Buccleugh Belle — Buccleugh Ned
— Buccleugh Trick

Capt. Bald's Susan

Liddell's Ninnie

Liddell's Ben — Liddell's Sam
— Barnett's Juno

Straker's Sal, 1891 — Fenwick's Dacre
— Straker's Nell, 1881

73

Pedigree chart:

- **Dual Ch. Banchory Bolo, 1915** (under the heading of Malmesbury's Tramp)
  - **Scandal of Glynn**
    - F.C. Peter of Faskally, 1908
      - Waterdale Gamester
        - Sherfield Spratt, 1900
          - Munden Sixty, 1897
          - Munden Scottie
        - Waterdale Twinkle, 1904
          - Munden Sentry
          - Venus
      - Birkhill Juliet
        - Munden Sovereign
          - Brayton Sir Richard
          - Munden Single
        - Capt. Bald's Susan
          - Buccleugh Bruce, 1896
          - Liddell's Ninnie
    - Shelagh of Glynn
      - Scamp of Glynn, 1906
        - Bragg
          - Bob
          - Barnett's Snail
        - Jet
      - Shelagh
        - Munden Sentry
          - Munden Sixty
          - Munden Scottie
        - Munden Sceptre
          - Brayton Sir Richard
          - Munden Psaltery
  - **Caerhowell Nettle**
    - Foxley Kennett
      - Ranger
        - King Richard
        - Bess
      - Bendysh Bess
        - Prince
        - Black Bess
    - Baker's Nora

74

Dual Ch. Staindrop Saighdear (Y)
(under the heading of Malmesbury's Tramp)

- Knappies Lass
  - Ch. Kinpurnie Kam (Y)
    - Ch. Orchardton Donald
      - Ch. Ingleston Ben
        - Duke of Kirkmahoe (Am. imp.)
        - Ingleston Nancy
      - Orchardton Dawn (Am. imp.)
        - Ch. Brocklehirst Donner
        - Hardie's Choice
    - F.C. Kinpurnie Kate
      - Kinpurnie Joe
        - Nith of Halleaths
        - Kinpurnie Gypsey
      - Catter Betty (unreg.)
        - Soot of Keavil
        - Lady Betty of Struthers
  - Glenhead Jimmy
    - Dual Ch. Bramshaw Bob
      - Ch. Ingleston Ben
        - Duke of Kirkmahoe
        - Ingleston Nancy
      - Bramshaw Brimble
        - F.C. Kirkmahoe Rover
        - Ch. Balbeardie
    - Glenhead Bess
      - F.C. Ledsham Peter
        - St. Mary's Donson, 1915
        - Dalbeattie Rose
      - L'Ile Bouncing Girl
        - Ingleston Don
        - Heather Belle
- Glenravel Glynter
  - F.C. Glenravel Nimrod
    - F.C. Tag of Clava
      - Dual Ch. Titus of Whitmore
        - Twist of Whitmore
        - Teazle of Whitmore
      - Ch. Drinkstone Gyp
        - Wolferton Dan
        - Ch. Pride of Somersby
    - Queen of the May
      - Black Hawk
        - Great Scott
        - Craigetta
      - Liddly Kingfisher
        - Ch. Tar of Hamyax
        - Liddly Vanity
  - Our Lil
    - Eng. & Am. Ch. Towyriver James
      - Ch. Banchory Bolo's Trust
        - Dual Ch. Banchory Bolo
        - Beaulieu Nance
      - Towyriver James
        - Dual Ch. Titus of Whitmore
        - Towyriver Bead
    - Wild Wisper
      - Ch. Banchory Danilo
        - Dual Ch. Banchory Bolo
        - Munden Scarcity
      - Ch. Reyen Lass (Y)
        - Storey (Y)
        - Helen (Y)

Pettistree Dan

Dual Ch. Banchory Painter
- Peter The Painter
  - F.C. Ledsham Peter
  - Dinah
- Glenhead Bess
  - F.C. Ledsham Peter
  - L'Ile Bouncing Girl

F.C. Quest of Wilbury
- Ch. Ingleston Ben
  - Duke of Kirkmahoe
  - Ingleston Nancy
- F.C. Muntham Raven
  - Banchory Corbie
  - Beningbrough Tansey

Greatford Pettistree Shadow

Withington Sam
- F.C. Withington Nith
  - Nith of Somersby
  - Withington Judy
- Boathouse Bess
  - Redesmere Bruce
  - Withington Tactful

Scotney Doushka

Scotney Dinah
- Withington Victor
  - Nith of Somersby
  - Siddington Judy
- Withington Tact
  - Withington Hemp
  - Countess of Somersby

Eng. Nat. F.C. Greatford Teal, 1955
(under the heading of
Ch. Ilderton Ben)

Colwill Diamond
- Pettistree Dan
  - Dual Ch. Banchory Painter
  - F.C. Quest of Wilbury
- Salesbury Trustful
  - F.C. The Plodder
  - Saleburt Tactful

Countryman of Chrishall

North Dyke Kirstie
- F.C. Banchory Donald
  - Ch. Brocklehirst Donner
  - Ingleston Nancy
- F.C. Kinpurnie Kate
  - Kinpurnie Joe
  - Catter Betty

Mackland Honeysuckle

Hiwood Shimey
- Ch. Ingleston Ben
  - Duke of Kirkmahoe
  - Ingleston Nancy
- F.C. Hiwood Chance
  - F.C. Beningbrough Tanco
  - Rockstead Swift

Mackland Panter

Glastry Dainty
- F.C. The Plodder
  - Lochar Mac
  - Kinmount Juno
- Broadhill Dainty
  - King of Hearts
  - Thankerton Juno

76

Eng. & Am. F.C. Staindrop Murton Marksman

Shavington Ted

Shavington Ben

Shavington Jet — Ch. Liddly Jonquil / Nork Amber (Y)

Shavington Tees — Shavington Troop / Chesswardine Jane

Adderley Thought

Adderley Ted — F.C. Balmuto Hewildo / F.C. Adderley Tax

F.C. Adderley Bee — Banchory Benhmore / F.C. Adderley Trim

Brackenbank Jessie

F.C. Brackenbank Jasper

Sudborough Ben — Greatford Sinner / Venus

Banchory Murton Mystic — Glenhead Jimmy / Staindrop Hycup Dusk

Brackenbank Belle of Auburn

Banchory Jack — Ch. Kinpurnie Kam (Y) / Dunkeld Duchess

Quail of Auburn — Gorse of Romanidale / Jet of Romanidale

Nat. Ch. Galleywood Shot, 1957, 1958 (under the heading of Malmesbury's Tramp)

Dual Ch. Staindrop Saighdear (Y)

Glenhead Jimmy

Ch. Kinpurnie Kam (Y) — Ch. Orchardton Donald / F.C. Kinpurnie Kate

Knappies Lass — Dual Ch. Bramshaw Bob / Glenhead Bess

Our Lil

F.C. Glenravel Nimrod — F.C. Tag of Clava / Queen of the May

Glenravel Glynter — Ch. Towyriver James / Wild Wisper

Hiwood Peggy (Y)

Cheverell's Sally

Cheverell's Denny (Y)

Braeroy Rab (Y) — Hielant Laddie (Y) / F.C. Braeroy Roe (Y)

F.C. Cheverell's Amber (Y) — Grey Plover / Kefton Vanilla (Y)

Cheverell's Busybody

F.C. Balmuto Hewildo — Balmuto Tanco / Balmuto Kate

F.C. Cheverell's Bustle — Ch. Ingleston Ben / Xmas Nora

77

Bench

- **Dual Ch. Knaith Banjo**
  - Poppleton Golden Russett
    - Ch. Poppleton Golden Major
      - Ch. Poppleton Black Lancer (B)
      - Golden Gleam of Poppleton
    - Poppleton Golden Dawn
      - Ilton Roger (B)
      - Poppleton Black Lilac (B)
  - Knaith Brilliantine
    - Knaith Boom
      - Knaith Bogey
      - Amber
    - Knaith Brill
      - Knaith Busby
      - Knaith Shrimp
- **All Gold**
  - Ch. Poppleton Golden Flight
    - Poppleton Golden Russett
      - Ch. Poppleton Golden Major
      - Poppleton Golden Dawn
    - Modney Crocus (B)
      - Folkingham Solo
      - Bestwood Belle (B)
  - Dalwaht Dawn
    - Knaith Boom
      - Knaith Bogey
      - Amber
    - Kirkland Reconnaissance
      - Rustoil
      - Craigmalloch Lad

F.C. Zelstone Moss (Y), 1956 (under the heading of Ben of Hyde)

- **Ch. Zelstone Leapyear Lass**
  - Braedrop Bruce
    - Dual Ch. Staindrop Saighdear
      - Glenhead Jimmy (B)
        - Ch. Kinpurnie Kam
        - Knappies Lass (B)
      - Our Lil (B)
        - F.C. Glenravel Nimrod (B)
        - Glenravel Glynter (B)
    - F.C. Braeroy Fudge
      - Banchory Jack (B)
        - Ch. Kinpurnie Kam
        - Dunkeld Duchess (B)
      - Braeroy Chips
        - Braeroy Duke
        - Braeroy Mitre
  - F.C. Zelstone Darter
    - Durley Bracken (B)
      - Thatcher (B)
        - Toi of Whitmore (B)
        - Drinkstone Stella (B)
      - Liddly Ouzel (B)
        - Liddly Blackcock (B)
        - Judy of Rook (B)
    - Glenmorag Parella of Podington
      - Neptune of Hinwick
        - F.C. Hawkesbury Jupiter
        - Manor
      - Polka of Podington
        - Six Mile Rock
        - Six Mile Melody

5

Yellows

COLORS recognized by the British and American standards today are the Yellow and the Chocolate or Liver. Yellows may vary in shade from the lightest cream to the darkest fox red, either as solids or intermittently shaded, with a lighter undercoat covered by dark outer coloring.

Records of many old gundog breeds point out that these coat colors were evident and common long before any recorded breeding was the rule. Spaniels, Poodles, Setter-Retriever crosses, and even certain strains of old Pointers and some of the large old Newfoundlands were described as having often been "red, brown, brown and white and occasional yellow specimens" (Gordon Stables).

So far as one can ascertain, there have been no written accounts nor descriptions of "small water dogs" arriving at Poole from St. John's having been other than "jet black, rarely liver hued" (Stonehenge). An odd exception to this might be taken from the Scott-Middleton book in which Major J. A. Joicey writes that "Susan was a yellow woolley dog, not a Labrador," in reference to an individual in a pedigree. Lord Joicey owned the well-known Scottish affix of Flodden.

The early history of yellow Labradors may have a certain

PARENTS	Puppies pure black	puppies appear black but carry Y	puppies Yellow
BB × BB	● ● ● ● ● ● ●		1.
BY × BB	● ● ● ●	◐ ◐ ◐ ◐	2.
BY × BY	● ●	◐ ◐ ◐ ◐	◐ ◐ 3.
Y × BY		◐ ◐ ◐ ◐	◐ ◐ ◐ ◐ 4.
BB × Y		◐ ◐ ◐ ◐ ◐ ◐ ◐ ◐	5.
Y × Y			◐ ◐ ◐ ◐ ◐ ◐ ◐ ◐ 6.

THE YELLOW COLOR
A Simple Recessive in Labradors

BB—Black genes (Dominant)
yy—Yellow genes (Recessive)
By—Black and Yellow genes

1. Only black puppies possible, as neither parent carries yellow.
2. All black in appearance, but half carry yellow.
3. Two thirds of the black puppies carry yellow; ratio approximately 3 blacks to 1 yellow.
4. Can have no "pure" blacks, as one parent is yellow.
5. Can have no "pure" blacks, as one parent is yellow.
6. Only yellow puppies possible, as neither parent carries black genes.

Proportions of yellows and blacks and also blacks carrying yellow can vary either way from the expected ratio in breeding, 1/2, 1/3, 1/4.

Small litters are inconclusive. The larger the litter the nearer the breeder approaches the expected ratio.

Actual examples of pedigrees relating to No. 3, are those of Ben of Hyde and Staindrop Saighdear. Sire and dam of both these dogs were By's.

Examples of No. 4 can be illustrated by the pedigrees of Burnham Buff and Galleywood Shot. Sires of both were By's, and dams of both were yy's.

amount of tantalizing mystery surrounding it: if so, there is no valid reason for it, as it is no longer a disputed fact that there appeared in the early days before color establishment yellow or "brown" puppies in litters fully expected to produce the orthodox black. These off-color puppies were just not appreciated at the time and consequently were done away with. "While it cannot be said," comments Mackay Sanderson, "that color faddism dominated the situation to any extent, it is nevertheless substantially true that the dubiety which characterises the general attitude to any color removed from the ordinary, to a certain extent acted as a deterrent to rapid Yellow advance."

Nevertheless there came to the fore, in the early part of this century, breeders who did become keen on cultivating the color, among them Maj. C. E. Radclyffe, Col. Swan, Mr. F. Straker, Mr. A. Clark, Lord Wimborne, and the late Lord Feversham. All these gentlemen owned dogs of that color and, through the interbreeding of their strains, eventually firmly established the Yellow Labrador.

One may divide the ascent of the Yellows into three phases of development from approved yellow lines, starting with the first recognized yellow Labrador, Ben of Hyde.

Ben was whelped in 1899 (KC55698), bred from two black parents, Neptune and Duchess (owned by Major Radclyffe), both of which stemmed from original black imports taken off the fishing boats that docked at Poole. The last of these was a black dog called Turk, who arrived in 1871. Generations were bred from Turk until Ben arrived. Major Radclyffe recalls old Turk as being "short on the leg with a broad head and chest. His coat was thicker underneath than now seen on bench Labradors and he had a small white patch on his chest and his ears were inclined to be pricked, unlike the flat ears of today."

Ben of Hyde sired many Yellows through black bitches brought to him; however, his yellow litter sister, Juno, failed to produce any at all when bred to black dogs. Ben's sire, Neptune, may well be distinguished as the keystone to the present Radclyffe Zelstone kennel—"The gateway," as Mr. Sanderson puts it, "from which all the Yellows which have achieved distinction on the bench and in working circles converge,—the recognized fountainhead of excellence and the first to register the advance of the color in emphatic fashion."

Field Ch. Zelstone Darter (Durley Bracken ex Glenmorag Parella of Podington), bred and owned by Mrs. A. Radclyffe.

Ben of Hyde (Neptune ex Duchess), bred and owned by Major C. E. Radclyffe, was the first yellow Labrador registered with the Kennel Club (England).

Through the kindness of the present Col. Radclyffe, and of Mrs. Radclyffe, I have an informal description of the early Radclyffe dogs, before their prefix became Zelstone. "Ben of Hyde," writes Mrs. Radclyffe, "was born of course at my husband's old place near here in Dorset. He remembers Ben well; Ben was a stocky dog, with a wonderful coat and tail but rather short in neck. Ben got almost all yellow puppies but his sister none. There were only black bitches to breed to him then and one did hear of black occurring in early yellow bred litters but none as far as I know since those times. Lord Ilchester's dogs were all Golden Retrievers; the Radclyffes bred only for work and never had a great many dogs at a time nor showed nor ran them much. I first ran a dog called Zelstone Sandy in 1937 and got a CM. Sandy was a great grandson of Foxdenton Neptune; pedigrees would have been easier to follow had the Radclyffes registered a prefix at the time, but no, they just called their dogs Ben, Nep, Turk, Duchess and the like and it gets very complicated.

"Alas, I lost my Sandy's blood in the last War. There were quite a lot of good Blacks that go back to Zelstone Sandy including those of Mrs. Heywood Lonsdale's Shavington kennel. In the last war my husband bought a yellow bitch puppy on my recommendation while he was serving up north, called Parella of Podington. Parella was a granddaughter of Fld. Ch. Hawkesbury Jupiter and a bitch called Manor who was by Knaith Monkboy. From her we bred a very good litter including Zelstone Jet (black) and my Fld. Ch. Zelstone Darter (yellow); we then most unfortunately sold her to Major Malcolm of the Glenmorag prefix who of course bred some beauties from her. Darter was really a first class bitch in every way and dam of Fld. Ch. Hockham Victoria, Ch. Zelstone Leap Year Lass and Am. Ch. Zelstone Kate. Lass has won nine CC's, several reserves and many field trial awards. Jet, Darter's litter sister was also very good, but we sold her because of her color. Your lovely bitch Pokey has a head almost exactly like her granddam Jet; the black strain comes through Durley Bracken. Bracken was a good looking dog and would have made his mark at trials but for the War. Hawkesbury dogs were excellent workers—many not good to look at, too light in bone. Jupiter was first class. Mrs. Wormald's kennel of Knaith is the oldest kennel of true dual purpose yellow blood there is, of real Labrador type and all workers. She set her

84

face, at the beginning against crossing with as little black blood as possible and few kennels can say the same."

Mrs. Arthur Wormald became one of the staunchest supporters of the color in 1910. Her prefix today is still as active as ever and a household word in the annals of Yellow history. She saw her first Yellow in Col. Swan's Pink and was determined to own one herself.

Pink was a dog called Sportsman, pedigree unknown, but described as a "red" dog and owned by a Mr. Campbell.

Eventually Mrs. Wormald was able to breed a litter from Velvet, a black granddaughter of Pink, and produced two Yellows of quality in Mannie and Sam. One of her early bitches, called Knaith Lady, was bred to Major Portal's well-known Field Ch. Flapper, and although the litter resulted in ten black puppies, subsequent generations from this crossing carried the yellow factor.

Another Yellow enthusiast of this period was Mr. E. Dawson, head keeper to Mr. Straker, long identified with the Angerton kennel. Among all the game keeper owners, no one has adhered more faithfully to the color, nor has anyone had as many field trial wins with Yellows as he.

The late Lord Lonsdale also had many Yellows from Major Radclyffe. By this time many other sportsmen were drawn to the Yellows and, in the interest of furthering it publicly, were approached to support the first Yellow bench show classes in 1913 at the National Dog Show held at Olympia. Many, including Major Radclyffe, entered dogs, and the winner was Nereid, a bitch bred by Mrs. Wormald. According to Mr. J. Alexander, a great trainer and judge of gundogs and long associated with the Dutchess of Hamilton's Dungavel Kennel of Labradors and Spaniels, Nereid could hold her own with the best of the Blacks. In a letter to me, Mrs. Wormald wrote: "Nereid was a lovely bitch by Major Radclyffe's Foxdenton Neptune but got distemper at the show and I lost eleven out of my twelve dogs. I only saved Mannie who figures prominently in the early pedigrees. Mannie was then bred to Lord Feversham's Nawton Brownie, described by some who knew her as having been a liver whelp, turning black at maturity; others spoke of her as a Black with brown markings. Subsequently Nereid was given to Captain Lucas, a brother of Major Lucas, and it was from this great working strain of Hawkesbury that Kettledean was founded."

Mrs. Wormald's bitches were of high standard and include Knaith Shrimp, Limekiln Rhoda, Muntham Pepper, Knaith Brill, Knaith Bass and many others. Outstanding were five of her dogs— Bliss, Bounce, Bogey, Field Ch. Brock and Dual Ch. Banjo. Banjo was considered by many to have been one of the finest Yellows ever bred, apart from his working credentials. His was a rugged, masculine character, yet tempered with real quality. He was Mrs. Wormald's constant companion for fifteen years, and there is an emptiness at Glenstuart today that will never be filled again. One of the most graciously written tributes to a dog and owner appeared in the 1961 *Dog World,* written by Mr. Gilliat on the passing of Dual Ch. Knaith Banjo:

"Little did I know when I embarked on my first Championship show judging assignment at the Labrador Club of Scotland in 1947 that I would find there a young yellow Labrador which was to make breed history. In a Junior, and I think Undergraduate class, there appeared a clear cut winner handled by Mrs. Wormald. Before awarding the CC, this unbeaten dog was sent for and despite the great merit of the placed dogs in the Open class, I had no doubt whatever that this Junior yellow dog was the first, and he was duly awarded his first Challenge Certificate. Subsequently I discovered the name of this youngster to be Knaith Banjo, of impeccable Knaith breeding. Mrs. Wormald will remember that I there and then named her dog "The Bumptious Boy" as he was so full of fun and vigor, and when two years later he won the coveted title of Dual Champion, I was delighted to receive a telegram from this Bumptious Boy and his owner, giving me the wonderful news.

"Banjo (always Jo to his owner) lived to a grand old age and when he died after a second heart attack, he had just celebrated his fifteenth birthday. Banjo was the last living dual champion and was the only Labrador dual champion to have been bred, trained, and handled at field trials by his owner. His show record includes 12 CCs (all gathered under different judges), four best of breeds, and seven times reserve best of sex. At field trials he collected the stupendous total of forty-one awards and never disgraced himself or his owner by a run in (break). He clinched his dual title by winning the Kennel Club's Open stake in 1949, a really great achievement for his sporting owner. To me there appeared to be a distinct similarity in the character of both owner and dog.

Dual Ch. Knaith Banjo (Poppleton Golden Russet ex Knaith Brilliantine), bred and owned by Mrs. V. Wormald.

A group of Knaith dogs with Major Arthur Wormald and a friend—a Border terrier and Pekingese cross.

"It is one thing to understand your dog, but if your dog understands you equally well (preferably better), the road to success is made simpler, and this is how things appeared with Mrs. Wormald and Jo. All of us dog lovers know the awful pang of bereavement when an especially valued dog leaves us, and of course after fifteen years the grief is all the greater. Labrador folk, and I am sure other breeders will wish Mrs. Wormald to know how sorry they are to bid farewell to a very wonderful dog; but what a superb partnership Jo and his owner enjoyed for so many years."

The second stage of development in Yellows may be placed after 1918, when strong kennels came into prominence and reached their peak all through the '20's and '30's. Some of these can be estimated as having been pure yellow; although outstanding Blacks occurred among them, they were far enough away from black dominance to be firmly established as yellow lines. Although many of them are no longer functioning, and their prefixes are nostalgically beginning to be seen as far back as the fourth generation in the majority of pedigrees, it is essential to know about them and realize that most of what is of value today derives directly from their influence.

Apart from Knaith and Zelstone, which are currently in the forefront, the three most highly regarded kennels were Major T. C. Lucas' Hawkesbury, Dr. Stanton's Folkingham, and Mrs. M. K. MacPherson's Braeroy. Major Lucas held an unequaled dual purpose record for that period with Field Ch. Hawkesbury Jupiter and Sherry of Kettledean. The latter proved a dominant sire through his daughter, Hawkesbury Joy, who was the first Yellow to gain a bench title, while a litter mate, Chum of Boghurst, owned by Major Doyne Ditmas, produced Golden Morn, one of the most forceful studs of the late '20's. Golden Morn's pre-eminent get include Mrs. Wormald's Field Ch. Knaith Brock and Mr. Allbones' distinguished Ch. Alby Twink, and he was also instrumental in modeling the future of the Poppleton kennels.

For aggregate field trial honors, Dr. Stanton's Folkingham Labradors take precedence over all others during the latter part of the '20's. Over a score of dogs carrying his prefix won or placed in Open stakes consistently from year to year, and produced their like in such immortal names as Swimmer, Solo, Spud, Bexter, Speedy, and many others.

Braeroy Maid (Buro of Strichen ex Golden Nada), bred by Mrs. M. Mac-Pherson and exported to America to Miss Agnes Fowler.

The Scottish Braeroy kennel of Mrs. MacPherson was of the first magnitude on the Yellow working scene. Mrs. MacPherson has had an array of field trial champion bitches second to none in Roe, Ruddy, Fudge, and many stake winners. Field Ch. Braeroy Ruddy has the distinction of having been the only yellow bitch to ever win six Open stakes. Field Ch. Fudge, acquired by Lady Hill Wood, and dam to Mrs. Radclyffe's Field Ch. Zelstone Darter and granddam to her Ch. Leapyear Lass, was trained to her title by Mr. Hallett, head keeper of Great Windsor Park, who also bred his late Majesty George VI's Windsor Bob, who was by Dual Ch. Staindrop Saighdear ex Fudge.

Glencoe Mac was Mrs. MacPherson's first Labrador. Whelped in 1923 by Remus ex Pins, from the old red strain of Lord Feversham through his prolific brood bitch, Scarlet, Mac was trained first on sea gulls, the only feathered game available. He subsequently ran in trials and won several CMs. Mrs. MacPherson's prefix, Braeroy, meaning "Red Hill," was named after the moors where she once lived. She had excellent stud dogs in Western Reiver, Hielant Laddie and Braeroy Rab, the latter being one of the strong forces behind many contemporary kennels of that period. Her most important successes occurred just prior to World War II, and after the loss of her husband, Capt. MacPherson, she limited her trial activities. Her strategic win in October, 1962, with her black homebred, Rivington Braeroy Swift, at the Championship stake at Cromlix, was a success in the arena of competition and breeding she so wholeheartedly supported in prewar times. Captain MacPherson, a devotee of sheep dog trials, often handled the Braeroy dogs in stakes and used his handling skill to great advantage with them. The Yellows have always been pre-eminent with Mrs. MacPherson, but she has also bred some deserving Blacks. She feels that Yellows are more pliable and simpler to manage for amateurs than some of their more impetuous black counterparts.

Other Yellow kennels of pre-World War II merit were Worlington, Kinmount, Kettledean, Birdshall, Boghurst, and the Hon. Lady Ward's Chiltonfoliat, where occasional livers were bred, and which housed a liver bitch bred by Mrs. MacPherson, Darry of Chiltonfoliat (formerly Braeroy Darkie), a granddaughter of Western Reiver. Here it may be well to explain to American readers that prior to a postwar English Kennel Club ruling on registered dogs' names, anyone could change the name of a dog they bought. The new ruling indicates that a registered dog's name may be changed *once* by the new owner, but only by *adding* a prefix or affix to the original name. Such instances as Braeroy Jack becoming Banchory Jack and the above-mentioned Darkie are examples which no longer hold. This seems to be a much fairer approach, wherein a breeder, even when relinquishing his dog, will always have the mark of distinction through his kennel name for posterity.

Prejudice against the color was still to be felt at dog shows as late as the late 1920's, and in Mrs. Wormald's letter to me one can sense the predicament. "My Knaith Bogey," she writes, "was a fine dog and unlucky not to have become a champion. The judges in those days were very prejudiced; I showed Bogey's sire Bounce at the Kennel Club show and the stewards tried hard to turn me out of the ring, as they said I'd entered in the wrong variety—as my dog was a Golden Retriever! But I stood my ground and got third that day!" After this incident it was decided to take matters into hand and the Yellow Labrador Club was formed, of which the late Lord Lonsdale was its first president. It guaranteed support of Yellow classes at shows, inaugurated annual field trial meetings for the color, and has ever since held an annual Open Show, also restricted to the color. The supposition that Yellows required a club of their own and trials of their own because they could not compete with the Blacks is only a partial truth. To foster any new enterprise, special efforts have to be resorted to in the beginning and such was the case with the yellow Labrador. Their record speaks well for the fact that when they are of the best they can win with the best, and to point out that many of the best Yellows have stemmed from black genealogy is beside the point.

A Yellow standard was drawn up as any standard has to be, to list the correct points and draw attention to the undesirable features prevalent at the time of setting up a standard. There was such a divergence of type, make and shape in those days that it became imperative to establish it for the sake of the color's future—for uniformity of type and the elimination of as many structural evils as possible.

The following faults were supereminent: ears badly carried, often too large, sometimes near-prick and poorly set; overly short necks and upright shoulder placement, resulting in a stilted, paddling front gait, topaz eyes, which, even if they did upon occasion "harmonize" with the coat, had an ill-disposed look that is alien to the breed. Colors were uneven; there was great "flecking" or patches of darker on lighter or vice versa: large white patches on the most unconventional places. There were poor feet and other flaws.

In order to compete on equal footing with the classic Blacks, much work and careful breeding had to be done. During this time some breeders made great efforts to divide the colors at shows completely, by applying for separate Challenge Certificates for each color. Lady Howe wrote on this that "this would mean to all intents and purposes that they would be two distinct breeds. When it is stated that at that particular time there were two Labradors, father and son competing at shows, the father being a Black and a big winner of C.C.s, the son, a Yellow, being his runner up for the certificates, the absurdity of father and son being two distinct varieties can be easily realized. . . ." The dogs in question were Ch. Banchory Danilo (black) and his yellow son, Ch. Badgery Richard.

Before any of the Yellows competed at their own trials, one notes that as early as 1908 Mr. Straker's Sandy, by Rover ex Lady, placed reserve at the Northumberland trials, one of the earliest Yellows to gain recognition in working competition. Mr. Straker's Rust, breeding not given, won the All Aged stake at the same trial two years later.

An early yellow field champion bitch was Field Ch. Janet, owned by Sir E. Sprigges, by Babs ex Floss, both unregistered. Whelped in 1926 and entering competition in 1928, she won four stakes in top black opposition, which embraced the Kennel Club stake in 1931 and the Labrador Club's All Aged event in 1934. Other brilliant workers were Mr. Heaton's Field Ch. Cheveralls Amber and Mr. Johnstone's Belle of Halleaths, Scottish bred.

A review from the weekly column of Richard Anderton, correspondent for Labradors in a 1936 issue of the *English Kennel Gazette,* touches on some of the breeding problems of the day and reports on the Kennel Club Show, judged by Major T. C. Lucas of the yellow Hawkesbury prefix:

"Major Lucas who judged Labradors at the K. C. show says he was surprised at the variety of type in the Junior classes, and the percentage of real Labrador jackets was small. He only goes on to mention six individual dogs in his report, so that it is not possible to gather in which direction the majority failed, although he does say that variations in size, length of body and throatiness were noticeable. Taking the latter point it has always been a matter of considerable surprise to me that the standard of the Yellow Labrador Club should specifically mention this feature in a permissive sense, giving the impression that in the Yellow it is not a serious fault. Of all breeders of Yellows, very few are better qualified than Major Lucas to give light on this subject. For those who may not have the words, they are, 'the neck should be stocky and may be inclined to be throaty.' It is rather significant that under such a noted Yellow breeder the highest positions were all occupied by blacks, and all six worthy of comment in his report are of that color. Can it be that the inclination to throatiness in the Yellows places them at a disadvantage and if so what can the Yellow Labrador Club do about it?"

Mr. Anderton then goes on to say, "there seems to be no good reason why throatiness should be tolerated in Yellows any more than in Blacks; in fact I am not personally convinced of the tendency and can name quite a long list of throaty Blacks."

However, the next decade did see immense strides in overall improvement and in 1959 we were informed that under pressure from the A.G.M. the Yellow standard has been abandoned and that the Black standard would be henceforth followed.

Actually, up to the present day occasional throatiness in certain individual dogs and in some lines is as strong as it ever was, as far as my own experience and observations have taken me. Blacks can be as throaty as Yellows; it is a definite feature in Labradors, but in varying degrees. A perfectly clean neck such as a Pointer's is rare. As a matter of fact, I have found that such rare occurrences tie up with other characteristics of the Pointer—in a sleek coat, tails with little semblance to the otter shape, and a generally finer, racier build, which of course is not typical. To me, it is only when a neck is too *short* (and this again usually goes hand in hand with badly placed shoulders), in that it has no reach, that throatiness becomes more obvious and annoying. In this instance, one is weighing one fault against the other: a short neck, which is a structural handicap, against some throatiness, which, if the neck be of ample length, is a minor evil, and certainly would not stand in the way of a dog's doing a good day's work. This is not to give breeders of show animals a loophole in which to neglect efforts to eliminate throatiness and poorly laid shoulders; for, in so neglecting, one is inadvertently turning faults into virtues. Eradicating one or two drastic faults cannot be done at the expense of incurring others, either. The present fashion for extremely short backs, with the corresponding short, thick tails, is a step towards balance, but it will take extensive breeding care to combine and keep this quality of balance intact without the aforementioned defects that seem so often to go hand in hand with it.

The quality of balance must be obvious when a dog moves, as well as when he is standing in repose. Balance or imbalance is even more apparent when a dog is gaiting, for at that time one can observe shoulders at their best or poorest advantage. One cannot repeat too often that a Retriever's gait should be free and effortless and ground covering. A static "stay in one place" stride, where forelegs are picked up in a choppy hackney movement, and hindquarters, especially at hocks, fail to show drive or propelling action, is a working fault, and also, from a "show" angle, is, in many judges' opinions, considered to be unsound.

As the popularity of the color expanded, Field Ch. Haylers Defender, by Peter Popperly ex Borisdemain, became the first Yellow to achieve a field trial title, in 1927.

The first Yellow Labrador Club trial was held in 1925, at Wooten near Bedford, with twelve entries in the All Aged stake. It was won by Major Callender's Littlebourne Mac, a grandson of Knaith Monkboy. The Club's last prewar trial was held in 1938, and was won by Mrs. MacPherson's Field Ch. Braeroy Ruddy. Haylers Defender won it in 1926 and 1927. Mrs. Wormald's Knaith Brock, appearing as winner in the Puppy stakes in 1929, won the All Aged stake in 1931. The year 1947 saw a dual win for Mrs. Radclyffe's kennel, with Brig. Trappes-Lomax's Hockham Victoria winning the Junior stake, while her dam, Field Ch. Zelstone Darter, was awarded the All Aged win. Hockham Victoria became a field champion in 1950.

Among Yellow winners at the British National Championship stake, the first of which was held in 1909, open to all Retrievers, including Interbreds and Crossbreds, one notes that the first Yellow to place in what was hitherto a monopolization of the Blacks was the bitch, Field Ch. Sienna, by Field Ch. Hayler's Defender ex a

Two examples of the need for a Yellow standard: Many early Yellows showed hound-like heads, weak feet, sparse coats, light leg bone, thin tails, and white on muzzles.

Field Ch. Hayler's Defender (Peter Opperly ex Borisdemain), owned by Mrs. L. Stewart, was the first Yellow field trial champion (1927).

daughter of Golden Morn. Sienna's placement of third in this 1934 event was repeated in 1936. In 1935, Mrs. MacPherson's Field Ch. Braeroy Ruddy was awarded third, and 1938 marked the first year wherein a Yellow *won* it—again a bitch, Mr. Heaton's Field Ch. Cheverell's Amber, with equal third going again to Ruddy. Mr. Hallett's Field Ch. Braeroy Fudge was second in 1946, with Mr. Winter's Staindrop Saighdear third. In 1948, Mrs. Radclyffe's inimitable Field Ch. Zelstone Darter went second, and in 1958 her Field Ch. Zelstone Moss was second to the black winner, Field Ch. Galleywood Shot. Moss, a granddaughter of Dual Ch. Knaith Banjo ex Ch. Zelstone Leap Year Lass, was subsequently bred to Galleywood Shot, and produced Mr. Wilkin's Field Ch. Sendhurst Zelstone Tinker; from this litter are two more well on the way to their field titles, Dr. Acheson's Ballyduff Zelstone Broom, and Mr. Cock's Sendhurst Zelstone Bright. Thus Mrs. Radclyffe has had an unprecedented record—stemming from the original Ben of Hyde— of having bred four field trial champions in Hockham Victoria, Darter, Moss Tinker and 1964 Fd. Ch. Zelstone Bonnie; and in Ch. Leap Year Lass, a qualified worker and producer. As one can observe from the pedigrees, it is unadulterated working blood.

The most recent success among the Yellows was the 1962 Kennel Club Open stake, won by Major F. C. Howlett's bitch, Venmeth Valerie (Venmeth Venture ex Lind o' the Carse). Venmeth Valerie, a three-year-old, Scottish bred, stems from the black line of Mrs. Heywood Lonsdale, being great-granddaughter to the yellow Brackenbank Peril, owned by Mrs. Fraser Horn. Peril is litter brother to Mr. John Olin's Field Chs. Staindrop Murton Marks-man and Staindrop Ringleader; on the sire's side of these dogs the line ties in with Mr. Corbett's Adderley kennel through Adderley Thought.

Other Yellow workers of exceptional merit have been Miss Hyde Harrison's Pavenham Virginia; Mrs. H. Taylor's Field Ch. What-standwell Hiwood Brand; Major Malcolm's Field Ch. Minstrel of Glemorag; and Lord Middleton's Field Ch. Birdshall Vesper.

Two sires of pre-eminence belonging to the second period were Ch. Badgery Richard and Ch. Kinpurnie Kam, both stemming from long black parentage. Richard was a very prepossessing dog in his day, a grandson of Lady Howe's Bolo. His imprint was felt in many of the best of Folkingham blood, also siring Major Peacock's Great-

Ch. Badgery Ivory shows a head of strength and character with a kindly expression.

Ch. Badgery Richard (Ch. Banchory Danilo ex Coodenbeach Nell), bred by A. Cundell and owned by Miss Buller.

ford Nan, Mr. Dinwoodie's Lochar Polly, and several from Mr. Coleman's Nork prefix.

Without prejudice for or against, one can name Ch. Kinpurnie Kam, whelped in 1939, as a Yellow force of first rank for future generations. He was the first Yellow to appear in four generations of Blacks, by Ch. Orchardton Donald ex Field Ch. Kinpurnie Kate, thus carrying the immortal blood of Ch. Ingleston Ben and providing a pivotal link in the best of the Poppletons through Golden Charm, Sherry, and Pilot; he was above all the impetus behind Banchory Jack and Mr. Annand's Glenhead Jimmy. Mr. Dewar, Saighdear's breeder, who knew Kam well, had good reason to believe that, but for World War II, Kam would without exception have become the third Yellow dual champion in England. As it was, he was only entered in competition in 1938, but was making his mark as a brilliant worker. Kam was handled to his bench title by the late Bob Gilchrist, who succeeded Jimmy Coates at Sir Cayzer's Kinpurnie Kennel.

Again, one must reiterate the stimulus of Dual Ch. Staindrop Saighdear. No Yellow did more in his allotted span than he to bring appreciation and consideration of the color to so many fronts, and to a point of international reckoning between Yellows and Blacks in working circles. To Mr. Winter goes the distinction of having developed him into the incomparable dual product he became. He refused astronomical figures for him, including concentrated efforts on the part of Lady Howe to add him to her formidable kennel. Saighdear was really in a class by himself, a rare and elegant dog.

Early Yellows of note at shows were Major Lucas' Hawkesbury Joy and Mr. Allbones' Alby Twink, the first of each sex to gain their bench titles. Others were Reyen Lass, bred by Mrs. Wormald; Chs. Badgery Richard and Ivory of Miss Buller's; Tessa of Hamyax; Mr. Manson's Scottish Gold Gleam of Glengour, by Knaith BoBoy; and many of the successful Yellows from Mrs. Outwaite's Poppleton prefix. While starting with the Blacks, Mrs. Outwaite soon developed a dominant yellow type during the late '30's which was to influence most of the postwar stock; to mention some of her best are Chs. Stormer, Golden Flight, Golden Russett, Major, Dawn, and Sherry.

One can reiterate the odds that presented themselves to breeders

Major F. C. Howlett, with his bitch, Venmeth Valerie, winning the Kennel Club's Open Stake at Norfolk in October, 1962.

Mrs. A. Radclyffe with Field Ch. Zelstone Darter at the I.G.L. Championship stake in 1948 where Darter placed second.

Mr. Edgar Winter, Miss Joan Winter, and Dual
Ch. Staindrop Saighdear.

Ch. Zelstone Leap Year Lass (Braedrop Bruce ex Field Ch. Zelstone
Darter), photographed at the Bath Ch. Show in 1961 at the age of ten.
She was Best of Breed out of an entry of ninety-eight dogs.

after the war, and, in the comparatively short span of seventeen years, they demonstrate the steady advance made in the color regarding coats and tails and substance at shows generally.

The third period of Yellow development may be placed at the time when new kennels emerged through the '50's and into this decade. Regarding the Yellows, this embraces the turn of events which has reversed the popularity of the color at shows. Today the Yellows in England find themselves in the position that was held by the Blacks during the '20's and '30's. The Blacks predominate at trials, and no doubt will always do so in the long run, but at shows the percentage of Yellows is at least as high as ten to one.

In comparing Labrador show status here and abroad, one must realize that they have always been one of the most powerful of bench forces, possibly because the Kennel Club has been composed to a great degree of Retriever enthusiasts; at this writing, Labradors are fourth in popularity in all breed registrations at the Kennel Club.

Show kennels in any breed usually depend upon, as their main outlet, a "pet market" for members of individual litters that do not measure up to show standard. Labrador show kennels in England have three effective markets: shows, for top material; pet- or companion-gundogs, which include picking up at shoots and the ever expanding Working Test competitions; and the community-minded Guide Dogs for the Blind. Other outlets are the armed forces and the London police force. The Labrador is a lucky breed, as so many breeders of other breeds are well aware; with Labradors one never need resort to the distressing avenue of having to "put down" perfectly healthy, sound puppies because no other way of life can be found for them.

Kennels of long standing are known by the following prefixes: Landyke of Mr. Keith Hart. Mr. Hart, following in the footsteps of his well-known father, the late Mr. John Hart, has bred such prominent and typical dogs as Chs. Poppy, Sheba and Velour, the latter the property of Lady Howe, and the champions, Stormer and Lancer; Kinley of Mr. Fred Wrigley, with American champion Kinley Comet; his quality bitches, Melody and Classic, and his current winners, Ch. Skipper and Ch. Copper; Diant of Mrs. Wilson Jones, under whose prefix Mr. Tillson's Ch. Swandyke Creamcracker has dominated the type set at shows for the last ten years, and whose daughter Ch. Diant Juliet, winner of over fifteen CCs, was considered one of the best yellow bitches in the late '50's. Others that have profited by the stud forces of Creamcracker and Ch. Whatstandwell Coronet, are Col. and Mrs. Venn's dual purpose Corsican prefix; Mrs. Saffel's Rookwood, her distinctive bitches and multiple CC winner, Ch. Petergold; Mrs. Underwood's Barra; Mrs. Rae's Cornlands; Mrs. Wynyard's Braeduke; Mrs. Kinsella's Brentchase; and individual winners such as Ch. Artistry Laffah, Dobrudden Baron, Ch. Lady of Tring, and Ch. Charlotte Queen, all having made their marks in high measure. Many of these owners are championship show judges and demonstrate their high standards in the show ring as they do in the obvious success of their breeding stock. Yellows are now at home in traditionally black strongholds, and one can look forward to their future without qualms.

The Yellow British Standard
(Obsolete)

General Appearance

The general appearance of the Yellow Labrador should be that of a short coupled, strongly built, active dog, deep through the heart and well ribbed up, with strong loins and hindquarters.

Detailed Appearance

COAT. The coat should be short, thick, without wave, and practically a double coat, the undercoat being thick and woolley, the overcoat being smooth.

COLOR. May vary from fox red to cream, without white except on the chest or extreme tips of toes. The coats should be of a whole color, and not of a flaked appearance.

HEAD. The skull should be broad, with brow slightly pronounced, with long powerful jaws, but free from snipiness. The nose should be wide and nostrils well developed, black in color, or may harmonize with the coat. The eye should be dark brown in color, or to match coat, with dark rims. The ears, small and slightly elevated, and should hang close to the head; in color they should be darker than, or the same color as the coat.

NECK and CHEST. The neck should be stocky and may be inclined to be throaty. The chest wide and of good depth. Shoulders square in front, running well back from the point.

LEGS and FEET. Legs should be short and straight from the shoulder with plenty of bone and not back at the knee. The feet compact, circular and strongly made with pads well developed.

TAIL. The tail should be thick at the base, gradually tapering, round or otter like in appearance, and may curl slightly or droop.

Ch. Kinley Copper (Ch. Kinley Skipper ex Kinley Tango), bred and owned by Mr. Fred Wrigley.

Ch. Rookwood Silverdew (Roncott Shandy ex Rookwood Honeysuckle), bred by Mrs. Marion Saffell.

Dank of Siltpit (Folkingham Solo ex Liberum Beauty) exhibits a rugged masculine character and a typical Labrador look.

Ch. Reyen Lass, one of the earliest Yellow bench champions and descended from Ben of Hyde.

Mr. Guest's dog

Mr. Montagu Guest's Sweep II

C.J. Radclyffe's Rover, 1875

C.J. Radclyffe's Turk (imp.)
C.J. Radclyffe's Duchess

Major Radclyffe's Neptune (black), 1892

C.J. Radclyffe's Rock, 1880

C.J. Radclyffe's Dinah

C.J. Radclyffe's Bob, 1873

C.J. Radclyffe's Nell, 1887 (given to Mr. Guest)

C.J. Radclyffe's Countess

C.J. Radclyffe's Dido

from imported dogs but no particulars.

Ben of Hyde (Y), 1899

Col. C. Hambro's dog (from Milton Abbey)

Mr. Tapper's Duchess (black) (bred by Lord Wimborne)

Lord Wimborne's bitch

Pedigree of Major C. E. Radclyffe's BEN OF HYDE, 1899 (K.C.55689)

The First Yellow Registered Labrador, from whom descend the Kennels of Knaith, Zelstone, Folkingham, Boghurst, Hawkesbury, Kettledean, Braeroy and others.

6

Livers or Chocolates

THE origin of the Liver or Chocolate is no more misty than is that of the Yellows. Liver is a very old color and has appeared in all the Retriever varieties, as well as in Pointers, Setters, Spaniels, Irish Water Spaniels and Poodles.

The recessive genetic factor in the liver color (or chocolate or dark brown, or whatever one chooses to call it) was evidently present in one of the two Newfoundland puppies shipwrecked off the coast of Maryland, according to the well-known story of the beginning of the Chesapeake Bay Retriever. "The dog puppy was a dingy red," so the description goes, "and the slut pup black." No doubt there were many unrecorded dogs of such dingy red, or liver, or blacks carrying the factor among the dogs unloaded at the fishing ports of England and Scotland. An old description from Gordon Stables, quoting an unknown writer explains that "It would seem that in the earlier years of this century the color of the Newfoundlander was considered a matter of no importance, except by sportsmen who preferred for obvious reasons those of a darker and less conspicuous shade. Red, brown, brown and white and even yellow dogs were being landed at the quays at Poole. . . ."

As far back as 1892, two liver-colored whelps were known to have been born at the Buccleugh Kennel at Dalkeith. The Duke of Buccleugh wrote to Hurn Court, seat of Lord Malmesbury, for information on pedigrees, but the keeper could give little light on the subject.

Many of the Flat- or Wavy-coated Retrievers of Mr. Shirley, and also of Mr. Reginald Cooke of the well known Riverside prefix, were of the liver shades. Lee, in *Modern Dogs,* states that "the latter (brown Retrievers) are repeatedly produced from black parents and are equally useful and handsome as any other.

"Personally," he adds, "I have a great fancy for this pale chocolate Wavy Coated retriever. He is a novelty and if he shows the dirt more than his black parents his coat is equally glossy and he is quite as good tempered and sociable. The white or pale primrose colored eye is objectionable as it is in the black."

Gordon Stables, in his treatise, *Our Friend The Dog,* says: ". . . since the days when shows first started (the first being in 1859) great improvement has taken place in this breed of dogs. At large shows four different varieties usually exhibited are the Flat-coats, the Curley coated blacks, and reds or livers or the same style coats. There are sandy colored Retrievers and I have seen pure white Retrievers. . . . I have also seen pure white blackbirds and starlings and that is all I have to say about either!" He goes on to mention that "the Livers should in every respect be the same as the Blacks but that they are very seldom seen so good, either in coat or shape, that they are excellent water dogs and are even more lively than the black Retrievers and are more easily excited."

His description of the Norfolk Retriever bears retelling here, if for the color alone: "My readers have heard of the Norfolk Spaniel but few I daresay know that there is supposed to be a breed of Retriever common to the same county. For this dog there is no class at our shows which is equivalent to saying that he is not recognized by the Kennel Club. I never saw the dog myself, although I hope someday to make his acquaintance. I therefore cull the following description of the animal from my friend Hugh Dalziel in his British Dogs, but I must premise that the description is really by 'Saxon,' a well-known writer on British sporting subjects:

"The color is more often brown than black and the shade of brown rather light than dark, a sort of sandy brown in fact. Coat curly of course but the curls hardly so close and crisp as the show retriever of the present day but inclined to be open and woolley.

"The coat is not long however, and across the back there is often a saddle of straight short hair. In texture the coat is inclined to be coarse and it almost invariably looks rusty and feels harsh to the touch. This, however may be in some measure due to neglect.

"The head is heavy and wise looking, the muzzle square and broad: ears large and somewhat thickly covered with long curly hair; the limbs stout and strong with large and webbed feet. The tail is usually docked like a spaniel's but not so short. This seems to be quite a keeper's custom, and probably originated in the fact that to an inexperienced eye the tail of a puppy generally appears too long for the dog. However, although docking improves the appearance of a Spaniel, in my opinion it completely spoils the symmetry of a Retriever. I remember once asking a Norfolk keeper's opinion of a very handsome Flat-Coat that I had. After examining the dog very carefully the man said, 'Well, sir, he would be a rare nice looking dog if you'd only cut half a yard off his tail!' When white appears on the chest it is more frequently in the form of a patch or spot than a narrow streak. They are usually rather above than below the medium size and are strong, compact dogs. As a rule they are exceedingly intelligent and tractable, capable of being trained to almost anything both in the way of tricks and to the gun.

"In temperament they are lively and cheerful making excellent companions and it is rare that they are found sulky or vicious. When only half trained they are apt to be head strong and impetuous and though with a strong retrieving instinct are inclined to be a little hardmouthed. This defect can be traced to two causes—the result of injudicious breeding from hardmouthed parents or it may arise from slovenly handling in their younger days. However when they are wanted most exclusively for wild fowl shooting, this failing is not so much of the moment for they will be used principally for retrieving birds that have fallen in water and as fowl for the most part are very tough birds, the rough grip as a dog seizes a duck will not cause much mischief, and whilst swimming, the most inveterate 'biter' will seldom give his birds a second nip. . . . When accustomed to seashore shooting they will face a rough sea well and they are strong swimmers, persevering and not easily daunted in their search for dead or wounded game."

Many of the early trial winners in England were liver-colored Retrievers. The first trial, in 1900, was held at Havant on October 12th with an entry of ten dogs. The winner was Abbot's Rust, a Wavy-coated liver bitch—"what is still described as an old game-keeper's dog," writes Charles Eley, whose Flat-Coat, Bergholt Dale, was one of the contenders.

Less disdained in Labradors after the turn of the century, the liver shades made a little progress as time went on. The Hon. Lady Ward of Chiltonfoliat bred some, and one of hers was imported to the United States by Mrs. Marshall Field; this was Diver of Chiltonfoliat (Hayler's Joker ex Hayler's Fantasy), who was a grandson of yellow Field Ch. Hayler's Defender. Mr. Severn of Tibshelf has bred many over the years and Metesford, Blaircourt and other kennels have often produced the color.

That the majority of livers lack consistency of type, substance and the true "Labrador look," is unfortunate, and the prejudice they engender stems more from the above faults than from their color. The first liver bench champion was Am. Ch. Invail's Pogey Bait in 1956, bred by the late C. V. Brokaw and owned by Mrs. R. Haggerty. Coming from generations of blacks headed by the noted National Champion, Major VI, Pogey was a delightful Labrador with a soft, kindly expression from eyes that were dark golden instead of the more usual and baleful greenish-topaz. A second American champion has recently been made of Mr. R. Willey's Indian Valley Raed Wulf, the result of an imported mating of Altiora of Blaircourt, a black daughter of Ch. Ruler of Blaircourt, by Bart of Blaircourt. The only liver field champion to date is Mrs. R. Lewis's Can., Am. F. & Am. F.C. Kimbrow's General Ike, bred in Canada by Mrs. L. Robertson.

1964 gave England its first liver bench champion, Cookridge Tango, bred and owned by Mrs. Pauling and one of the most beautiful Labradors of today. She is a daughter of Ch. Sandylands Tweed of Blaircourt and has given the color great impetus. If livers could be guaranteed to reproduce in hers and Pogey's manner, their future would hold promise.

Mr. Lee Fisher of Alvaleigh kennels bred a few litters. Of one dog he wrote: "Chocolate Soldier, a solid black for six generations, when bred to Black Widow, whose dam was a yellow, produced 4 black, 3 yellow, 1 chocolate, arriving in the order of their dominance, black, yellow, chocolate."

Regarding other rare colors, an interesting report from a 1933 issue of *The Gamekeeper* mentions a strain of "white Labradors" that was treasured by Mr. Austin MacKenzie at Carradale, Argyleshire. They originated from a dog owned by Mr. Fenwick, called Sam, whose grandsire was Stag, the sire of Major Portal's Flapper. Sam came from the Duke of Buccleugh's imported strain of Blacks, yet three litters by Sam were all buff-colored except one bitch which was pure white. This bitch was later mated with Lord Lonsdale's Blanco, a bluish-white dog by Capt. Radclyffe's Ben of Hyde; the result was eight white puppies, and the color was apparently fixed.

One reads occasionally of black Labradors carrying Gordon Setter markings. The Standard abroad and here does not sanction such markings. Other varieties of Retrievers have also been known to show this idiosyncrasy, including the Curly Coats of which Brig. Lance, in an article on his breed in British *Our Dogs* in 1960, writes, "I have also had Curleys showing a distinct tan on the muzzle and under the tail. I can only think it may be a throwback to a Spaniel or Gordon Setter." This may be true to a certain extent with our Retrievers, which are still so close to the variations and compositions of what made them up in the past, whether in coat length, wave or curl, a "saddle back" or color. Such markings are similar to dogs of other breeds which the eminent geneticist, Dr. E. Fitch Daglish, described in British *Dog World* in 1961. When a Labrador breeder wrote of a litter in which there were seven Blacks and one Yellow, the ninth puppy being black-and-tan, Dr. Daglish listed such recognized breeds as Dachshunds and Dobermans, with black-and-tan marking which they normally have. He adds, "The factor for tan markings may be carried by an animal of any top color. In dogs it is frequently associated with black, blue, or chocolate when the contrast is clearly apparent such as chocolate Dobes or Dachshunds. If it is carried by a red or yellow animal the markings are inapparent as they blend closely with the general coat color. Theoretically therefore, there is a possibliity that black Labrador with yellow in its ancestry might receive the tanning factor from a yellow forebear in which its presence was totally unsuspected."

The importance of stressing the aberration of mismarking cannot be overemphasized. Although it is rare, it does occur, and in the hands of unknowledgeable back yard breeders, whose main outlets for sales may be pet shops, department stores or laboratories, it can do insidious harm to the breed. Such animals that consistently produce this deviation should first be test-mated with a completely divergent bloodline, and if the defect persists, they should be discarded for breeding. Whatever progeny is mismarked should be given away without registration papers and with adequate explanation for so doing.

We have had Yellows that, when whelped, sometimes had a white spot the size of a quarter on the top of their heads, a slight white slash on the muzzle, a white foot, etc. If the yellow was not too dark, much of this tended to disappear with age and a few castings. In blacks or fox reds, however, the white will persist and often spread and grow larger, and for show purposes this is not permitted.

We have also noticed that some Blacks (usually good-coated ones) tend to show a "pepper and salt" shading at casting time and some of them will have a permanent "ring" of a few whitish hairs (completely indiscernible outwardly) somewhere along the middle of the tail if the outer hair is ruffled back. This ring can also be seen on yellow tails, especially those of the darker shades.

Black on yellow is very rare indeed, but those who knew a well-known yellow champion in England, with generations of yellow behind him, remember that he had a black spot on his rib that could only be noticed if the outer coat were well pushed back. We had a yellow stud puppy by Ch. Lockerbie Blackfella similarly marked; we first thought he had gotten in grease under the car; the dark spot disappeared with his second coat but there were always a few black hairs among the yellows in that spot.

Interbreds

In England the Kennel Club recognizes Retrievers under one heading or breed, but classes them as different varieties. Under this heading one finds (besides the Goldens, Flat-Coats, Curly-Coats and Labradors) the Interbreds and, upon occasion, the Cross-breds.

111

Before the formation of the Labrador Club of England, the Kennel Club used to record puppies under the breed of the parent each puppy most resembled. For instance, in the case of a Labrador dog bred to a Flat-Coat bitch, some puppies might have been registered as Labradors, the rest as Flat-Coats. This however, proved most unfair and unsatisfactory for all varieties concerned, especially when members of the same litter might be winning in one ring as a Flat-Coat and in another ring as a Labrador.

A turning point in Labrador history was the inauguration of the British Labrador Club in 1916, after which the Kennel Club classified the Interbreds separately under the following rules:

1. "A dog from parents of the same breed but of different varieties must be registered as an Interbred. In all cases the names of the varieties making the interbreeding must be stated."

2. The rule for Cross-breds is: "Any Retriever or Spaniel ineligible for registration as Purebred or Interbred may be registered under the heading of Retriever Crossbred, or Spaniel Crossbred."

3. "A dog bred from a parent registered as Interbred must be registered as Interbred but provided the Interbred ancestors are registered at the Kennel Club a dog can be registered in a Breed register if in each of the first three generations of its pedigree one of the parents making the interbreeding is eligible for entry in that Register."

4. "For Gamefinders: this to include any dog whose owner wishes to run it at Trials, no matter what the variety, all dogs pedigree unknown, crosses between any variety of dog and Retriever, dogs ineligible for registration due to mixed parentage, etc. Subsequently the word 'Gamefinder' was changed to 'Retriever Outcross.'"

There were six Interbred field trial champions in England during the late 1920's.

DAZZLE—sire, Start (Lab.); dam, Duchess (I. B.); owner, C. Alington; breeder, C. Tunnard.

FLASHY—sire, Start (Lab.); dam, Jubilee Daisy (I. B.); owner, C. Alington; breeder, Capt. Duberly.

STOURHEAD NERO—sire, Never (Lab.); dam, Stourhead Satan (I. B.); owner, S. H. Hoare.

HAULSTON BOB—sire, Call Boy of Wolley (Golden); dam, Haulstone Jenny (I. B.); owner, J. Eccles.

BLACK DRUCE—sire, Bardolph John, (Lab.); dam, Dinah, (I. B.); owner, G. Homer.

GREATFORD QUICKSTEP—sire, Twist (Lab.); dam, Stanthorne Serula, (I. B.); owner, H. Peacock.

There were eight breeding combinations used during this period, and the facts prove that when interbreeding was resorted to it was to the Labrador that breeders of the other varieties turned for improvement in work such as speed, drive, pick-up and style. Their tabulation is:

Labrador dog and Interbred bitch	15
Golden dog and Interbred bitch	5
Interbred dog and Flat-Coat bitch	2
Labrador dog and Flat-Coat bitch	2
Yellow Labrador dog and Golden bitch	2
Flat-Coat dog and Interbred bitch	2

The kennels most interested in this breeding experiment were those of the late Mr. C. Alington, owner of Bright, whose line within five generations was to influence American dogs through Odds On and Peggy of Shipton; Mr. J. Eccles, of Haulstone Golden Retrievers; Sir Henry Hoare; Sir S. W. J. Marriot; Mr. Wood Homer, and Mr. Peacock (later Major Peacock of the Greatford Labrador prefix).

The Retriever Championship was won two years running (in 1921 and 1922) by Mr. Alington's Flashy, and five stakes were won by his Dazzle. In 1921 a Scottish Interbred, Logan Darkie, won the Kennel Club stake and was second in the National stake.

Dr. Stanton of Folkingham, who, within the past week of this writing, died at the age of ninety, also had a share of success at that time with his yellow Folkingham Blanco, who was by yellow Labrador Invergarry Sam ex Folkingham Budge. Budge was by a yellow Labrador ex a Golden dam. Both dogs won second and third in two Open stakes in 1925.

However, since that period, and through the period prior to and after the Second World War, Interbreds have ceased to be of importance, and although one notices occasional registrations of them in the Stud Book, whatever advantages may have been sought through them seem no longer of value.

Interbreds in America were few and far between; however in the

1930's, one of the leading trial dogs of the day, Tyke of Barrington, who had eleven points, was an Interbred. Tyke was by Dev of Devonshire, a grandson of an imported Flat-Coat bitch, Ashington Banter, bred by Mr. James Dickie. Tyke's dam was the renowned Kitty of Barrington, by Banchory Roger ex Balbeardie. Tyke's litter was accepted for the purpose of information for future registrations by the F.D.S.B. (Field Dog Stud Book), but the F.D.S.B. would not register the offspring as Labradors until Ashington Banter did not appear in a three-generation pedigree. The puppies were to all purposes typical Labradors and, but for thoroughly scanning the pedigree, one could not have known about the breeding.

In the pedigree of Dual Ch. Shed of Arden, one notes his dam (Field Ch. Decoy of Arden) has in her fourth generation the Interbred bitch, Jubilee Daisy. Jubilee Daisy was also dam of Mr. Alington's Interbred Flashy and is listed in the British Kennel Club as unregistered, as there is no information concerning her own forebears.

The British Royal Kennels: Wolferton and Sandringham

It is surprising that many contemporary breeders, even in England, know so little about the background of the Royal Kennels.

The traditional love of dogs always associated with the British people manifested itself throughout the Kingdom ever since Henry the Eighth, and royal records make mention of money "paid for hair cloth to rub Spaniels with," as well as "Robin, the King's Majesty's Keeper."

In more recent times, King George V's grandmother, Queen Alexandra, exhibited various breeds at Cruft's Dog Show in 1891. Both during his mother's reign, and after his succession to the throne, the late King Edward VII also exhibited at Crufts.

The greatest dog lover of them all, Queen Alexandra, was the first to use the Royal prefix Wolferton, the name of a little village on the Sandringham estates. The Kennels were built around 1879.

In later years, King George V adopted the Wolferton prefix and began breeding and exhibiting black Labradors. He had many outstanding dogs, including Wolferton Ben, winner of six Challenge Certificates, but who never became a champion because at that time Royal dogs never competed at field trials.

The fine working qualities of the Sandringham dogs were attributed to His Majesty's personal supervision and interest, and the supremacy of the Sandringham inmates rested on Sandringham-bred dogs and no others. Many of the Royal lines were based upon Whitmore and Banchory blood.

The head game keeper at that time was Mr. F. W. Bland, who was in Royal service for forty-four years, and to whom King George V made the gift of a choice bitch: Sandringham Soda (Ch. Toi of Whitmore ex Wolferton Solo), who subsequently proved herself an invaluable matron.

The King's three favorites were Scrum (so named because a touring Australian rugby team was paying a visit to Sandringham just as he arrived as a new puppy), Simon, and Bob (he always liked to have a "Bob" among his personal dogs). These dogs not only led a separate existence from the others, under a selected keeper, but were the only dogs to accompany His Majesty to Balmoral. "A rare old philosopher is Scrum," observes a contemporary article, "calm and businesslike, and as indifferent to outside people and events, as he is apparently unmoved by the high position he holds!"

They were all first-class workers, as the King insisted that every dog in the Royal Kennel be first and foremost of an active, tireless working type.

The late King George VI's preference leaned towards the Yellows; they were treasured shooting companions, but never shown on the bench. His winning entry at the Kennel Club's Open Stake at Sutton Scotney, in 1948, was Windsor Bob, yellow son of Dual Ch. Staindrop Saighdear ex Mrs. MacPherson's Field Ch. Braeroy Ruddy, bred and handled by Mr. George Hallet, head keeper at Windsor. Mr. Saunders of Liddly was one of the judges; he remarked on the excellent performance of Bob: "You just wouldn't have known Hallett carried a whistle at all."

Queen Elizabeth II's tastes are more for the Blacks, and the choice of contemporary bloodlines at Sandringham today are of the highest caliber. A promising ten-month-old litter we saw there in the winter of 1962 was by Field Ch. Roffey Dunlop, a son of Field Ch. Glenhead Zuider out of a trim black bitch, Sandringham Mask, a daughter of Field Ch. Harpersbrook Poacher ex Sandringham Mint. Mint is a granddaughter of Zuider, through her sire, Field Ch. Hiwood Don. This was a repeat mating of a previously successful one, which is currently represented by F. C. Sandringham Ranger, a good-looking dog, which won the 1962 All Aged Stake at the Essex Field Trial Society, handled by Mr. Curtis.

It was a great privilege for us to visit the Kennels at Sandringham. They are beautifully laid out, built of red brick and black iron palings over eight feet high. Each run is square and roomy.

Nearby is a large training paddock, with the young rabbits running free, and a long, narrow, wired-in area containing five jumps of graduated heights, the highest of which I should estimate as being about five-and-a-half feet. Because British trials and shooting are run naturally in open country and around farms, it is essential that all dogs learn to jump well carrying game, and as many of their retrieves are over five-barred gates, hedges and even barbed wire, all training kennels are equipped with a group of hurdles.

Mr. Curtis kindly brought out many individuals for us, giving them all retrieves, and then all were sent over the jumps and back again. It was a rare pleasure to see such a lot of good-looking workers; they were all of a type, of good size, with great drive. They ought to bring immeasurable satisfaction and continued success to Her Majesty in the future.

Labradors as Police Dogs in England

In 1937 the Home Office started an experimental training school at Wastwater, near Newbury, under the direction of Mr. H. S. Lloyd, who is well known over the world as the owner of the "Ware" cockers. Mr. Lloyd's task was to ascertain which breed of dogs would be most suitable to the Police Force.

After experimenting with a number of breeds, the Labrador was chosen as the best dog for accompanying constables on their rounds and for doing liaison work. Since 1946 they have been useful members of the Metropolitan Police Force, apprehending criminals as successfully as other breeds used for this purpose. Because of their super-sensitive noses they are used exclusively for picking up elusive clues of human scent and following their leads to culprits.

Lady Simpson, owner of the Foxhanger prefix of dual-purpose Labradors, writes of the dogs trained for this work:

"Here is a Labrador with a London policeman. I have attached

Foxhanger Otter and bobby, P. C. Scogings.

His Majesty's favorite dogs, Scrum, Bob and Simon.

to the photo a press cutting of the arrest he made at the time the photograph was taken, which is considered to be particularly good dog work. This dog, Foxhanger Otter, P.D.ex., T.D.ex., known as 'Simon,' is by my dog, Foxhanger Mascot, P.D.ex., T.D.ex., W.D.ex., U.D.ex., C.D.ex., out of a good type of working bitch, bred from gamekeeper's stock. Mascot is the fourth generation of owner-bred-and-trained 'Foxhanger' Labradors and has 32 awards in Retriever Field Trials and 16 awards in Championship Trials for Police and Tracking Dogs as well as numerous Championship Show awards. Otter has a number of awards in Championship Trials for Police and Tracking Dogs. He joined the Metropolitan Police at fifteen months, has a number of other good arrests to his credit, and is considered to be one of the best of the breed in the Service. In efficiency, the Labradors are very highly thought of, and all those on patrol work have a good record of arrests.

"Labradors trained for Tracking do extremely well in our Championship Working Trials, where they compete against professional Police dogs of all breeds. The Ch. Stake now consist of: ½ mile track, 3 hours cold, to find 3 articles left by the tracklayer; search an area (free) of 25 yds. square of foiled ground to find 4 articles in five minutes. Articles are often as small as a button or latch key; Scale Jump, 6 feet; Long Jump, 9 feet; and Clear Jump, 3 feet; a small amount of Obedience work. There have been only three Labradors in history to become Working Trial Champions of which I owned the first, my well-known post-war foundation bitch, Working Trials Ch. French Court Ripple, T.D.ex., and bred the second, Working Trials Ch. Foxhanger Maize, T.D.ex. Two wins are necessary to become Champion."

As War Dogs in England

In World War II, the Labradors were credited with doing a superb job of detecting land mines, reputedly accomplishing the work faster and with more intelligence than any other breed.

Mr. Lloyd was also in command of the training branch called "The War Dog School of Great Britain." In connection with the progress the breed made in absorbing the intricate training involved, Mr. Lloyd remarked: "The mere fringe of a dog's mentality has yet only been touched upon, and it is a subject of the deepest interest in research for the benefit of the nation. The latent capa-

A mascot of Her Majesty's Armed Forces.

Learning to parachute in the airforce.

bilities of the dog are unpredictable and such experimenting is of little value if undertaken in a small way.

"One cannot form any worthwhile opinion with any degree of certainty unless many dozens of dogs are examined and trained— or the exception—the super dog, confounds the whole issue. Much has been discovered about 'scent' during the training of War Dogs, which has completely scrapped pre-conceived ideas on the subject and should have far reaching effects on the training and judging of field and hound work in the future."

The tenacity and determination of the Labrador character has shown itself to be of value in many fields, including the current course in parachute jumping, recently instigated by the Air Force.

Guide Dogs for the Blind

In Britain the Labrador is used in great numbers for leading the blind. The breed's stable nature and innate dependability have gained it top rank there as a guide dog. Over 70% of the dogs housed at the beautiful kennels of the Guide Dogs For the Blind Association at Leamington Spa are Labradors, mostly Yellows, very good-looking, many of them show quality.

Guide dog work for the breed in America is also reaching large proportions: there is a school in California composed entirely of Labradors. As far back as 1935, the late Mrs. Harrison Eustis, who founded the "Seeing Eye" in Morristown, New Jersey, wrote to Mr. Franklin Lord, who was then carrying the Labrador Club column for the *American Kennel Gazette,* about a black bitch given for training by Mr. Wilton Lloyd-Smith. Mrs. Eustis wrote, "We had some difficulty in breaking down her belief, as she had already been field trained, that she had to stay at heel and wait for commands.

"Once she got it into her head that she could and would have to *use her own initiative* in solving problems, all went well and her schooling followed smoothly."

The Buccleugh prefix, owned by the present Duke of Buccleugh, has not been included in the previous listing because it is still unique in not having ever been associated with commercial markets or public competitions. It is the only kennel of its caliber, as far as I know, that has been kept completely to itself, as a private and personal pursuit, in exactly the same manner as when it was first started in the 1800's.

Through Lord Malmesbury's Tramp, from which the most influential group of Labradors is descended, one finds Buccleugh Avon, commonly accepted as the ancestor of all modern Labradors. A son of Tramp, he was the forerunner to the Munden Kennels, down through consecutive channels to the present day. Buccleugh Bachelor gave impetus to the Adderley dogs and their subsequent generations, and the influence was sustained through another pivotal sire, Malmesbury's Sweep, a contemporary of Tramp, in whose line we finally approach Field Ch. Flapper, grandson of Buccleugh Jock, and great-grandson of Buccleugh Ned.

Stemming from these original lines, with as few outcrosses as possible—and those resorted to only to freshen the blood and protect against becoming too inbred—the Buccleugh dogs we were privileged to see in 1962, on our visit to Scotland, were a handsome, uniform lot. Out of the twenty-odd dogs we saw, only three were yellow; they had been brought in from outside lines, and were much on the stamp of Braeroy Maid, pictured on page 71.

Dogs required on the Buccleugh estates number anywhere from 90 to 130, and are used chiefly in Scotland, almost continually throughout the year, in all types of terrain, including moorland, dense cover and water. Physique and endurance are insisted upon for their high standard of performance, and only the ones that have these requisites are used for breeding.

The dogs we watched work were rugged, medium-sized, well-balanced, good coated, and classically headed, with the proverbial manners of the British shooting dog. It was quite a sight to see this large group emerge from the kennels, in perfect unison at heel with the trainer, whose voice was so low in his commands that only the dogs could hear it. There has never been any attempt to show the dogs nor enter them at trials; they have always been kept solely for work on the estates. According to the old, carefully preserved records, kindly shown me by Lord Dalkeith, their pure strain throws only Blacks, and essential breed characteristics have been adhered to throughout the years.

Only occasionally is stock sold and then it is only to those who appreciate this particular line and have an interest in keeping it up to the standard it has always maintained. The Buccleugh prefix is a rarity in our contemporary times.

7

Labradors in America

WHAT was known as an "English Retriever" in America at the end of the nineteenth century, was not seen in great numbers until the 1920's. Occasional pen-and-ink drawings, reproducing such specimens as "Paris and Melody," were printed in contemporary dog books, mostly facsimiles from Stonehenge editions. It is not until 1885, at the "Annual New York Dog Show"—held at the old Madison Square Garden from April 28th through May 1st, with an entry of 950 dogs—that one finds an "English Retriever."

In a class for dogs and bitches, a certain Edward Dexter's "Belle Tinker," breeding not given, appears in the catalogue. One may take it for granted that she was a Flat- or Wavy-coated variety, as Curlies made their appearance over here later.

In *The Dog Book* (1906), Watson writes, in his chapter on Retrievers: ". . . there seems to be little prospect of the English Retriever gaining a foothold in this country, although in Great Britain and Ireland he is of great use, as Setters and Pointers are preferred not to touch dead game. To avoid calling upon a Setter or a Pointer to retrieve, the Englishman takes another dog afield with him, whose duty it is to retrieve wounded and dead game. At the present time the usefulness of the Retriever is made still more apparent owing to the change in style of shooting, by walking up the game, the battue, and the driving to the guns. In such cases, the Retriever is a necessity, and as it is likely to be a long time before any appreciable amount of American shooting will be done along these lines, the day of the Retriever is yet dim in the future for us. . . . On the Rutherford estate at Allamuchy, at Fisher's Island, and at the estate of the late Mr. Moen, and Mr. Bayard's preserve at Massachusetts, where English pheasants are reared for battue shooting, a few Retrievers are kept, and we occasionally seé a few others at the New York Dog Show; these are mainly of the smooth variety, but from time to time a rough coated or curly specimen has been shown. The case is very different in England, where Retrievers are frequently the best represented at Shows and much attention is paid to their improvement."

J. A. Graham's book, *The Sporting Dog* (1904), mentions only Chesapeakes and Irish Water Spaniels. "We have been advised," he writes, "that a number of Retrievers have been imported for use in some of the southern preserves, but throughout the country at large, Americans prefer the Setter or Pointer, broken to retrieve as well as point back. . . . Retrieving from water is in a bad way as part of American sport. A glance at the benches at any show tells how feeble is the interest. Unless it is one of the stronger Eastern events, there are no Chesapeakes and only a few ordinary specimens of the Irish Water Spaniel."

American Kennel Club registrations for Retrievers in 1926 (they were all grouped together at that period) were three in all, compared to England's breakdown for the same year: 71 Curlies, 371 Flat-Coats, 400 Goldens, 16 Interbreds, 35 Crossbreds, and 1,247 Labradors.

Whatever few were sporadically brought over by sportsmen at the turn of the century, the first official, registered A.K.C. Labrador arrived in 1917, the year after the British Club was formally inaugurated.

This was a Scottish bitch, "Brocklehirst Nell," by Brocklehirst Bob ex Stewardness, a bitch of strong Munden blood on the distaff side. She was dam of Brocklehirst Daisy and Field Ch. Nith of Halleaths, who was later to become sire to Mr. Robert Goelet's American trial-winning dog, Nith's Double. Both were by Dual Ch. Banchory Bolo, and bred by the late Mr. Dinwoodie.

123

From that date on, imports began arriving from various points in greater numbers, and from the late '20's through the '30's one saw the first great influx—the backbone and future of the breed in this country.

The interest in Retrievers, and in Labradors particularly, centered around a small group of sportsmen in the East, accustomed to shooting in Scotland and on the continent with Labradors. Their ambition and fancy soon gave impetus to the idea of enlarging their scope at home by developing this breed and gradually holding field trials among themselves, patterned after those they were familiar with abroad.

"For services rendered" the Labrador in America, the following are the earliest prefixes of importers and active breeders of that day:

CAUMSETT, Mr. and Mrs. Marshall Field
BLAKE, The Hon. Franklin P. Lord
ARDEN, The Hon. W. A. Harriman
WINGAN, J. F. Carlisle
GLENMERE, Mr. Robert Goelet
EARLSMOOR, Dr. Samuel Milbank
MEADOW FARM, C. L. Lawrence
BARRINGTON, T. M. Howell

The greatest credit in acquainting the Americans with Retriever training is due the Scottish trainers that came over in that period: Dave Elliot for Wingan; Colin Macfarlane for Glenmere; Tom Briggs for Arden; Douglas Marshall for Caumsett; Jim Cowie, (who arrived in 1920); Jock Munro; Lionel Bond; and the family Hogan —Martin and his two sons, Francis and James—who pioneered Retriever trials throughout the West.

The Hon. Frank Lord's *American Kennel Gazette* column, representing the American Club in its initial stages, was of invaluable aid to those who knew little about the history of the breed.

Mr. Lord was a close friend of Lady Howe and acquired many dogs from her; among them was Boli of Blake, the first American Bench Champion, who was by Ch. Ingleston Ben ex Banchory Trace, bred by Lady Howe in England and whelped in the U.S.A. Subsequently Mr. Lord brought over Boli's dam, Trace; Banchory Student; and Middlecoate Endeavour, who was by Dual Ch. Bramshaw Bob ex Tutsham Brenda, a Beningbrough Tanco daughter.

124

Mr. Lord's correspondence through his *Gazette* articles was voluminous at the time, with new fanciers from all parts of the country eager to learn about the "new" Retriever. In October, 1933, he wrote: "A Dr. George Patton of Greeley, Colorado, says he has a good dog and hopes someday to be able to begin breeding Labradors. As one knows, this resulted in Dr. Patton's well-known Bankhurst prefix, workers and bench dogs of excellent type.

"Another Coloradan sends in news that he has 'just gotten a yellow dog, a year old, a grandson of Eng. Field Ch. Hayler's Defender.'" Mr. Lord ends this article on a humorous note: "I have had some rather amusing experiences in the last ten days with the fox hunting people of Syosset, Long Island. My kennels adjoin those of the Meadowbrook Hunt and I have been exercising four or five Labradors behind a horse. At the same time every groom in the countryside is firmly convinced that I am trying to collect a pack of black Foxhounds! All sorts of questions are asked; the Labradors make a friend of everyone who sees them, packed up and trotting along behind my horse."

In 1936, Mr. Lord visited England as a guest of the late Mr. McCandlish, then chairman of the Kennel Club. He gives us a vivid picture of his journey: "My first visit was to Mr. Heaton's place, where I saw his great producing matron, Xmas Nora. She is the dam of Lady Howe's Ch. Cheverell's Ben, also of Cheverell's Don, now in our country. Mr. Heaton goes to Scotland with his dogs in August and works them there and upon his return, he says he can get home in the afternoon by five o'clock and kill twelve to fifteen partridges before dinner, so that the dogs get their daily work on game. This is a tremendous advantage to what we have here. I also spent a day with Lord Ashburton, whose shooting experiences and knowledge of guns always makes it a privilege to talk with him. He has seen most of the great Labradors at work, from Flapper down, and was a great friend of Lord Chesterfield, who often loaned him Field Ch. Beningbrough Tanco for a day's shoot.

"On the following day at Lady Howe's at Idsworth, we went to the Kennel Yard and Gaunt brought out Cheverell's Ben, his sire Ch. Ingleston Ben, Towyriver Don, a son of Mrs. DuPont's Ch. Towyriver James, and Dual Chs. Bramshaw Bob and Banchory Painter. . . . I gave Gaunt a 'silent whistle' which neither he or

Lady Howe believed would work. If they prove practical, it will certainly be a great blessing at trials not to hear a handler yelling for his dog and blowing a very annoying, shrill whistle. We then returned to the Kennels to see the dogs exercised.

"The large exercising run is a quarter of a mile round; all the Setters and Pointers were placed in the run. Then Gaunt appeared with a Labrador called Banchory Trailer, whose greatest joy in life seems to be running around the outside of the run, while all the dogs shut up in it run after him. As it was a hot day, he was allowed to do only three circuits, when he was stopped. The Labradors were then placed in the run and Trailer started out again. This time, Mr. McCandlish, who was present, timed him and he ran the half mile two laps, in one minutes, five seconds.

"This trip of mine was for the purpose of learning more about Labradors and also more about the methods of training. One thing about Labradors in England at shows; they seem to be more keen, and were shown on a loose lead, rather than held up by the head and tail on a block the way they are shown in this country. I wish more Labrador judges in America could go over and see what a *real* Labrador is—for I fear we shall get away from correct type if we go on as we are now; above all, they are shortcoupled with an otter tail!"

The efforts and absorbing interest of J. F. Carlisle, his participation in trials and at shows, and his generous offering of dogs at stud to new breeders gave the breed a tremendous push forward in this period. He helped to form a nucleus of good material to build upon, together with the superb group of imports that included Banchory Nightlight, Jetsam and Trump, Orchardton Doris and Dawn, Liddly Bulfinch and Drinkstone Peg, all champions, with the latter's famous "Britishbred-American whelped" litter by Dual Ch. Bramshaw Bob. All this gave the breed the right start, and it was not long before history repeated itself, so that the Labrador was on its way to overtaking all the other Retriever varieties in the New World, as it had in the Old.

Among Mr. Carlisle's imports, the most successful was the above mentioned Field Ch. Nightlight, by Blackworth Midnight ex Dinah of Wongalee. Midnight was by Wilworth Rip, one of the foundations for the Sandylands kennels in England. Nightlight won the 1937 Field and Stream Trophy, trained and handled by Dave

Ch. Orchardton Doris of Wingan with Mr. J. F. Carlisle after winning the Amateur Stake at the Club's fifth trial in 1935.

Field Ch. Glenairlie Rover, flanked by his two sons, left to right, Field Ch. Freehaven Jay and Field Ch. Glenairlie Rocket.

Elliot; another was Field Ch. Banchory Varnish, by Dual Ch. Banchory Painter ex Hawkesworth Glimmer, a Glenhead Bess daughter. All these dogs carried Mr. Carlisle's Wingan affix. Varnish was later acquired by Mrs. Kathleen Starr Fredericks, and sired American Field Ch. Firelei of Deercreek and Field Ch. Meadow Farm Night, bred and owned by Mr. C. L. Lawrence, who had earlier imported the latter's dam, Cheverell's Dina, a product of an Ingleston Ben-Xmas Nora mating.

Soon to follow these leading lights were Mr. Howell of Barrington; Mr. and Mrs. Wagstaff of Ledgelands; Gerald Livingston of Kilsyth; Mrs. H. S. DuPont of Squirrel Run; and the late Mr. J. Gould Remick's Marvadel, whose first allegiance was to the Curlies and Chesapeakes, but who gave unstinted support and encouragement to the Labrador and its future activities.

Western interest was on a par with eastern activities at this period. One of the most prominent sires of the day was Field Ch. Glenairlie Rover (Dalbeattie Tango ex Lady Matilda), bred by gamekeeper P. Coleman in Scotland and imported by Harold Ward of Woodend Kennels in Minnesota. Subsequently, Rover was acquired by Fletcher Garlock, who already owned his outstanding son, Field Ch. Glenairlie Rocket.

Rover was not only a brilliant worker but an invaluable sire, and two of his sons, Rocket, and James Lamb Free's Field Ch. Freehaven Jay—both ex Mr. T. M. Howell's Spot of Barrington— added enormously to the quality of American trial history. Mr. Howell was an importer of note, and his Barrington affix was enhanced by the purchase of the prolific brood bitch, Ch. Balbeardie, sent over in whelp by Banchory Roger. Balbeardie produced his great bitch, Kitty of Barrington, which when bred to another Howell import, Fresco Smut (in direct line to Peter of Faskally), produced a strong rival to Glenairlie Rover in Field Ch. Nigger of Barrington. Nigger was a highlight at trials in the '30's, and a worthy sire. Spot of Barrington's dam, Wendy of Barrington, was little sister to Nigger. Spot's sire, Duke of We Twa, was by another import of Mr. Howell's, Withington Banter, ex Ch. Balbeardie. Balbeardie figures strongly as granddam to Rover and Peggy of Shipton.

Rover also sired Glenairlie Blackjack, Eve, and Freehaven Molly,

Peggy of Shipton (Roland of Candahar ex Gehta), bred by Colonel J. Sleeman and owned by the Hon. W. A. Harriman, arrived in the U.S.A. in July, 1929.

Grouped here are four field champions handled by Francis Hogan at the First National Retriever Club Championship Stake at Quogue, Long Island, Dec. 5–7, 1941. Left to right are: Glenairlie Rocket, Orchardton Dorando, Goldwood Tuck, King Midas of Woodend and Orchardton Dale.

all litter mates; their dam, Langbourne Darkie, was a granddaughter of Ch. Banchory Trueman ex Stourhead Gilda, an interbred.

Field Ch. Nigger, handled by Frank Hogan, who also included him in his famous group of Labradors exhibited at sportsmen's shows throughout the country, had many top wins east and west. Not the least of these was the Labrador Club's eighth trial, in November of 1938, whose judges included F. P. Lord, F. Squires, and the Hon. Joan Hill Wood, her first venture among us. Nigger won the 1938 Field and Stream Trophy under the ownership of Gordon P. Kelley, handled by Frank Hogan.

At the ninth Labrador Club trial in November of the following year, he won the Open stake with Blind of Arden second, Rip (Golden Retriever) third, and Braes of Arden fourth. At the Annual meeting that evening, a cable was sent to the directors of the Labrador Club in England, expressing the hope that Retrievers over there would come through the present troubled period, and a discussion followed of the possibility of bringing over some of their leading dogs for safe-keeping. This was unfortunately not followed up, and irreparable losses to the breed were the result.

Dr. Samuel Milbank spent his boyhood in close proximity to Chesapeakes, extensively bred by his late father, Dr. Milbank, Sr., but he had never owned a Labrador. His Earlsmoor prefix had long been associated with the best in Terriers, and he had great experience in Spaniel circles, as shot, judge and amateur handler. A famous Scottish surgeon, Dr. J. Wilson, owner of the well-known prefix of Solwyn, which was later to enhance the breeding stock of Ledgelands Kennels, met the doctor on a visit to the States and suggested he acquaint himself with a Labrador, promising to find him a first-class one.

The subsequent importation of Raffles, who was bred in Scotland by W. Farquarhson, and chosen as suitable by Dr. Wilson, started a collaboration for Dr. Milbank and W. A. Harriman that molded the fortunes of the Arden kennel, setting a precedent for quality that has never been equaled by any other Labrador Kennel in America.

Raffles, incidentally, was a litter brother to L'Ile Airman, a big winner in his day, sire of Mr. Twyford's Field Ch. Adderley Tax and Mrs. MacPherson's Braeroy Rock. The stroke of fate that occasionally occurs just at the propitious moment, bringing forces of

Ch. Raffles of Earlsmoor (Thatch of Whitmore ex Task of Whitmore) pictured winning the Fourth Annual Club Specialty in 1936.

Major K. J. Malcolm receives a pheasant from his Scaltback Nell of Glenmorag at the Midlands Counties Retriever Club's Open Stake, November, 1961. This field of sugar beet is an example of the kind of field that British land tests offer in heavy cover.

good together, manifested itself with the importations of Odds On, by Mrs. Marshall Field, Peggy of Shipton, by Mr. Harriman, and Raffles by Doctor Milbank.

Mrs. Field was the former Mrs. Dudley Coates of Ballathie, Perthshire, Scotland. As early as 1922 she was interested in furthering the cause of the Yellows, in conjunction with Col. Swan, the Marquis of Granby and Major Lucas, from whom she acquired Hawkesbury Jade, also owning a prominent working Yellow in Kinclaven Bob, by Invergarry Sam. She was prominent in postwar trials, her most outstanding dog at the time being Troop of Faskally. Her handler, until she moved to England, was David Seath, cousin to John Annand of Glenhead.

This trio of dogs, in the unification of their bloodlines, proved to be one of the proverbial "nicks" in breeding that occur only once in many generations. What Banchory Bolo was to England, certainly Raffles became to America; a beautiful dog in his own right, superbly bred, an excellent worker as well as a bench winner, he was soon to exert influence as a gifted stud force. The old saying that "good ones rarely come from anything but good ones" was never more clearly demonstrated than with Ch. Raffles of Earlsmoor.

We may digress here for a moment to mark the organization of the Labrador Club in this country, incorporated in 1931 with its first slate of officers as: President, Mrs. Marshall Field; Vice-president, Mr. Robert Goelet; Secretary-Treasurer, Mr. Wilton Lloyd-Smith.

The first field trial for Retrievers in America was that of the Labrador Club's own inaugural trial, held in December of the same year at Glenmere, Mr. Goelet's estate at Chester, New York. Judges were Dr. Milbank and Mr. David Wagstaff.

In the American-bred stake of eleven starters, three were placed: Sam of Arden, Moose, and Glenmere Monarch.

One of Mr. Harriman's earliest Labradors was Sam of Arden, whelped in 1929, by an import of Mr. Clarence Mackay—Duke of Kirkmahoe ex Peggy of Shipton. Moose, whelped in 1927, was not registered, but was by a dog called Moose of Idaho ex Scottish Lassie. He was owned and trained by Tom Briggs, Mr. Harriman's trainer, and won very well for him. Monarch was from two imports of Mr. Franklin Lord's—Banchory Minority ex Neighla.

The Open stake at this first trial had sixteen starters; all but one were imports:

1. Carl of Boghurst (yellow), by Corona of Boghurst ex Hayler's Linda;
    breeder, S. Watson; owner, Mrs. Field
2. Odds On, by The Favourite ex Jest;
    breeder, Mr. Alington; owner, Mrs. Field
3. Sab of Tulliallan, by Sam of Invertrossachs ex Dinny;
    breeder, Mr. W. Black; owner, Mr. Goelet
Equal 4. May Millard (bitch), by Kinmount Diver ex Corporal's Daughter; breeder, Mr. Lightfoot; owner, Mr. Field
Equal 4. Glenmere Joe, by Sab of Tulliallan ex Peconic Vixen; breeder and owner, Mr. Goelet

The following list of pedigrees will be of use for reference in tracing the prominent lines that have consistently had the most direct bearing upon contemporary American dogs. The great old names, as one can observe, invariably follow through, repeating their dominance to the present day.

Due to a limit on the number of pedigrees I may include, I have tried to give a broad view of as many different bloodlines as possible, by choosing individual dogs in such a manner, so as not to have a repetition of names that appear again and again in so much of the genealogy. Dogs such as Peggy of Shipton, Ch. Balbeardie, Shed of Arden, Hiwood Mike, Odds On, and others, reappear so frequently that it is unnecessary to have separate pedigrees for them, due to the advantage of having five generations on most, and thus showing in many instances of their influence being felt in the subsequent generations that have followed. Raffles of Earlsmoor is an exception, as I felt that, to breeders, it would be informative to point out his complete Whitmore background, as an example of a dog almost continually bred from one kennel's entire line.

I also considered the importance of including Smudge of Prairie Creek Farm, who, but for his untimely passing, would have, through authoritative opinions, no doubt taken his place as one of the outstanding American-bred sires. Massies Sassy Boots was not used at stud as extensively as for instance Cork of Oakwood Lane, nor were many of the old highlights of former days, but that does not in the least take away from their unassailable value. I consider it fortunate to be able to include three dual champions in Bracken Sweep, Little Pierre, and Grangemead Precocious; the inclusion of the four bitches, whose records as workers and producers speak for themselves, illustrate to advantage the principle and ideal of the George W. Holmes Trophy, for the furtherance of training and development of bitches in this country.

This first success pointed the way to annual club trials and the gradual formation of other clubs throughout the country.

An outstanding litter was bred at Arden in 1933, by Odds On ex Peggy of Shipton. Two in the litter were destined to make their mark on future generations: Decoy and Blind of Arden, both of which became, respectively, the first American field trial champions of each sex. They made their first appearance at trials as puppies in the fourth Labrador Club trial in November, 1934. In a Puppy stake of seven starters, Decoy was first, Blind second, Bulga Brant (a litter mate) third, and a dog called Dasher of Glenmere fourth, who was bred by Mr. Goelet. Also at this period Mr. Goelet bred Michael of Glenmere, who was to become the first American Dual Champion. Michael was by Ace of Whitmore ex Vixen of Glenmere, the Whitmore here being a Canadian prefix.

Regarding this particular trial, Mr. Lord in one of his monthly *Gazette* columns observed, "I met Udo Fleischmann, one of the judges, on the train and he said that the work of the dogs was very good, but that he did not believe it was fair to the judges to give them 3 stakes which included a pheasant drive and a water test, of so many dogs in one day. He suggested that the club hold a two-day trial, if possible to be held at some place like Fisher's Island, and the birds walked or hunted with Pointers or Springers, as he thought this was a better test of a Labrador than the present method.

"In the Open stake," he continued, of the 24 starters there were several new imports to be seen, including many of Mr. Carlisle's, Wagstaff's Solwyn Juniper, Mrs. Wagstaff's Della of Knocke, Dr. Milbank's Raffles of Earlsmoor, and Mrs. Schiff's Peter of Cookhill."

Stake winners were:
1. Decoy of Arden
2. Blind of Arden
3. Ch. Raffles of Earlsmoor
4. Drinkstone Pons of Wingan

It will be observed that, from that date on, per Mr. Fleischmann's suggestion, all future meetings were of two or three days' duration.

There follows a written report by Mrs. Walton Ferguson about the 1935 Labrador trial, where the Open stake placings went to Blind of Arden, Decoy of Arden, Bugla Brant, and Orchardton Doris. It is reminiscent of the valuable critiques that are still assiduously written each year abroad for the annual Bench Show and Trial meetings in the British Club's useful little year books.

"The Labrador Retriever Club," wrote Mrs. Ferguson, "deserves all the praise for the conduct of its trial at Bedminster on Mr. Pierpont's estate. The ground could not have been better, giving the Retrievers a chance to demonstrate their ability in different kinds of cover; the beats were excellently chosen and excellently laid out and marked. The method of releasing birds could not have been improved upon and the birds were wonderful—strong flying, heavy, healthy birds, all of them. The guns were adequate in number, fine trial shots and most understanding of trial requirements. Beginning with the Open All Age, the work of the various dogs was marked as follows: Blind of Arden, winner of the stake. This dog is a brilliant trial performer, nothing less can be said of him. He has pace, style, drive and dash. He is the keenest Labrador I ever saw, is a perfect marker, has beautiful pick-up, carry, and delivery, and with all his keenness and quality, he is under the most absolute control. In short, on the day, Blind was faultless and even in that hot company, won easily. If his handler spoke to him I did not hear it. A motion of the hand or low whistle was all he needed, and that perfect control has taken away nothing from his natural qualities, only enhanced them by making them subservient to his handler's wishes. Blind is a model of perfect training with none of his own initiative lost thereby, which is as it should be. Blind was down three times and each time down, his work was perfect.

"In the first series he did an excellent piece of work in marking at a distance the fall of a bird another dog was sent to retrieve. He remembered the fall for a considerable length of time while the other dog quested unsuccessfully. On being ordered to retrieve when the other dog was taken up, Blind went at great pace at once to the fall he had marked and remembered, found at once and made a perfect fast retrieve. On his third time down, a bird was shot which scaled over the top of a hill a long distance away, and fell out of sight. Blind marked the line of flight, and on being ordered to retrieve from where he stood, he raced to the top of the hill and over out of sight. The judges and his handler then started to walk up the hill when Blind suddenly appeared on the hilltop looking towards his handler. A motion of his handler's hand sent him on again and before judges had reached the top, Blind came back again at full speed with his bird. It was evident that as he was able to mark only the line of flight and not the fall, he missed the bird on his first cast, and wished to make sure of his handler's position, and also possibly wished to reassure himself of flight direction through a signal from his handler. Seeing him, he was at once reassured and he made a further cast out of sight, and found his bird.

"Such a dog is using his intelligence and he will not waste his time nor his handler's time in being uncertain of either of their positions. I have never seen a better Retriever than Blind, or a more intelligent dog, or a better trained one. On the day he was perfect.

"Decoy of Arden, second. Another high class performer, losing to Blind only in the matter of real brilliance. . . . Decoy marks the fall as does Blind and does not mark short of it and start questing too soon. Both Blind and Decoy were handled and trained by Thomas Briggs, and the great performance they both gave in this stake is a tribute to Mr. Briggs' training and handling ability.

"Bugla Brant, third. Here is a dog without the finished training of the two placed above him but he is a dog of great natural ability. Brant is slower than the winners, with not quite their dash and style but he is a keen dog of great intelligence, an honest, thorough worker, and he had a chance to prove his nose. . . . He did one of the most beautiful pieces of work on a runner I have ever seen. A bird was shot, the fall of which Brant could not mark. The bird hit the ground running, and Brant took the direction of the fall, acknowledged it at once, from the fall, took the line with no hesitation whatsoever and went off on the line at a great pace over a hill, into a wood and out of sight. He was gone from five to eight minutes out of sight of his handler, who, to his great credit, remained perfectly silent, showing by that silence, his confidence in his dog. In due time Brant came back over the hill with a big pheasant in his mouth, which was apparently enjoying the ride, head up and looking around. He delivered the bird perfectly to his handler, not a feather ruffled, and be it remembered that Brant had to catch a strong running bird to pick it up from a long distance; that piece of work stamps him as a dog of great ability; his other work was uniformly good in every department.

"Orchardton Doris of Wingan, fourth. This import is a high class bitch with beautiful style, great pace and very keen. . . . She and her handler, Dave Elliot, gave a beautiful exhibition of giving and taking direction to an unmarked fall by hand and whistle, without undue disturbance of ground on either side. She has an invariably excellent pick-up, carry and delivery. The second time down, Doris went a little wide of a fall she should have marked and did not obey her handler's whistle at once, but made a good find of a bird shot a long way out and an excellent retrieve. Doris is a bitch that should be near or at the top in any company.

"All these dogs took the water test with ease. Blind picked up his bird and turned in the water like a high powered cruiser, giving consistent brilliance in this test as he did in all the others. I was told afterwards, that Blind, Decoy, and Brant are all of the same litter, which is a record any breeder may well be proud of. I only wish it were possible for an American bred and trained dog to compete in trials in England, for from what I saw today, I feel sure that they could give a good account of themselves in any company."

In the early days field trials were very different from those of today. Mr. Dave Elliot was very kind in offering to write me a detailed description of what constituted an American trial at that period:

"Many changes have taken place in the conduct and proceedings of running early field trials in the United States. The small entries in those days put no pressure on the clubs either in regard to time or finances, so both could be completely ignored.

"Almost all tests started with a single bird released from a trap planted in cover on the course. These traps had wire netting placed around them so that when the trap was sprung, the pheasant would fly, when it ran up to the wire; a long string was attached to the trap which released it when pulled, and a man was assigned by the judges to do this.

"All such tests were walk-ups, and clubs did not look for uniform cover. More often than, not, we worked in low brush, cover that was well over your dog's head and dotted with cedar and pine. All you could do was watch the cover ahead, and try not to get caught behind some of this tall stuff. You were not picked up after having retrieved your single bird, but would be kept in line until the judges were satisfied that they had seen enough of your dogs. I should mention here that we had two judges and they would have two dogs under them at one time—one on their left and one on their right.

"They would call the lowest number first on the first time round. However, after each dog had worked, they would call whichever number they wanted, as there was no longer any running order. No previous notice was given as to what the tests would be, how many birds you would get, or in what order.

"If you failed to find a bird, your bracemate would be sent to look for the same bird; very embarrassing if he wiped your eye! This failure would not put you out of the trial if the rest of your work had been respectable; you could go on and even score—and it was even still possible to win. After all the dogs had been tested, the judges would change dogs; each one would take what the other had had in the first round, so therefore they had separate scores. Only if a dog broke (ran in) or was proved hard-mouthed by both judges, would they know until the end of the series, what each other's dogs had done. On a break or hard-mouth, one would immediately notify the other.

"The Labrador Club always had a pheasant drive in the Open All Age stake. All dogs still in the stake would be brought up to the stand at one time, and if you had more than one dog in competition you brought them all to heel. When the drive was over, the judge would indicate what dog to run. You never knew how many birds you would be asked to pick up. If very few birds were shot at your stand, they would move you up to where there were more.

"These jobs today would be called 'blind retrieves.' You just sent your dog in the direction indicated, and let him hunt. It must be remembered that handling as understood today was unknown at that time. I handled mine in the first trial and was not given a very favourable reception. Much more admiration was felt for dogs *able to do their own work*, without outside assistance.

"In all landwork, more than one dog would be sent out to work at the same time, in fact, in these drives, three or four dogs would be working simultaneously. There was no such thing as a 'bad fall'; everything down was considered fair game, seldom did you get an opportunity for accurate marking; you or your dog would see the bird in the air, and if he did not see it, you sent him out and left him alone to hunt. In view of the fact that handling was in its infancy, there was nothing else they *could do;* and that is one thing those dogs were wonderful at! Experience taught them how to *hunt,* it taught them *self reliance,* they knew how to follow a cripple, they seldom if ever looked for help, and most of them stuck well in the area.

"It was common practise for one handler to have two dogs in line during a walk-up, and again, the judge would designate which of the two dogs was to be worked.

"All water work in Open stakes was conducted over *live decoys,* and if your dog retrieved one, you could just count him out. You would always get one long bird shot into open water from a boat, or into reeds. However, one or more would be shot over these live decoys and this could prove a difficult test, depending on the roughness of the water. Long Island Sound and the Great South Bay were popular sites in those days, and could be very choppy. If the water was choppy and your decoys were tossing on the waves, it was often difficult for your dog to distinguish between the shot bird and the decoy, especially if your shot bird was still kicking and active in close proximity to a decoy.

"You prayed for a stone-dead duck, but you prayed even harder if you got a cripple who was parading around among the decoys; you just prayed your dog would know the difference! In this instance, the guns, would however, shoot the cripple for you, but often your dog would have been sent before you realized just how active your bird was, and the damage would be done before your guns got a chance to finish him off. It is then that you would most willingly shoot the guns! Their faces are red, but yours is white!

"While you are doing all this, your open water duck has either come ashore or headed out to sea, depending on the wind and tide. If he has come ashore, then all you have to do is to be able to put your dog down the shore. If your duck had come ashore, the wind would have to be an inshore wind, and therefore blow the scent in to your dog. If your bird has gone to sea, he will be well off the boat from which he was shot, and no doubt will look like a very small cork if you can see him at all.

"This is where a dog used to rough water excels. Such a dog would head out to sea, then rise in the water, look around, spot his bird, and off he'd go. He would keep doing this until he had his bird in view. A low swimmer was at a decided disadvantage, and in view of the fact they did not handle, this type often failed.

"This is where my ability to handle pulled me out of many such situations. I think I did much to prove to the skeptics that handling had its good points. All your ducks in those days, were shot, so you never quite knew what your fall would be.

"Many of the duck blinds of the early 30's had no look-out for the dog; he may have seen his bird in the air, but not down. In some cases a make-shift blind was made on the spot, with brush and reeds, and as a rule your dog had to go out from the back of the blind, as the front would be too high for him to jump from a sitting position.

"Very little if anything was done to make the tests uniform; everything was run as a real ordinary day's shoot. You prayed for luck, and if your prayers went unanswered, it was just too bad. You were not given another opportunity if you got a bad fall or a bird was a cripple. Those birds were there for your dog to *find,* and if *he* couldn't do it, they would get one that *could.* The element of luck was strong.

"Any dog in those days which did not possess a full measure of *natural ability* was sorely handicapped. If they could not accomplish 90% of the job by themselves—they were out; in those days very few handlers suffered from cold hands! They just kept them in their pockets!

"Through it all, there was very little griping. You would hear some remarks among the handlers to the effect that *some* people were damned lucky when *they* had been getting all the bad breaks; all in all, it was good fun, and one did see *natural* dog work. Dogs had full rein to develop their natural instincts, and the job was theirs alone.

"To compare the dogs of yesterday with the dogs of today, I have no hesitation in saying that the former were better game finders. They ruddy well had to be, as they got no help from any quarter.

Because they had to find the cripples as well as the dead, more training was given towards this goal. I am afraid today that we are much too ready to give them a helping hand, and too many look for it. Also, in view of the fact that we are no longer permitted to pick up cripples at our trials, little interest is given to teaching them this phase of work. We are no longer putting them through the apprenticeship that teaches them *self-reliance.* They depend too much upon *us,* and would be much more independent if they were still 'the poor man's son.' We are too generous and expansive with our help; we give them a college education, but hand them the books with the answers.

"Our Derby dogs of those days had it easy compared to the ones today. As in the Open stakes, each judge had two dogs in line; tests were simple single birds on land, a double in water, and occasionally a double on land in the last series. The youngster was judged on his natural ability, hunting his area with style and speed, and staying out there and not running back after a couple of casts. If he showed keen interest in all his work, good clean retrieves to hand and was fearless in the water, he would get the vote over one which may have been more accurate than he, but showed little enthusiasm in his work.

"I believe that judging the Derbies in this manner had much to do with so many at that time, coming through and making worthy Open All Age material. In comparison to the number of dogs put into training today, I believe we came through to Open All Age stakes with a *better percentage.* I am confident that if we judged our Derby dogs on natural ability, put less stress on how many birds he can mark, how well he can be lined out to the falls, how far he can swim in a straight line, or in fact—how far he can walk on the tight-rope; if we would ease off in the rigid manner in which all these things must be accomplished and bring him through that period of his life by giving him encouragement in bringing to the top his natural gifts, instead of trying to put an old head on young shoulders, I am positive more young dogs would become worthy as All Age contenders. As it is, our present day demands burn out too many before they reach maturity. In training a Derby dog today, one has to be prepared for any eventuality.

"Some parts of the country demand more of Derby dogs than others. Of course, it will be pointed out, that Derby dogs today are equal to the tests given them. This is true, for no matter what tests are given in Derbies, there will always be dogs equal to them, but what percentage? I would say, very small. Is it worth it to ruin so many to suit the few, especially when such work is not necessary?

"We would be doing our respective Retrievers a great favour if we confined our ambitions to developing our young dogs more slowly. If race horse trainers demanded the same from their young stock as we do, I am afraid they would not come through with many good two year olds. We have too many failing, both in the physical and mental tests, and it is only because such tests are beyond the realm of reason. Sacrificing so many youngsters brings the same penalty as cutting down a forest before the timber is mature. Both labour and material is a complete waste.

"Age is another point where many young dogs are ruined. A puppy, seven or eight months of age shows a great desire for retrieving, is fast, hits the water, in fact does everything in such a pleasing way, he has his owner purring like a kitten, and he never misses an opportunity of working his pup and showing him off.

"After a month or so this pup begins to show less enthusiasm, but seldom do we think that it is our own doing. We come to the conclusion that the pup is not as bright as we thought he was, and instead of honouring the danger signal and easing off, we take it out on the puppy by *forcing* him to do it; thus we pile one wrong on top of another. By now, however, it is beginning to dawn on us that perhaps we are pushing too hard, but boy, oh, boy, you'd better have a pup with a very sensible disposition and not too sensitive, if you ever hope to recapture the ground you've lost. *We never ruin the mediocre puppy;* it's always the brightest that feels the weight of our over-zealous efforts.

"I believe in taking a six months old puppy or even younger, and giving him little things to do, but not in any sense of the word asking him to accomplish these little things in all seriousness. By this I don't mean that if he is retrieving an object he should be allowed to play with it; he should be taught to bring it to hand. Such playfulness in retrieving can lead to some very bad habits, such as hard-mouth. If you are going to teach him to sit, do so gently; don't use force at this time. You want him to do all these things smartly, but he must *enjoy* doing them. There is plenty of time, when he is 10 months old to a year to impose more pressure.

142

If you instill fear and boredom in a puppy, you will have little more than the physical left to work with.

"As to sex, I actually prefer a bitch as a worker. Except for the times when they are in season, I think a well trained bitch puts her mind to her work better than a dog and they are not interested or upset by other smells. I also think that in many ways they are more loyal. The general lack of interest in developing bitches is understandable, as they seem to have the habit of coming into season at the most inconvenient times, and can upset a whole kennel during field trial season.

"We can seldom train a bitch in the same manner as a male. However, your own temperament and your general outlook towards the animal you are training has much to do with success or failure. If you don't favour a bitch, then leave them alone. She would have to show tremendous promise before you could believe in her. There are confirmed bachelors among trainers when it comes to female Retrievers. Nevertheless, if more interest were taken in developing bitches, we should know a little more about what we are breeding. Since most people are agreed that the bitch contributes at least 75% to the quality of a litter, I feel it is important that they have sufficient training to demonstrate the required characteristics, for without such training, we are whistling in the dark, just hoping that what we want will be reproduced. Training is the only way I know it can be done; you cannot judge a book by it covers."

The name of Arden will always take pride of place in the annals of American Labrador history. Through its unique triumphs in having bred all of its illustrious inmates it has become an American hallmark, and its genuine prestige is still acknowledged today.

Decoy won her field championship in 1936 and was bred the following year to Ch. Raffles of Earlsmoor. This was the first of two rare litters by Raffles. There were seven black puppies, and they were to be known as the "Scottish" litter, their names being, Moor, Braes, Banks, Heather, Burn, Loch, and Gorse.

Dr. Milbank preferred choice of litter to a stud fee, and selected Moor when he was about six months old. Two others were sold. Loch went to a man named Laidlaw in Toronto. He was in training with Jim Cowie and was showing great promise, when he suddenly succumbed to an acute infection. The other, Burn, went to Mrs. William DuPont, and only had been exhibited once, going best of breed at the old Baltimore show, when he too died. Gorse was given to Mrs. Morgan Belmont and the other three, Banks, Braes and Heather, remained at Arden.

The record of this litter at shows and trials is unique. Braes and Gorse became dual champions, the only Labradors of their sex to do so until recently; Heather, Banks, and Moor were bench champions of high caliber, Moor carrying the distinction of being the first Labrador in this country to win best in show. His record was five best in shows, twelve groups, twenty-seven placings, and forty best of breeds. Handled exclusively by Jim Cowie and exhibited only forty-two times, he was owned throughout his bench career by Dr. Milbank. Far-flung campaigning, on the scale to which we are now accustomed, was not pursued then for the purpose of maintaining a fashionable record.

Moor also holds a very special record, probably not equaled by another breed—that of having won the Annual Specialty *five times,* from 1938 through 1941, and again in 1943. Although Moor did not attain a field title, he was an intelligent worker and placed in Open All Aged stakes.

Contemporary with this litter was the one which produced another outstanding Arden bitch, Field Ch. Tar of Arden. Tar was by Hiwood Risk, a dog imported from Lady Hill Wood by Mrs. David Wagstaff, and her dam was Peggy of Shipton. Tar passed into Paul Bakewell's ownership when still quite young, and gained her title and her successes under the Deercreek banner. Apart from her illustrious trial career, she, like her kennel mate, Decoy, has earned lasting fame as a matron of first magnitude in having produced five field trial champions, four of them bitches. The combination of Tar and Hiwood Mike brought out Field Ch. Black Magic of Audlon, owned by Mr. and Mrs. Mahlon Wallace (and who, until 1962 was the only Labrador bitch ever to win the Nationals); Confusion at Deercreek; and Dual Ch. Little Pierre of Deercreek. All three were littermates.

When bred to Field Ch. Banchory Varnish of Wingan, Tar produced Field Ch. Firelei of Deercreek. She was next mated to her son, Little Pierre, and got Field Ch. Mary-Go-Round at Deercreek. This last-named was a lovely and stylish little bitch; we shall always remember her, working in such unison with Dolly Marshall at some of the Long Island trials.

A successful breeding will not always repeat itself. In this instance it did, in 1939, with almost all of the best concentrated in one individual. This was the Arden "Fish" litter, with such names as Bass, Marlin and Shad given to the puppies. By a typographical error on the registration blank, *"Shed"* emerged instead, but, as a contemporary critic put it: "Even as Shed, this Lab was as a fish in water, and it was his fearlessness in ice-coated lakes that so often won him the approval of the judges. . . ."

Bass and Marlin became bench champions, the latter going as choice of litter to Dr. Milbank, proving herself a good worker by qualifying twice for the Nationals.

Shed's first appearance at trials was at the Labrador Club's tenth meeting, in 1940, when he was twenty months old. Judges were Henry Ferguson, Robert McClean, and Sherburne Prescott. The Derby winners were:

1. Hiwood Tossa of Wingan (imp.)
2. Shed of Arden
3. Butch of Sing Sing
4. Bass of Arden

Shed was acquired shortly after by Paul Bakewell and was developed by him and "Cotton" Pershall, gaining his dual title and earning his greatest honors under the Deercreek colors.

Shed of Arden's qualities were of the highest; he epitomized an ideal. Certainly during his long and brilliant heyday—and even today, when we regrettably find him receding farther and farther back in pedigrees—he captured not only the imagination of the American dog public at large, but also of everyone else who had anything at all to do with Retrievers. By those who are knowledgeable, he was considered to have embodied the greatest qualities a Retriever can possess in equal parts: looks, performance, and the priceless gift to transmit these from generation to generation. He was truly Arden's crown jewel. Following is a list of all the dogs at Arden:

1942, 1943, and 1946 Nat. Ch. & Dual Ch. Shed of Arden.

The "Fish" litter which included Dual Ch. Shed and Chs. Marlin and Bass of Arden, taken at eight weeks. (Ch. Raffles of Earlsmoor ex Field Ch. Decoy of Arden.)

Dual Champions	*Field Champions*
Shed of Arden****	Peconic Pyne of Arden (Import)
Bengal of Arden**	Blind of Arden***
Braes of Arden** (bitch)	Tar of Arden** (bitch)
Gorse of Arden** (bitch)	Decoy of Arden (bitch)
	Gun of Arden**

Bench Champions

Echo of Arden* (bitch)
Buddha of Arden** (bitch)
Quail of Arden (bitch)
Earlsmoor Moor of Arden*
Banks of Arden*
Heather of Arden (bitch)
Earlsmoor Marlin of Arden** (bitch)
Bass of Arden

  * Placed in Open stakes.
 ** National Qualifiers.
*** First American Field Trial Champion.
**** Three times National Champion, a still unbroken record.

From these dogs, and especially from this superlatively strong bitch line, have descended over seventy field champions and stake winners—grandget and great-grandget of Shed of Arden.

An import destined to make an indelible mark on the fortunes of American stock was English Field Ch. Hiwood Mike. Mike was sent over to Mrs. John Williams by Lady Hill Wood in 1940. He was already five years old at the time. Dave Elliot re-trained him for American competition, and he won his U.S. title in 1941 and qualified for the Nationals the same year (handled by Dave). The following year he qualified again and was run by Jim Cowie. He was a well-bred-looking dog of great character and could have become a dual champion. American lines were enormously enriched by his advent, for he exerted notable influence through many kennels such as Grangemead and Deercreek, and on individual dogs such as Good Hope Smoake and Angus, who in their roles as producers were invaluable.

The celebrated name of Deercreek belonged to Mr. and Mrs.

147

Paul Bakewell, III. Starting in trials in 1939 with his renowned Golden Retriever Rip (the first Retriever he ever owned), Paul Bakewell proved himself an astute and gifted amateur handler not only in winning the first Open stake with a Golden Retriever but also by being the first amateur to win an Open stake over professionals. He won the Field and Stream Trophy three years in a row: in 1939 and 1940 with Rip, and in 1941 with the intrepid Tar of Arden, handled at that meet by the popular and talented "Cotton" Pershall.

The year 1942 marked the holding of the National Championship as it has been held ever since, and Mr. Bakewell piloted Dual Ch. Shed to victory there. The following year, Shed repeated this win under the able guidance of Cliff Wallace, as his owner, Lt. Bakewell, was far away doing a job with the Navy. The year 1946 brought the owner and this sterling dog back for a third triumph, Shed being six years old at the time.

Deercreek's fourth victory was in 1949, with Field Ch. Marvadel Black Gum, also owner-handled. Deercreek bred an outstanding dog at this period in Dual Ch. Little Pierre of Deercreek (mentioned earlier) by Hiwood Mike and Tar of Arden. The threesome, Shed, Mike and Little Pierre, constituted a formidable trio of stud forces whose combined talents reached a high-water mark in American trial breeding. Still another dog bearing the Deercreek affix was Dual Ch. Matchmaker for Deercreek, bred by Bill Rook, whose Bigstone kennel has given nine homebred field champions to the American scene, including the 1962 National winner, Field Ch. Bigstone Hope, a bitch. Bigstone has invariably carried a very strong bitch line through Tops and Little Tops of Bigstone.

Deserved prominence is due Mr. Thomas Merritt's Grangemead kennel. The dual purpose principle embraced here is second to none, and rather intensifies the power in descent, as far as working competition is concerned. Mr. Merritt writes, "We first ran in trials in 1940. At the start I did the training and running, but after we had acquired several young dogs, it took more time than I could give. We never had yellows—only blacks. One of our first puppies was Grangemead Angel, a daughter of Freehaven Jay. We bred her to Hiwood Mike, and Sharon was one of that litter. Precocious was a bigger dog than Shed. He was a good marking dog, especially in water and especially strong in water triples."

English and American Field Ch. Hiwood Mike
(Pettistree Dan ex Pettistree Poppet).

An Arden group—left to right: Scotch, Decoy, Blind, Joy, Sam, Pyne, and
Banks.

This kennel is perhaps best known through its most distinguished inmate, Dual Ch. Grangemead Precocious, trained and brought to his title by Harold Berentsen, and one of Shed's brightest contributions to the breed. Precocious was so named because at the tender age of *seven months* he sired Dual Ch. Cherokee Buck, Field Ch. Medicine Man, and Mr. James Lamb Free's Field Ch. Freehaven Muscles, all litter mates. The irony that sometimes accompanies such events was that Grangemead Sharon, their dam, was given away and lost track of before the litter was old enough to prove itself—and thus was lost to the breed the probable and possible repeat matings of a rare quality.

Grangemead's reputation is worthily sustained in its unequaled record of four Dual Champions in four consecutive generations, namely, Shed of Arden; his son, Grangemead Precocious; his grandson, Cherokee Buck; and his great-grandson, Alpine Cherokee Rocket. Buck was originally owned by Robert Darlington of Chicago. Harold Berentsen also handled him to his field title, and the bench championships of all four dogs was under the handling of Hollis Wilson.

Timbertown Kennel of Mrs. Kathleen Starr Frederick was started in 1930, although as early as 1925 she owned a dog called Black and Blue Jett, British bred, by Beechgrove Dick ex Beechgrove Gypsey, and a bitch called War Bride, also imported, by Diver of Liphook ex Ridgeland Black Diamond. Diamond was imported in the late 1920's by Mr. J. Redmond, and was one of the foundation bitches of the Liddly Kennels of Mrs. Saunders at Newbury. Old Peter of Faskally is in the background here.

Between 1932 and 1940, Mrs. Frederick had imported quite a few blacks, some of which carried the prefix of Mr. David Black. Partial to the Blacks, Mrs. Frederick bred out the yellow and chocolate colors that accompanied some of these lines for her own particular purposes and concentrated upon lines of Hiwood Mike and that of her homebred Field Ch. Timbertown Clansman. Clansman was trained by Paul Svane, whose Woodcroft prefix figures in many pedigrees, and attained his field title under Cotton Pershall. His breeding stems from Mr. Carlisle's Pons Jr. of Wingan and Orchardton Doris. A daughter of his, Bracken of Timbertown, a wonderful producer in her own right, was dam of Mr. Pomeroy's mettlesome Dual Ch. Bracken Sweep.

150

Clansman also figures in some of the dogs bred under the West Island prefix of Mr. and Mrs. Junius Morgan—to be specific, Field Chs. West Island Whiz, Tramp, and Comet, litter mates, by Mr. Edward Spaulding's exceptional import, Dual Ch. Treveilyr Swift, ex a Clansman daughter. Mrs. Morgan also bred a field champion bitch, West Island Raven, by Ch. St. Jones Blackie ex Deercreek's Baby Cakes, owned by Charles Hook. The aforementioned Comet was also an Amateur Field Champion under the late Mr. C. V. Brokaw's ownership.

The Dolobran prefix of Mr. C. A. Griscom III; the Marvadel prefix of the late Mr. J. Gould Remick; the Black Point prefix of Mr. Daniel Pomeroy; and that of Kingswere, were prominent in working circles in the postwar years.

One of the first Labradors owned by Miss Frances Griscom was imported in 1934—Cheque of Glencove, by Banchory Don ex Choice of Glencove, she by Peter of Faskally. Mr. Griscom bred four field trial champions in Dolobran Little Ash, Spook, Streak, and Smoke Tail. A fifth, Angus, became an Amateur champion under Mr. Brokaw. Spook and Streak were little brothers, by Field Ch. HiTail of Wyandotte ex Dolobran Lassie. HiTail was a grandson of Banchory Nightlight of Wingan and of Hiwood Mike, while Lassie stems from the yellow Dunottar lines of Mrs. Catherine Morgan's Dunottar prefix. All but Angus were National qualifiers. Field and Am. Field Ch. Dolobran Smoke Tail won it in 1960; he was a son of Spook, and was always handled in his four years of National competition by his owner, Richard Hecker.

One first notices mention of Mr. Remick's interest in the breed through a litter he bred in 1934 by a black import called Hayler's Fort. Fort was Scottish-bred, by Fort of Kinclaven ex Borisdemain. The litter was mixed in color and Mr. Remick registered Dinky and Hayler's Girl, Yellows, and Marvadel Peter, a Black who was the first of his Labradors to carry his prefix.

The outstanding inmate of this kennel was the 1949 National winner, Marvadel Black Gum, by Mint of Barrington ex Marvadel Cinders. Mint was a son of Field Ch. Glenairlie Rover, and Cinders a daughter of Dr. Milbank's Ch. Raffles. Black Gum, acquired by Paul Bakewell, was trained and handled by him to his championship. Black Gum holds the record for the number of years of National qualification, which was *eight;* he qualified for

151

the first time in 1946 and the last time in 1953. An excellent Marvadel brood bitch was Topsy, bred by Mrs. David Wagstaff by Ledgelands Donne ex an imported bitch, Solwyn Duchess. Topsy was granddam to three field champions.

The Black Point kennel of Mr. Daniel Pomeroy was based on Glenhead Sweep, imported from John Annand, Perthshire. Sweep, by Banchory Benmhore ex Glenhead Biddy, carried Adderley blood on his dam's side; his sire, Ingleston Nith, was by Lochar Mac ex a Dinwoodie-bred dog. Whelped in 1943, Dual Ch. Bracken Sweep was a Canadian bred, ex Mrs. Frederick's Bracken of Timbertown, and was acquired by Mr. Pomeroy at the age of two, when he had already won his Canadian field title. He made history at American events.

His American field championship was won in 1946, his dual title followed, and his National win came in 1947. He was retired in 1952, one of the six Retrievers up to that time to accumulate in excess of 100 points (111). Cotton Pershall was usually at the helm with him, and he also did well for his owner in Amateur stakes. He was a dog of keen, brilliant temperament, and a good-looking bench specimen. He was considered a smooth, manageable worker, with great style. He had a vitality that took him far beyond the allotted span of a dog's life, for he lived to the age of sixteen and was a National qualifier for seven years. His get include Field Chs. Black Point Dark Destroyer, Sweep's Chance, Field and Am. Field Ch. Nilo Senator, Field Ch. Woodcroft's Inga's Bonus, and 1950 National Derby Ch. Black Point Dark Tiger. In addition, he was grandsire of 1955 National Ch. Cork of Oakwood Lane.

Kilsyth prefix was owned by the late Mr. Gerald Livingston. Beginning in 1916, he was connected with various breeds of gun-dogs and hounds and was, in addition to being president of the Westminster Kennel Club in the 1930's a well-known field trial and bench judge. An early import of his was Maize of Kilsyth, by Kin-purnie Joe ex a Withington Flapper daughter. He owned three National qualifiers: Field Ch. Cliff's Patrick, by Itaska's Black Prince ex Queen of Bismarck; Field Ch. Black Prince of Sag Harbor, by Marvadel Flash ex Smokey of Northwest (Flash being by Good Hope Angus, a Hiwood Mike son); and Field Ch. Kilsyth Cleo, by Field Ch. HiTail of Wyandotte ex Hiwood Tern of Wingan. Tern was litter sister to Hiwood Tossa, a brilliant young Derby winner, both of which were sent over as puppies by Lady Hill Wood. They were by Hiwood Mike ex Field Ch. Adderley Tax.

The Kingswere kennel was owned by Mrs. Mariel King, who at the start was connected with Golden Retrievers through her brother-in-law, the late Samuel Magoffin. She became interested in Labradors through close association with Mrs. Sarah Edmiston, former professional handler at shows, and an all-round judge since 1924—one of the first women judges in this country. Mrs. Edmiston made quite a few trips to England with Mrs. King, and her active period in the breed was in the middle '30's. During that time she brought over two litter sisters, Jewel and Jean of Sandylands, by Jerryslad of Sandylands ex Jetta of Sandylands. Jean was an excellent worker, especially in water, and Mrs. Edmiston bred her to Mr. Riley McManus' Good Hope Smoake, a Hiwood Mike son. Jean produced two promising males, both of which were given to Mrs. King; one was killed in an accident, and the other became Field Ch. The Spider of Kingswere.

Dave Elliot came in to take charge of the Kingswere dogs at the time, and upon arrival was told by the kennel-man that Spider was no good and no time should be wasted on him. Dave decided otherwise, considered him the best of the lot, and developed him until he left, whereupon Cotton Pershall continued with him and completed his field championship in 1949. Spider qualified for and completed four Nationals, two under the ownership of Kingswere and two under Leonard Florsheim, with whom he also won his Amateur title. He was retired in 1952 after gathering sixty-two Open stake points. Whelped in 1946, he died in 1958. His working record, plus his contribution as a sire, more than justified Dave's initial opinion of him. His get include Field and Am. Field Ch. Hal's Spi-Wise Zeke; Field Ch. Deercreek's Bewise; Field Ch. Jolor's Amigo, owned by Mrs. George Murnane; Dual Ch. Kingswere's Black Ebony; Field and Am. Field Ch. Webway's Crusader; as well as others of merit. Crusader in turn sired two Beautywood dogs (this prefix is owned by Dr. L. M. Evans). The dogs were Ch. Beautywood's Carbon Copy and his sister Peggydidit, both owned by Mrs. George Murnane, and a third dog from this line, John of Sandylands, a littermate to Spider, who sired Field Ch. Hot Coffee of Random Lake, owned by Mr. John Olin.

153

A royal foursome—Dual Ch. Grangemead Precocious and his three sons, Dual Ch. Cherokee Buck, Field Ch. Cherokee Medicine Man and Field Ch. Freehaven Muscles, all out of Grangemead Sharon.

I₤ is interesting to note that a kennel devoted to the purest in bench lines, such as Sandylands of Mrs. Broadley in England, should have inadvertently influenced, with such success, a line of trial dogs in America. This example may seem to contradict the principle of choosing working dogs from bench lines. Exceptions prove the rule, but one must be familiar with lines that make up the individual pedigrees. These dogs, although not of trial background, were good workers, and the unfortunate "stigma" of the bench cannot apply to them.

In listing the active kennels of today, it is simplest to tabulate the National Retriever Championship *winners*, their owners and kennel prefixes. As was mentioned previously, the first field trial for all Retrievers was held in 1931:

1932	2 trials	1937	10 trials
1933	2 trials	1938	18 trials
1934	4 trials	1939	15 trials
1935	5 trials	1940	20 trials
1936	8 trials	1941	21 trials

During the War years, while we in America were most fortunate in being able to breed or compete at all, the number of trials dropped in 1942 to fifteen trials, in 1943 to twelve, and in 1944 to sixteen. The year 1946 saw the gradual rise to thirty, and on upwards until, in 1961, there were 105 Open stakes held throughout the country. The Labrador Club itself offers two trials a year, a spring meet for all Retrievers, and a fall trial for Labradors only.

In view of the fact that the Labrador Club has, over the years, published five books encompassing the years from 1931 through 1956, with a 1959 supplement, and plans to edit others in the near future, it is unnecessary here to repeat and reprint all they contain regarding lists of judges, trials held, wins, and the dogs' breeding. These books are available through the club secretary and are to be found for reference also at the American Kennel Club library and at sporting book shops. The National Retriever Field Trial Club has also published two books of its own activities and history, also procurable through their secretary.

However, for the record, the manner in which the National Retriever Field Trial Club came into being may be explained here for those unfamiliar with trials in general.

As field trials became increasingly popular, Eltinge Warner, publisher of the sporting magazine, *Field and Stream,* donated a trophy to be offered annually to the "Outstanding Retriever of the Year," and 1935 marks the first year of competition and points towards winning it. Such points were to be gained in all licensed trials in their Open stakes, with the ratio of 5 for a 1st, 3 for a 2nd, 2 for a 3rd, and 1 for a 4th.

The 1955 club book explains in its preface that "annually the competition for the Trophy was most keen, and for a fair chance to win it a good dog would have to be run in as many trials as possible. In at least a year, the winner may not have accumulated a sufficient lead to insure the championship until the last trial. This uncertainty created a most unsatisfactory situation. Towards the end of the trial circuit, some owners with a good dog would hope that the points accumulated would hold up to win the championship and would not make the extended last trip to secure additional points; others would fight to the last ditch; this could and did develop into a very expensive procedure.

"A number of more experienced Retriever men felt the desirability of one great Championship stake to be held annually, at the conclusion of the regular season, in which proven dogs would be eligible to compete.

"At a meeting in New York in 1941 a committee was appointed to form a Club to conduct such a trial. The winner of the club's trial was to be awarded the title of 'National Retriever Champion of 19___.' As in every new venture there were skeptics—those too anxious to retain the status quo, who for the first year refused to go along with the title. . . . Consequently for 1941, confusion existed between the FIELD and STREAM Trophy and the club's award for first winner of this trial. This of course did affect the entries, but it was corrected, so that in 1942 and thereafter, the title has been awarded as decided on by the club. The FIELD and STREAM Trophy was also given along with the Championship Trophy throughout 1953, when it was finally retired as the club felt that more than one Trophy would be superfluous."

Following is the complete list, as of 1962, of National Retriever Club winners, their owners and kennel names:

Mr. and Mrs. Paul Bakewell owned the winning dog 4 times.

DEERCREEK: '42, '43, '46, '49.

Dr. and Mrs. L. M. Evans, owned the winning dog 2 years.
BEAUTYWOOD: '44, '50 (both Golden Retrievers).
Mr. and Mrs. George Murnane owned the winning dog 2 years.
MACOPIN: '57, '59.
Mr. and Mrs. John M. Olin owned the winning dog 2 years.
NILO: '52, '53 (And bred the 1958 winner).
Mr. and Mrs. Mahlon Wallace owned the winning dog 2 years.
AUDLON: '45, '51.
Other winning owners, listed chronologically, are:
Mr. E. N. Dodge, 1941 (Golden Retriever).
Mr. Daniel E. Pomeroy, 1947.
Mr. Clifford Brignall, 1948.
Mr. and Mrs. Fraser Horn, 1954.
Dr. A. H. Mork, 1955.
Mr. W. T. Cline, 1956.
Mr. K. K. Williams, 1958.
Mr. Richard Hecker, 1960.
Mr. L. J. Snoeyenbos, 1961.
Mr. and Mrs. Bing Grunwald, 1962.

FIELD AND STREAM WINNERS

Year		Breed	Sex	Owner	Handler
1935	Field Ch. Blind of Arden (Odds On ex Peggy of Shipton)	L	D	A. W. Harriman	T. Briggs
1936	Field Ch. Dilwyn Montauk Pilot (Prince of Montauk ex Sou West Sal)	C	D	D. Carpenter, Jr.	H. Conklin
1937	Field Ch. Banchory Nightlight of Wingan (Blackworth Midnight ex Dinah of Wongalee)	L	D	J. F. Carlisle	D. Elliot
1938	Field Ch. Nigger of Barrington (Fresco Smut ex Kitty of Barrington)	L	D	G. P. Kelley	F. Hogan
1939	Field Ch. Rip (Speedwell Reuben ex Speedwell Tango)	G	D	Paul Bakewell, III	Paul Bakewell, III
1940	Field Ch. Rip (Speedwell Reuben ex Speedwell Tango)	G	D	Paul Bakewell, III	Paul Bakewell, III
1941	Field Ch. Tar of Arden (Hiwood Risk ex Peggy of Shipton)	L	B	Paul Bakewell, III	C. Pershall

WINNERS OF NATIONAL CHAMPIONSHIP STAKE

1941	Field Ch. King Midas of Woodend (Rockhaven Tuck ex Glittering Gold)	G	D	E. N. Dodge	F. Hogan
1942	Dual Ch. Shed of Arden (Ch. Raffles of Earlsmoor ex Field Ch. Decoy of Arden)	L	D	Paul Bakewell, III	Paul Bakewell, III

157

Year	Dog	Col1	Col2	Owner	Handler
1943	Nat. Ch. Dual Ch. Shed of Arden (Ch. Raffles of Earlsmoor ex Field Ch. Decoy of Arden)	L	D	Paul Bakewell, III	C. Wallace
1944	Field Ch. Shelter Cove Beauty (Rockhaven Ben Boalt ex Happy of Willow Rock)	G	B	Dr. L. W. Evans	C. Morgan
1945	Black Magic of Audlon (Field Ch. Hiwood Mike ex Field Ch. Tar of Arden)	L	B	M. B. Wallace, Jr.	C. Morgan
1946	Nat. Ret. Ch. '42, '43 Dual Ch. Shed of Arden			Paul Bakewell, III	Paul Bakewell, III
1947	Dual Ch. Bracken Sweep (Glenhead Sweep ex Bracken of Timbertown)	L	D	D. E. Pomeroy	C. Pershall
1948	Field Ch. Brignall's Gringo (Freehaven Lucky ex Victoria Crescent)	L	D	C. Brignall	Roy Gonia
1949	Field Ch. Marvadel Black Gum (Mint of Barrington ex Marvadel Cinders)	L	D	Paul Bakewell, III	Paul Bakewell, III
1950	Field Ch. Beautywood's Tamarack (Beautywoods Buckshot ex Goldenwood Sunset Jill)	G	D	Dr. L. W. Evans	C. Morgan
1951	Field Ch. Ready Always of Marian Hill (Bushaway Rocket ex Lady Hance)	G	D	M. B. Wallace	B. Wunderlich
1952	Field Ch. King Buck (Timothy of Arden ex Alta Banchory)	L	D	Nilo Kennels	W. Pershall
1953	Field & '52 Nat. Ch. King Buck				
1954	Field Ch. Major VI (Field Ch. Ebony Bob ex Wardwyn Windbound)	L	D	Mrs. Fraser Horn	R. Staudinger
1955	Field Ch. Cork of Oakwood Lane (Coastal Charger of Deercreek ex Alona Liza Jane of Kingdale)	L	D	Dr. H. A. Mork	Tony Berger
1956	Field Ch. Massie's Sassy Boots (Shadow II ex Penny of Wingan)	L	D	W. T. Cline	R. Gonia
1957	Field Ch. Spirit Lake Duke (Smudge of Prairie Creek Farm ex Random Lake Black Ghost)	L	D	Mrs. George Murnane	J. Schomer
1958	Field Ch. Nilo Possibility (Field Ch. Black Prince of Sag Harbour ex Kingswere Black Widow)	L	D	K. K. Williams	W. Wunderlich
1959	'57 Nat. Ch. Spirit Lake Duke				
1960	Field Ch. Dolobran's Smoke Tail (Field Ch. Dolobran's Spook ex Dolobran's Mity Mite)	L	D	R. H. Hecker	Owner
1961	Field Ch. Del-Tone's Colvin (Nat. Ch. '55 Cork of Oakwood Lane ex Del-Tone Bridget)	L	D	L. Snoeyenbos	T. Berger

158

1962 Field & Am. Fld. Ch. Bigstone   L   B   Mr. and Mrs. B.   D. Walters
Hope (F.C. & A.F.C. Cork of   Grunwald
Oakwood Lane ex Bigstone
Ricky)
1963 F.C. & A.F.C. Del-tone Colvin   L   D   L. Snoeyenbos   T. Berger
1964 F.C. Ripco's V.C. Morgan (F.C.   L   B   J. Ott
& A.F.C. Ripco's Peter Pan ex
Peppy of Lopez)

In reviewing the breeding of these sixteen Labrador winners, from 1941 to 1964, one takes note of the fact that the old blood-lines coming through with the most consistency are those of Raffles, Glenairlie Rover, Peggy of Shipton, and Hiwood Mike.

The three "National" tabulations—of the National Championship stake, the Amateur Stake, and the Derby stake—are true keys to the sovereignty of the Labrador. A breakdown by breed and sex of the 290 individual dogs that have started in the Nationals since their inception are, through 1960:

LABRADORS	Dogs	185
	Bitches	45
	Total	230
	Dogs	34
GOLDENS	Bitches	8
	Total	42
CHESAPEAKES	Dogs	11
	Bitches	7
	Total	18

THE WINNERS	LABRADORS		GOLDENS	
	Dogs	12	Dogs	3
	Bitches	1	Bitches	1

ALL-TIME HIGH SCORING IN OPEN STAKES
(1931–1963, 50 Points and Up)

*Spirit Lake Duke	L.	180	Mrs. Geo. Murnane
Black Panther	L.	172½	Carl W. Carlson
*Massie's Sassy Boots	L.	147	Wm. T. Cline
*Major VI	L.	145½	Mrs. Fraser M. Horn
Black Boy XI	L.	125½	Lewis S. Greenleaf, Jr.
*Bracken's Sweep	L.	111½	Daniel E. Pomeroy

159

1952 and 1953 Nat. Ch. and Amt. Ch. King Buck.

Field and Am. Field Ch. Beau of the Lark (Ace of Whitmore ex Cedar Lake Trish). A grandson of Ch. Earlsmoor Moor of Arden, Beau accumulated more championship points (59½) than any other yellow Labrador in the history of the breed in America.

*Dolobran's Smoke Tail	L.	110½	Richard H. Hecker
*Brignall's Gringo	L.	110	Clifford N. Brignall
Dairy Hill's Night Cap	L.	108	Andrieus A. Jones
Rip of Holly Hill	L.	107	Mrs. Wm. P. Roth
*King Buck	L.	93½	John M. Olin
Ardyn's Ace of Merwalfin	L.	90	Eddie Salvino
Rick of Charlemagne	L.	89½	Mrs. Reginald M. Lewis
Cindy's Pride of Garfield	L.	88½	Mrs. Clifford V. Brokaw, Jr.
Shoremeadow Tidewater	L.	84½	Cyril R. Tobin
Butch's Bitterroot Smokey	L.	79½	Jos. Albertson
Little Pierre of Deer Creek	L.	79½	Mr. and Mrs. Paul Bakewell, III
Oakcreek's Van Cleve	G.	78½	Alfred H. Schmidt
Black Monk of Roeland	L.	75½	Mrs. D. L. Mesker
*Cork of Oakwood Lane	L.	75	Dr. A. Harold Mork
Oakcreek's Fremont	G.	73½	Cyril R. Tobin
Truly Yours of Garfield	L.	72½	John M. Olin
Bitterroot Chink-ee	L.	71½	Martha B. Burnett
Keith's Black Magic	L.	71	Daniel E. Pomeroy
Sprig of Swinomish	L.	70½	Cyril R. Tobin
Firelei's Hornet	L.	64	Joe Versay
Staindrop Murton Marksman	L.	63½	John M. Olin
The Golden Kidd	G.	63½	Mrs. Gerald M. Livingston
Glenairlie Rocket	L.	63	F. F. Garlock
*Marvadel Black Gum	L.	63	Mr. and Mrs. Paul Bakewell, III
Rip	G.	63	Paul Bakewell, III
Black Corsair of Whitmore	L.	62½	Sandy F. MacKay
Boley's Cascade	L.	62	Ernest J. Goppert, Jr.
The Spider of Kingswere	L.	62	Leonard S. Florsheim
Pepper's Jiggs	L.	60½	Robt. Pepper
Freehaven Jay	L.	60	James L. Free
Beau of the Lark	Y.L.	59½	Mr. and Mrs. Mahlon B. Wallace, Jr.
*Shed of Arden	L.	59	Paul Bakewell, III
Black Prince of Sag Harbour	L.	58½	Gerald M. Livingston
Slo-Poke Smokey of Dairy Hill	L.	58½	Andrieus A. Jones
Carr-Lab Hilltop	L.	57½	Glenn B. Bump
Gilmore's Peggy (Bitch)	L.	55	Dr. Leroy M. Evans
Stilrovin Nitro Express	G.	54½	Benj. L. Boalt
Bracken's High Flyer	L.	53½	Geo. L. Dukek
Marian's Timothy	L.	53½	Mrs. Chas. P. McPhail
*Ready Always of Marian Hill	G.	53½	Mahlon B. Wallace, Jr.
Tar of Arden (Bitch)	L.	53	Paul Bakewell, III
Macopin Expectation	G.	51½	Mrs. Geo. Murnane
Tar Baby's Little Sweet Stuff	L.	54	Kensyle L. Carpenter
Rip's Bingo	L.	51½	David Paper & Clifford W. Mortensen
Bengal of Arden	L.	51	Mrs. Albert P. Loening
Boley's Tar Baby	L.	50½	Bing Grunwald
Pitch of Timber Trouble	L.	50½	Guthrie Bicknell

46 Labradors (4 bitches)

7 Goldens

* (National Championships scored as 5-point wins)

161

Dual Ch. Bengal of Arden, first triple crown
winner. Dual and A.F.C. title, shown here
with owner, Mrs. A. Loening.

Field Champion Spirit Lake Duke, 1957 and 1959 National Champion and
all time high point winner.

Spirit Lake Duke, whelped in 1953, was bred by Paul Namvedt. He acquired his field title after a brilliant derby start in 1956. At this writing, he has been Eastern Champion five times (winning the Madeleine Austin Memorial Trophy), has qualified for the Nationals eight times, has run six times, was a finalist five times and a winner twice in 1957 and 1959. He tied for second place with Massie's Sassy Boots in the above point rating until February, 1963, when his record jumped to 174, and again at the end of April, 1963, at the Labrador Club trial, where another Open Stake win put five more points to his total. At the 1963 May trial at the Nutmeg Club, he ran, according to his sporting owner, Mr. Murnane, an almost flawless eight series, placing third, which brought his complete record to 180 points. At that time Mr. Murnane wrote, "he could probably run strongly for another year, but I want his companionship, and I hope he can endure mine and that we will have a few fine years together." Duke was not campaigned on a nation-wide scale, but was run almost exclusively in the Eastern zone, where competition is always keen. A handsome and prepossessing dog, he was ten years old in 1963.

Field Ch. Black Panther, whelped in 1944, by Blackout Nigger ex Dakota Princess, was, as his obituary in the *Wisconsin Field Trial News* noted, "a little bundle of dynamite, and always the dog to beat, from 1946 to his retirement in 1953." He held the all-time high point-winning record until the recent accumulation by Spirit Lake Duke. He qualified seven consecutive years for the Nationals —from 1946 through 1952—and produced one field champion bitch in Nico-Bet's Black Candy, also a National qualifier, ex Ch. Manzanal's Rain, a Freehaven Muscles daughter, bred by Mr. Ed. Spaulding. Candy was a stalwart little specimen, of lovely type and style—a dual champion missed.

Massie's Sassy Boots, whelped in 1948, bred by Joe de Loia, was 1956 National winner. Trained and handled at his early trials by his breeder, and owned at the time by Arthur Massie, he was just fifteen months old when, at the August 1949 Duluth trial, he won the Derby and the Qualifying stakes, and was top dog in the Open until the final test. Acquired by Mr. Cline, he finished his title under Frank Hogan's handling in 1951, qualifying the previous year for the Nationals. He was retired from active competition in 1957, to make his mark as a notable sire of six field champions.

163

Major VI, whelped in 1948 and bred by Graydon Topping, was a son of the late Howes Burton's Field Ch. Ebony Bob ex Wardwyn Windbound. Major was one of the most colorful and stylish workers of his time, and earned his greatest wins under the ownership of Mrs. Fraser Horn, handled by Ray Staudinger. A grandson of Little Pierre and Marlin of Arden, he was, besides being 1954 National winner, the first National Amateur winner in 1957, handled by his owner, John Fraser Horn. He was nine years old at the time.

Black Boy XI, whelped in 1950, bred by Fred Nissen, and owned throughout his spectacular career by Mr. and Mrs. Lewis Greenleaf, Jr., had a record that has put him among the top five black Labradors in American trial history. He qualified seven out of eight years for the Nationals, completing four. He ran in three Amateur stakes, completing one. In six of the Nationals he completed fifty-eight out of sixty-three tests. Retired in 1960, after winning his last trial in North Texas, he died in December, 1962, mourned by the Greenleafs, whose devoted house dog he had become. He was a grand type dog, on the order of the present Buccleugh or Sandringham stock—a real Labrador.

Lack of space precludes allotting paragraphs to each of these grand dogs so that the three following have been chosen for their relatively interesting positions.

1955 National Champion, Cork of Oakwood Lane, whelped in 1951, bred by John Cogan, has been consistently the most influential sire of the past nine years. The predisposition of his breeding on both sides has manifested itself in his roster of champion get from different bitches from year to year. The 1961 National was won by his son, Field Ch. Del-Tone Colvin, with *six* other dogs by him competing, and the 1962 National was won by a daughter, Field Ch. Bigstone Hope, with *nine* other of his get competing, a record for a producer. His only other contemporary rival as a sire has been the above-mentioned Massie's Sassy Boots.

Beau of the Lark, whelped in 1950, bred by Herman Stettler, and owned by Mr. and Mrs. Mahlon Wallace, deserves ranking here as a Yellow of outstanding merit. Just three years old at his first trial in 1953, he gave every indication that he would become a top-flight contender. He finished his title in 1954, and accumulated more championship points than any other Yellow in the history of the breed in this country. He qualified for four Nationals, completing two of them, the last in 1957.

Cruelly incapacitated all his life with crippling arthritis, Beau was the highest example of courage and tenacity. He was a wonderful dog in all ways, instrumental in awakening the fancy to the possibilities of Yellows as contenders equal to the Blacks, and a bright spot at trials that will take long to fill.

Bengal of Arden, whelped in 1944, bred at Arden by Good Hope Angus ex Burma of Arden, was trained alternately by Dave Elliot and Jim Cowie, the latter bringing him to his dual title. First owned by Claude Bekins and subsequently by Mrs. Madeleine Austin, under whose ownership he qualified three years for the Nationals with 51 points, Bengal will always be remembered as a dog of unusual character, charm, and moral fiber.

When Mrs. Austin died, her dogs passed into the ownership of Mrs. Sarah Loening. One cannot write of Bengal without writing of Sarah. Their colleagueship was an unbreakable bond, and he was completely responsible for getting her into the Retriever world. In reverse, it was he that brought his handler along, with perseverance, patience and love.

The following are the winners of the National Amateur Stake

NATIONAL AMATEUR

Year	Dog	Breed	Sex	Owner
1957	1954 Nat. Ch. Major VI (Field Ch. Ebony Bob ex Wardwyn Windbound)	L	D	Mrs. Fraser Horn
1958	Dual Ch. Boley's Tar Baby (King Chukker of Robinsdale ex Mem of Greeymar)	L	D	Bing Grunwald
1959	Field Ch. Bracken's High Flyer (Kingsdale Shadrack ex Bracken's Flight)	L	D	D. Dukek
1960	Field Ch. Queenie of Redding (Black Demon of Granton ex Robin of South Pass)	L	B	Rolland Watt
1961	Field & Am. Field Ch. Ace's Sheba of Ardyn (Field Ch. Ardyn's Ace of Merwalfin ex Xmas Holly)	L	B	Eddie Salvino
1962	Field & Am. Field Carr-Lab Hilltop (Marion's Duke of Benedict ex Carr-Lab Pride's Ad Lib)	L	D	Glenn Bump

1963 F. & A.F.C. Pepper's Jiggs (F. C.   L   D   R. Pepper
     Ardyn's Ace of Merwalfin of Black
     Magic ex Van Nola)
1964 Nat. A.F.C. Dutchmoor's Black   L   D   Nelson Sills
     Mood (Dual Ch. Calypso Clipper
     ex Jets Tammy)

Inaugurated in 1937 and held continuously since then, the National Derby Championship Trophy has been awarded to the Derby Retriever earning the most points in AKC-licensed trials run in the current year.

NATIONAL DERBY

Year	Dog	Breed	Owner
1937	Chesabob	Ches.	Dilwyne K's
1938	Glenairlie Rocket	Lab.	Mrs. Frances Garlock
1939	Gunnar II	Ches.	R. N. Crawford
1940	Laddie of Rockingell	Lab.	Foreman Lebold
1941	Stilrovin Nitro Express	Golden	Audrey Meyers
1942	Shelter Cove Beauty (bitch)	Golden	Dr. L. M. Evans
1943	Scoronine for Deercreek	Lab.	Paul Bakewell, III
1944	Black Magic of Audlon (bitch)	Lab.	M. B. Wallace Jr.
1945	Nigger of Upham	Lab.	Nick Bonovich
1946	Marvadel Black Gum	Lab.	M. B. Wallace Jr.
1947	Tussy of Mark	Lab.	S. L. Mark
1948	Webway's Dolphin	Lab.	W. W. Holes
1949	Deercreek's Cforcatl	Lab.	Joe Versay
1950	Black Point Dark Tiger	Lab.	D. Pomeroy
1951	Young Mint of Catawba	Lab.	F. Lebold
1952	Hal's SpiWise Zeke	Lab.	H. Shidler
1953	Nelgard's Counterpoint (bitch)	Lab.	H. Schultz
1954	Tanca's Rocky of Random Lake	Lab.	John Olin
1955	Stonegate's Ace of Spades	Lab.	John Olin
1956	Nodak Ardee (bitch)	Lab.	P. Alport
1957	Nodak Cindy (bitch)	Lab.	B. Grunwald
1958	Meg's Pattie O'Rourke (bitch)	Ches.	Dr. F. A. Dashnaw
1959	Ace's Sheba of Arden (bitch)	Lab.	E. Salvino
1960	Jet of Zenith	Lab.	Mrs. Sarah Loening
1961	Cream City Coed (bitch)	Lab.	Chas. Morgan
1962	Col-Tam of Craignock	Lab.	Mr. R. Bateman
1963	Mirk of Daingerfield	Lab.	B. Grunwald
1964	Mac Genes Fall Guy	Lab.	Gene T. Galyean

British-Bred Labradors that have qualified for the Nationals have been:

Field Ch. Hiwood Mike (Pettistree Dan ex Pettistree Poppet), completed 1941 and '42

Field Ch. Orchardton Dale (Orchardton Donald ex Tullymurdoch Spanker), completed 1944

Field Ch. Orchardton Dorando (Orchardton David ex Glenhead Nan)

Field Ch. Hiwood Fleet (Hiwood Braeroy Benger ex Hiwood Bustle), '51, '52, '53, '54

Field Ch. Treveilyr Swift (Penlaan Don ex Treveilyr Starlight)

Field Ch. Hiwood My Delight (Darky of Elmbank ex Paper Weight by L'Ile Go-Gettem)

Field Ch. Pinehawk Nigger (Dual Ch. Treveilyr Swift ex Lawreate Bess)

Field Ch. Staindrop Kam (Dual Ch. Staindrop Saighdear ex Staindrop Glenhead Wren)

Field Ch. Staindrop Murton Marksman (Shavington Ted ex Brackenbank Jessie)

Field Ch. Staindrop Spanker (Shavington Ted ex Brackenbank Jessie)

Field Ch. Maidscorner Paul (Dullingham Danger ex Chippenham Briar), completed 1958

Field Ch. Staindrop Striker (Field Ch. Staindrop Murton Marksman ex Staindrop Glenhead Wren)

Field Ch. Hiwood Storm (Eng. Field Ch. Greatford Teal ex Eng. Field Ch. Hiwood Gypsey)

Field Ch. Staindrop Ringleader (Shavington Ted ex Brackenbank Jessie) (yellow)

This has been a history of black field trial Labradors. When one considers, by percentage, the staggering number of Labradors bred for and run at all trials, one realizes that the popularity of the Yellows has never been spectacular in America.

A list of Yellow Labradors qualifying for the National Championship follows. As of 1962, only two of them, Honey Chile Trixie and Beau of the Lark, had completed tests for which they were entered. The number X10 denotes completion of the trial.

Field Ch. Sand Gold Terry (Selby's Sandy Brown ex Black Hills Goldie)

Field Ch. Sir Jock (Symington Jock ex Golden Bubbles)

Field Ch. Goldie of Goldielands (Palmyra Red ex Sandy) (bitch)

Field Ch. Honey Chile Trixie (Rusty of Navarre ex North Shore Trixie) (bitch), X10 in 19

Field Ch. Chevriers Golden Rod (Argus Leader ex Brookings Golden Penny) (Canadian Bred)

167

Field Ch. Beau of the Lark (Ace of Whitmore II ex Cedar Lake Trish), X10 in 19

Field Ch. Black Point Rising Sun (Zelstone Mr. Ben ex Field Ch. Honey Chile Trixie)

Field Ch. Boise Buckaroo (Tar of Idaho ex Sun Valley Greta)

Field Ch. Buffington of Yellowstone (Sandy of Avalanche ex Lady Luck VII)

Field Ch. Staindrop Ringleader (Shavington Ted ex Brackenbank Jessie)

Field Ch. and Can. Field Ch. Brandy Spirit of Netley (Croziers Silver Lance ex Bonnie Star of Netley) (Canadian Bred)

Dual Ch. Burnham Buff (Ch. Deercreek's Toddy Talk ex Taffy of Burmar Farm) (bitch)

The last-named on this list, Burnham Buff, whelped in 1956, holds the distinction of being the first yellow bitch in the history of the breed to become a dual champion. Mrs. Joan Davis, of the Ironwood Labrador Kennels in Minnesota, has been kind enough to send me a rundown on the qualifications of this grand little bitch.

"Buff was whelped September 1st, 1956. Her sire was Ch. Deercreek's Toddy Time II, by Field Ch. Marvadel Black Gum and Field Ch. Tar of Arden. Her dam was Taffy of Bur-Mur Farm, a granddaughter of Rusty of Navarre, who sired Field Ch. Honey Chile Trixie. Buff was bred by Mrs. Burrell Finch of Bur-Mur Farms." (Let me add here that Buff is, incidentally, a half-sister to the late Mr. C. V. Brokaw's Invail's Pennell, a Black, by Toddy Time, and another that surely missed a worthy bench title. H. W.)

"Buff's field record is very good and will soon make her one of the all time great yellow Labrador bitches.

"She acquired 19 points in her Derby year which placed her 4th in the country. Her field championship was completed with an Open win in October, 1961, which also qualified her for the Nationals that year. Buff ran the 1961 Nationals but made her mistakes early in the trial so did not finish. In 1962 she earned 21 Open points for a total of 40 Open All Age points, more than any other yellow bitch has accumulated and she is still running strongly and placing consistently. She qualified for the 1962 Nationals, and was all set to run the trial when Mother Nature took a hand and she came in heat just prior to the trial. Mr. McGee, her owner took this opportunity to breed her to a promising young black dog, Raven Mike of Stonegate . . . She has been trained and handled by her very capable owner, and Roger Reopelle.

"Buff's field work made it necessary to squeeze her bench appearances in between field trials, so that she was only shown sporadically by my husband and myself, with Hollis Wilson showing her to two of her points. Percy Roberts said she was a lovely bitch, despite her gay tail, so Buff deserves both her titles."

Buff is the second dual champion bitch in the breed's annals, the other having been the Scottish bred black, Lochar Nessie, litter sister to Ch. Woodie of Tibshelf, both owned by the late Mrs. Morris, of Newry, County Down, North Ireland.

What does the future hold for Buff as a producer? We wish her the best, regardless of color. Certainly in her breeding, she bears out the indelible marks left by Peggy of Shipton, Glenairlie Rover and Raffles. Were she to be spirited to England, over the burdensome quarantine (where she would get a royal reception, like as not), she would be put to black National Winner Galleywood Shot, current master at the hand of turning out the best in both colors—or the coming young stud, Sandringham Ranger, owned by Her Majesty, the Queen. Whatever may be her path, she has already made her imprint, and we hope she will further it for future generations.

Ironically, the first Labrador Club trial's Open stake was won by a Yellow—Carl of Boghurst, imported by Mrs. Marshall Field. Yellow Field Ch. Ming was the first import to gain an American field title, but neither of these dogs left any get of importance. Honey Chile Trixie, a yellow field trial bitch, has produced three winners (two black and one yellow) in Field Chs. Black Point Dark Tiger and Sweep's Chance—both by Bracken Sweep—and the Yellow, Black Point Rising Sun, by the yellow import, Zelstone Mr. Ben. Son was owned by the late Stuart Crocker, and the color lost a strong adherent in him, who might well have carried on a patient, constructive breeding program but for his untimely passing. He was one of the most genuine of people in American trials.

A glance at a few of the Yellow Labradors imported in the 1930's will give a sample of the bloodlines brought over from working kennels of the day:

169

English and American Field Ch. Ming (Cock Robin ex Velvet), bred by Lord Middleton and owned by F. T. Bedford, was the first English and American Field Ch.

Dual Ch. Burnham Buff (Ch. Deercreek's Toddy Time II ex Taffy of Burm-Mur Farm), the first yellow Dual Champion bitch of the breed.

Wratten Julian (Field Ch. Hawkesbury Jupiter ex Hawkesbury Jezebel)

Golden Glimmer (Golden Morn ex Saber, he by Field Ch. Hayler's Defender), bitch

Symington Jock (Alby Golden Corn ex Frodsham Brenda)

Jill Spratt (ex a Hayler's Defender daughter)

EARLY AMERICAN-BREDS

Hill House Lassie (Carl of Boghurst ex Beeding Lilac) (Lilac was by Western Reiver ex Amber Joy)

Dakota Bill (Itaska Blaze ex Dakota Boots); 4th generation to Hayler's Defender

Florestal Nico (Muirton Sam ex Kinpurnie Bess); bred in California

Toffee (Mick ex Hiwood Dora)

Kenjockety Pasadink (Caumsett Dan of Kenjockety ex Kenjockety Nellie)

Cay of Cotuit (Carl of Boghurst ex Golden Glimmer)

Cleopatra of Conquest (Hayler's Fort ex Our Girl); same early Remick litter

Wingan Primrose (Ch. Drinkstone Pons of Wingan ex Kitty of Hillwood)

Arden kennels had a few Yellows, one litter in particular by Ch. Drinkstone Pons ex Babe of Arden; two were called Scotch and Soda of Arden. There was also yellow Fizz of Arden, by Hiwood Risk ex Peggy Shipton. Fizz sired Dunottar Plush, when bred to a yellow litter sister of Field Ch. Ming, called Betty Brown. The Dunottar prefix of Mrs. Catherine Morgan figures in many pedigrees of that period in Dunottar Reep, Trace, Peter and Puffin.

Puffin was by an import, Birchhanger Macbeth ex a yellow bitch called Diamond Lil, bred by Miss Virginia Pennoyer. Diamond Lil was by Mick ex black Hiwood Dora, a daughter of Hiwood D'Arcy ex Field Ch. Hiwood Chance.

Excellent working Yellows did come over from Braeroy, Treesholme, Zelstone and others, but found their finest medium as shooting dogs, both here and in Canada. Miss Agnes Fowler, friend of Mrs. MacPherson and long associated with the Seeing Eye Dog School, imported not only Western Reiver, but Braeroy Mac, Maid, and Ashdale Primrose, who was dam to Mrs. Mac's Field Ch. Braeroy Roe.

171

The question is put so often to me abroad, as to why the Yellows have never been in great demand in America. One may find the reason (apart from perhaps a national prejudice against a "yellow dog") in that there has not been a homogeneous group over here that over a long period of time has espoused the color above all else, so that it could have been brought (with inevitable disappointments and frustration) first to a consistent, high working level, and second to a uniformity of type—both indispensable to the success of a new outlet that a breed may take. Without such a concentrated effort—with many people to subscribe to it and support it—few if any concrete results can possibly follow or endure. Such a group must have an objective such as was demonstrated by the Yellow breeders abroad—an uphill fight even for them, what with the Blacks in such ascendancy at the time.

Yellows at shows have also been comparatively sparse, remaining numerically small over the years. The first Yellow bench champion, as far as one can ascertain, was an imported dog, Sandylands Golden Harvester, by Derryclaw Donald ex Lady Elsabeth, sent over by Mrs. Broadley—although she was not the breeder—to Mrs. Sarah Edmiston, who handled him herself to his title, in 1948, then sold him. He was subsequently used locally at stud in South Dakota. The same year another Yellow, Chevrier's Lion, a Canadian-bred which figures in many working pedigrees, became a champion. The first champion American-bred bitch of the color was Mrs. Curtis Read's Chidley Almond Crisp in 1950.

The following year saw Ginger of Pyreshire awarded her title. Ginger was bred by Mrs. Burrell Finch, who also bred Dual Ch. Burnham Buff.

The first Yellow classes for Labradors were put on by the Labrador Club at their 1938 Specialty, with American-bred and Open classes for dogs and bitches such as Mr. Livingston's Kilsyth Goldie, Mr. Harriman's Fizz of Arden, Mrs. Junius Morgan's Amber, and Mrs. Jacob's Jacob of Chale.

Blacks continued to predominate, however, and it was not until 1957 at the Annual Specialty show that a yellow bitch, Mrs. Lambert's Golden Chance of Franklin, was the first of the color to win Best of Breed there, repeating the win in 1958. Judicial prejudice against the color has abated somewhat in the past few years, but there is much room for improvement. Whatever bias still exists may be laid on the doorstep of mediocrity.

An imported yellow bitch, Bickerton Salmon Queen (Dobrudden Buffer ex Bella Mischief), is so far the first yellow Labrador—as well as the first of her sex in the breed—to win a best in show, in 1962.

By and large, real show quality among Yellows has not been on a par with the best of the Blacks in the thirty-two years' span of the breed's activities in this country. The best of them have inadvertently been bitches, many from black lines; among these have included some owned by the late Mrs. Doherty of Canada, with her Breezy Brae and Holland Marsh stock based on Treesholme; individuals from Mrs. Read's Chidley prefix; Rupert's lovely bitch, Ch. Brookhaven Angell; Mrs. Anne Simoneau's Ch. Dunnottar Popcorn; Alvaleigh kennel's import, Ch. Zelstone Kate, who did a grand job in producing Mrs. Reginald Lewis' Field Ch. DiMundy's Danny; James Warwick's import, Ch. Ballyduff Candy; the aforementioned Ch. Golden Chance of Franklin, a lovely apparition at shows in the many groups she so justifiably won; young stock from Ch. Diant Jupiter imported by Mrs. N. Tuttle, and Mrs. Audrey Mitchell's superb yellow bitch, Ch. Lockerbie Siena, also a group winner.

It is unwise to generalize about the future on the basis of the past, and it will be interesting to see how the color fares, both at work and at shows within the next decade. Sound breeding projects take time, and one must know where one is going.

AMERICAN DUAL CHAMPIONS

Michael of Glenmere
    (Ace of Whitmore ex Vixen of Glenmere), wh. 1935; breeder, R. Goelet; owner, J. Angle
Braes of Arden (bitch)
    (Ch. Raffles of Earlsmoor ex Field Ch. Decoy of Arden), wh. 1937; breeder, W. A. Harriman; owner, R. McManus
Gorse of Arden (bitch)
    (Ch. Raffles of Earlsmoor ex Field Ch. Decoy of Arden), wh. 1937; breeder, W. A. Harriman; owner, Mrs. M. Belmont
Shed of Arden
    (Ch. Raffles of Earlsmoor ex Field Ch. Decoy of Arden), wh. 1939; breeder, W. A. Harriman; owner, Paul Bakewell, III

Matchmaker for Deercreek
(Dual Ch. Little Pierre of Deercreek ex Tops of Bigstone), wh. 1946; breeder, Bill Rook; owner, Mr. and Mrs. Paul Bakewell, III

Little Pierre of Deercreek
(Eng. & Am. Field Ch. Hiwood Mike ex Field Ch. Tar of Arden), wh. 1943; breeder and owner, Mr. and Mrs. Paul Bakewell, III

Cherokee Buck
(Dual Ch. Grangemead Precocious ex Grangemead Sharon), wh. 1947; breeder, Thomas Merritt; owner, R. Darlington

Grangemead Precocious
(Dual Ch. Shed of Arden ex Huron Lady), wh. 1946; breeder and owner, Thomas W. Merritt

Hello Joe of Rocheltree
(Snikeb's Ding Ding Ding ex Billy's Black Babe), wh. 1949; breeder, Wm. Bryant; owner, Paul Bakewell, III

Yodel of Morexpense
(Field Ch. Freehaven Jay ex Ch. Echo of Arden), wh. 1940; breeder, Mrs. M. Belmont; owner, L. Bartlett

Bracken Sweep
(Glenhead Sweep ex Bracken of Timbertown), wh. 1943; breeder and owner, D. Pomeroy

Boley's Tar Baby
(King Chukker of Robinsdale ex Mem of Greeymar), wh. 1951; breeder, I. C. Bolenbaugh; owner, B. Grunwald

Kingswere Black Ebony
(Field Ch. The Spider of Kingswere ex Stylish Patsy of Deercreek), wh. 1951; breeder and owner, J. Romadka

Alpine Cherokee Rocket
(Dual Ch. Grangemead Precocious ex Nelgard's Madam Queen), wh. 1955; breeder, J. Woodall; owner, Chas. Cook

Problem Boy Duke of Wake
(Ponto's Ponto of Wake ex Kavanaugh's Ripple), wh. 1957; breeder, J. Kavanaugh, Jr.; owner, J. M. Preston

Beau Brummel of Wyndale
(Field Ch. Rips Bingo ex Shady Lady IV), wh. 1952; breeder, J. McKenzie; owner, Mrs. L. McCue

Burnham Buff (yellow bitch)

Dual Ch. Grangemead Precocious.

Am. Ch. Ballyduff Candy (Dual Ch. Staindrop Saighdear ex Ballyduff Venus), bred by Dr. T. Acheson, imported by Lockerbie Kennels.

(Ch. Deercreek's Toddy Time II ex Tuffy of Bur-Mur Farm), wh.
1956; breeder, Mrs. B. Finch; owner, J. P. McGee

Dela-Winn's Tar of Craignook

(Dela-Winn's Mike ex Dela-Winn's Gilda)

Calypso Clipper

(F. & A.F.C. Yankee Clipper of Reo Raj ex Bigstone Bobber),
breeder and owner, John Van Bloom)

Bengal of Arden

(Good Hope Angus ex Burma of Arden)

Many newcomers to Retriever Trials have requested information
as to: (1) The exact definition of a "Qualified Dog" for a Limited
All-Age Stake in A.K.C. Licensed Trials. (2) How a Field Championship is acquired. 3) How an Amateur Field Championship is
acquired. (4) The qualification requirements for the National
(Open) Championship Trial. (5) Qualification requirements for the
National Amateur Championship Trial. (6) The method of determining the National Derby Championship. (7) The definition of
an amateur. Here are some of the answers:

Definition of a Limited All-Age Stake

A limited All-Age Stake at a Retriever Trial shall be for dogs
that have previously been placed or awarded a Judge's Award of
Merit in an Open All-Age Stake; or, that have been placed first
or second in a qualifying Stake; or, placed or received a Judge's
Award of Merit in an Amateur All-Age Stake carrying championship points.

(Editor's Note: This rule became effective June 10, 1957. Prior
to that date a Derby that had placed first or second was a qualified
dog. It was not intended to make the rule retroactive; hence, it is
our opinion any Derby that had placed 1st or 2nd prior to June
10, 1957, would still be considered a qualified dog.)

How a Field Championship Is Acquired

At present, to acquire a Field Championship a Retriever must
win a National championship stake or a total of 10 points, which
may be acquired as follows: In each Open All-Age, Limited All-
Age, or Special All-Age Stake there must be at least twelve starters,
each of which is eligible for entry in a Limited All-Age Stake, and
the winner of first place shall be credited with 5 points, second

place 3 points, third place 1 point and fourth place ½ point; but before acquiring a championship, a dog must win first place and acquire 5 points in at least one Open All-Age, Limited All-Age, or Special All-Age Stake open to all breeds of Retrievers, and not more than 5 points of the required 10 shall be acquired in trials not open to all breeds of Retrievers.

Acquiring an Amateur Field Championship

At present, to acquire an Amateur Field Championship, a Retriever must win: (1) a National Championship Stake, handled by an Amateur, or a National Amateur Championship Stake or (2) a total of 10 points in Open All-Age, Limited All-Age, or Special All-Age Stakes or a total of 15 points in Open All-Age, Limited All-Age, or Special All-Age, or Amateur All-Age Stakes, which may be acquired as follows: in each Open All-Age, Limited All-Age, Special All-Age, or Amateur All-Age Stake, there must be at least 12 starters, each of which is eligible for entry in a Limited All-Age Stake, and the handler must be an Amateur (as determined by the Field Trial Committee of the trial-giving club), and the winner of first place shall be credited with 5 points, second place 3 points, third place 1 point, and fourth place ½ point, but before acquiring a championship, a dog must win a first place and acquire 5 points in at least one Open-Age, Limited All-Age, Special All-Age, or Amateur All-Age Stake open to all breeds of Retrievers, and not more than 5 points shall be acquired in trials not open to all breeds of Retrievers.

The above revision is effective April 1 and replaces the present requirements.

Qualification for National Championship Trial

At the present time, a first place (5 points), plus a total of two (2) other points gained in Open, Limited or Special All-Age Stakes earns qualification. The dog may be amateur or professionally handled. The points may be earned in All Breed or Specialty Trials. Qualification period starts on January 1 of the year in which the trial is to be run. The winner of the National Championship in the year preceding the Trial and the winner of the National Amateur Championship in the year of the Trial qualify automatically.

Qualification for National Amateur Championship Trial

At the present time, a first place (5 points) plus a total of two (2) other points earned by a dog (amateur handled) in an Open, Limited or Special All-Age Stake or an Amateur All-Age Stake (all stakes must have at least twelve qualified dogs) earns qualification. The points may be gained in All Breed or Specialty Trials. The qualification period (new rule adopted at the 1958 National Amateur Meeting) runs from the weekend of May 31 to the weekend of May 31 the next year. For purposes of clarification, in any trial which starts at the end of May and continues into June, the Amateur Stake will count for points no matter what day it is run. The Winner of the previous year's Trial qualifies automatically.

The National Derby Championship

Each year since 1937, this championship trophy has been awarded to the Derby gaining the greatest number of points in the current year. Points are totaled on the following basis: 1st (5); 2nd (3); 3rd (2); 4th (1). Points are awarded only in Derby Stakes open to all breeds of Retrievers, and there must be at least ten starters in the stake. The use of game birds on land is not compulsory.

The Definition of an Amateur Handler

The National Amateur Retriever Club at their annual meeting July 1, 1958, defined an amateur handler as an individual who has not derived or attempted to derive any part of his livelihood from the training, handling or showing of field or hunting dogs.

Outstanding Producing Sires and Dams and Their Predominance from 1936 through 1962

Ch. Raffles of Earlsmoor

	Dams Bred to
Ch. Banks of Arden	Field Ch. Decoy of Arden
Dual Ch. Braes of Arden	Field Ch. Decoy of Arden
Dual Ch. Gorse of Arden	Field Ch. Decoy of Arden
Ch. Earlsmoor Moor of Arden	Field Ch. Decoy of Arden
Dual Ch. Shed of Arden	Field Ch. Decoy of Arden
Ch. Earlsmoor Marlin of Arden	Field Ch. Decoy of Arden
Marvadel Cinders	Marvadel Topsy

Odds On

Field Ch. Blind of Arden	Peggy of Shipton
Bugla Brant	Peggy of Shipton
Field Ch. Decoy of Arden	Peggy of Shipton
Ch. Joy of Arden	Peggy of Shipton

Glenairlie Rover

Field Ch. Freehaven Jay	Spot of Barrington
Field Ch. Glenairlie Rocket	Spot of Barrington
Glenairlie Eve	Langbourne Darkie
Freehaven Molly	Langbourne Darkie

Eng. & Am. Field Ch. Hiwood Mike

Dual Ch. Little Pierre of Deercreek	Field Ch. Tar of Arden
Field Ch. Black Magic of Audlon	Field Ch. Tar of Arden
Confusion at Deercreek	Field Ch. Tar of Arden
Good Hope Angus	Drulochman Dance of Timbertown
Grangemead Sharon	Grangemead Angel

Dual Ch. Little Pierre of Deercreek

Field Ch. Dolobran's Little Ash	Marvadel Cinders
Field Ch. Ladies Day at Deercreek	Tops of Bigstone
Field Ch. Mary-go-Round Deercreek	Field Ch. Tar of Arden
Dual Ch. Matchmaker for Deercreek	Tops of Bigstone
Ch. St. Jones' Blackie	Marvadel Cinders
Field Ch. Zipper of Sugar Valley	Highland Lass
Little Tops of Bigstone	Tops of Bigstone

Dual Ch. Shed of Arden

Dual Ch. Grangemead Precocious	Huron Lady
Field Ch. Firelei's Hornet	Field Ch. Firelei of Deercreek
Field Ch. Ardyn's Ace of Merwalfin	Cindy of Merwalfin
Field Ch. Bigstone Bandit	Little Tops of Bigstone
Field Ch. Jibodad Gypsey	Little Tar of Bigstone
Little Trouble of Audlon	Field Ch. Black Magic of Audlon

179

| Field Ch. Pickpocket for Deer-
creek | Peggy of Pheasant Lawn |
| Symphony at Deercreek | Field Ch. Tar of Arden |

Dual Ch. Grangemead Precocious

Dual Ch. Cherokee Buck	Grangemead Sharon
Field Ch. Cherokee Medicine Man	Grangemead Sharon
Field Ch. Freehaven Muscles	Grangemead Sharon
Earlyanna of Countrywood	Kay Dee of Lynn
Beautywood's Creole Jane	Field Ch. Gilmore's Peggy
	Field Ch. Earlyanna of Country- wood

Field Ch. Massie's Sassy Boots

Field Ch. Beau of Zenith	Can. Nat'l Ch. Belle of Zenith
Field Ch. Shoremeadow Tide- water	Shoremeadow Jemima
Field Ch. Jet of Zenith	Thornwood Rhea
Field Ch. Techako's Ranger	Nodak Tar Pride
Field Ch. Boocindy's Renegade	Cindy of Holly Hill

Smudge of Prairie Creek Farm

Field Ch. Black Boy XI	La Belle's Petite Kaydonne
Field Ch. Smudge's Bingo	Highland Jet
Field Ch. Spirit Lake Duke	Random Lake Black Ghost
Field Ch. Spirit Lake Bay	Random Lake Black Ghost
Field Ch. Spirit Lake Phantom	Random Hill Black Ghost

Dual Ch. Treveilyr Swift

Field Ch. Pinehawk Nigger	Lawreate Bess
Field Ch. Salty of Sugar Valley	Field Ch. Zipper of Sugar Valley
Field Ch. Swifty of Sugar Valley	Field Ch. Zipper of Sugar Valley
Field Ch. West Island Whiz	Black Point Inga's Interest
Field Ch. West Island Hobo	Black Point Inga's Interest
Field Ch. West Island Tramp	Black Point Inga's Interest
Field Ch. Manzanal Clover	Hiwood Ness
Field Ch. Galleywood Swift (Eng- land)	Staindrop Winkie
Field Ch. Hilldyke Simon (Eng- land)	Lawreate Bess

Pinehawk Black Tarquin of Claven (Imp.)	Flora Dora of Claven

Field Ch. Cork of Oakwood Lane

Field Ch. Ace-Hi Scamp of Windsweep	Queen Ace
Field Ch. Bay City Zany Jane	Bigstone Breeze
Field Ch. Roy's Rowdy	Beautywood's Creole Jane
Field Ch. Star of Fate	Kay's Own Fate of Boone
Field Ch. Del-Tone Colvin	Del-Tone Bridget
Field & Am. Field Ch. Bigstone Hope	Bigstone Rickey
Field Ch. Mom's Mink-Corky	Field Ch. Marten's Little Bullet
Field & Am. Field Ch. Del-Tone Ric	Marten's Jet
Field Ch. Pomme de Terre Pete	Del-Tone Lass
Field Ch. Nodak Boots	Spider Wise
Field Ch. Sandburr Pete	Beautywood's Emdee's Nugget
Field Ch. Ace Hi's Lone Star	Queen Ace
Field Ch. Lord Beaver of Cork	Marten's Lady Jane
Field Ch. Crowder	Beautywood's Creole Jane
1956 Derby Ch. Nodak's Ar Dee	Spider Wise
Field Ch. Oakwood's Jane's Delilah	Beautywood's Creole Jane
Am. Field Ch. Nodak Playboy	Spider Wise

Dual Ch. Bracken Sweep

Field Ch. Black Point Dark Destroyer	Interest of Timbertown
Field Ch. Black Point's Sweeps Chance	Field Ch. Honey Chile Trixie
Field Ch. Woodcroff's Inga's Bonus	Interest of Timbertown
Field Ch. Nilo Senator	Field Ch. Mary Go Round Deercreek
Field Ch. Toto of Audlon	Little Trouble of Audlon

Field Ch. Ardyn's Ace of Merwalfin

Field Ch. & A.F.C. Pepper's Jiggs	Black Magic of Van Nola
Field Ch. & A.F.C. Ace's Dike of Winnaway	Black Pantheress of Ming

181

Field Ch. & A.F.C. Ace's Sheba of Ardyn	Chanbar Christmas Holly
Field Ch. & A.F.C. Storm of Winnaway	Black Pantheress of Ming
Field Ch. & A.F.C. Ace's Shed of Ardyn	Chanbar Christmas Holly

Ch. Reanacre Mallardhurn Thunder (Ch. Sandylands Tweed of Blaircourt ex Mallardhurn Pat), bred by N. Robinson, owned by J. Johnson.

Ch. Courtcolman Jess of Glynwood (Zelstone Tramp ex Courtcolman Honey), bred by gamekeeper, A. C. Wood, owned by Major A. W. Jones.

The Favourite, 1925

The Limit

Start

Mr. Alington's Bright, 1911

Mint (unreg.)
Jep (unreg.)
F.C. Peter of Faskally
Juniper (F.C. Flapper)

Gwendoline

Simon (unreg.)

Belle of the Rhins

Madge

Glenmuir Nero
Fraulein

Choice of Kirkmahoe

Dual Ch. Banchory Bolo

Scandal of Glynn

F.C. Peter of Faskally
Shelagh of Glynn
Foxley Kennett
Baker's Nora

Caerhoell Nettle

Kirkmahoe Dina

Kinmount Don

Brocklehirst Bob
Stewardess

Murrayfield Nora

Ch. Ilderton Ben
Murrayfield Kate

Odds On, 1928
(Under the
heading
of Bright)

Timothy

Start

Bright

Mint
Jep
F.C. Peter of Faskally
Juniper

Gwendoline

Jubilee Daisy (Interbred)

Jest

Bess

March

Judy

183

F.C. Nigger of Barrington, 1931
(under the heading of
Malmesbury's Tramp)

- Fresco Smut (imp.)
  - Tickford Blackie
    - Kiamil
      - F.C. Peter of Faskally
        - Waterdale Gamester
        - Birkhill Juliet
      - Munden Saba
        - Warwick Collier
        - Munden Single
    - Missi
      - Joe
      - Bess
  - Ebony Lady
    - Prince John
      - Joe
      - Jessie Flirt
    - Princess Juno
      - F.C. Peter of Faskally
        - Waterdale Gamester
        - Birkhill Juliet
      - Juniper
        - F.C. Flapper
        - Sandhoe Juno
- Kitty of Barrington
  - Banchory Roger
    - Dual Ch. Banchory Bolo
      - Scandal of Glynn
        - F.C. Peter of Faskally
        - Birkhill Juliet
      - Caerhowell Nettle
        - Foxley Bennett
        - Baker's Nora
    - Patience of Faskally
      - Robertson's Gourkha
        - Munden Scrambler, 1912
        - Gyp
      - Robertson's Queen
        - Page's Dock (F.C. Flapper)
        - Nancy
  - Ch. Balbeardie
    - Muto
      - Glenmuir Nero
        - F.C. Flapper
        - Jill
      - Fraulein
        - Lochnoris Roy
        - Glenmuir Jean
    - Balmuto Pinkie
      - Wemyss Nero
      - Camilla Maggie

F.C. Glenairlie Rover, 1933
(under the heading of Malmesbury's Tramp)

Dalbeattie Tango

Dalbeattie Don

Brave Ben

Ch. Withington Ben — Banchory Don / Withington Dinah

Bess of Helaugh — Leader of Warter / Yorkshire Venus

Westwood Judy (unreg.)

Nell

Tim of Whitmore

F.C. Peter of Whitmore, 1911 — F.C. Peter of Faskally / Logan Lorna

Wildridge Jet

Fairgirth Bell

Ch. Brayton Swift — Brayton Sir Richard / Betty

Stoneleigh Quality (Flatcoat)

Lady Matilda

F.C. Kirkmahoe Rover

Dual Ch. Banchory Bolo

Scandal of Glynn — F.C. Peter of Faskally / Shelagh of Glynn

Caerhoell Nettle — Foxley Kennett / Baker's Nora

Kirkmahoe Dina

Kinmount Don — Bracklehirst Bob / Stewardess

Murrayfield Nora, 1917 — Ch. Ilderton Ben / Murrayfield Kate

Ch. Balbeardie

Muto

Glenmuir Nero — F.C. Flapper, 1902 / Jill

Fraulein

Balmuto Pinkie

Wemyss Nero

Camilla Maggie — Lochnoris Roy / Glenmuir Jean

185

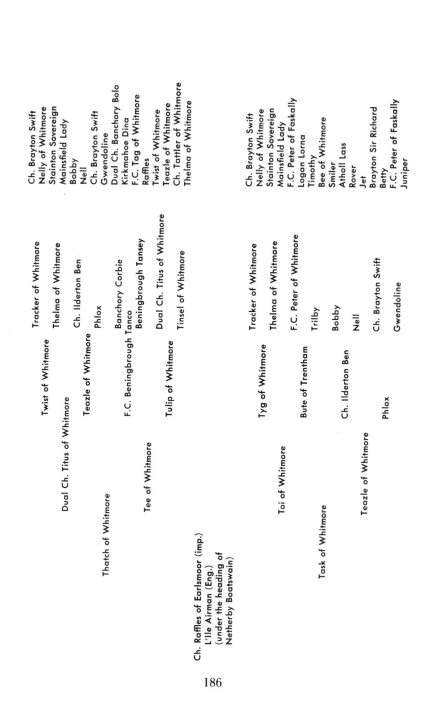

Ch. Raffles of Earlsmoor (imp.)
L'Ile Airman (Eng.)
(under the heading of Netherby Boatswain)

- **Thatch of Whitmore**
  - **Dual Ch. Titus of Whitmore**
    - **Twist of Whitmore**
      - Tracker of Whitmore
        - Ch. Brayton Swift
        - Nelly of Whitmore
      - Thelma of Whitmore
        - Stainton Sovereign
        - Mainsfield Lady
    - **Teazle of Whitmore**
      - Ch. Ilderton Ben
        - Bobby
        - Nell
      - Phlox
        - Ch. Brayton Swift
        - Gwendoline
  - **Tee of Whitmore**
    - **F.C. Beningbrough Tanco**
      - Banchory Corbie
        - Dual Ch. Banchory Bolo
        - Kirkmahoe Dina
      - Beningbrough Tansey
        - F.C. Tag of Whitmore
        - Raffles
    - **Tulip of Whitmore**
      - Dual Ch. Titus of Whitmore
        - Twist of Whitmore
        - Teazle of Whitmore
      - Tinsel of Whitmore
        - Ch. Tattler of Whitmore
        - Thelma of Whitmore
- **Task of Whitmore**
  - **Toi of Whitmore**
    - **Tyg of Whitmore**
      - Tracker of Whitmore
        - Ch. Brayton Swift
        - Nelly of Whitmore
      - Thelma of Whitmore
        - Stainton Sovereign
        - Mainsfield Lady
    - **Bute of Trentham**
      - F.C. Peter of Whitmore
        - F.C. Peter of Faskally
        - Logan Lorna
      - Trilby
        - Timothy
        - Bee of Whitmore
  - **Teazle of Whitmore**
    - **Ch. Ilderton Ben**
      - Bobby
        - Smiler
        - Atholl Lass
      - Nell
        - Rover
        - Jet
    - **Phlox**
      - Ch. Brayton Swift
        - Brayton Sir Richard
        - Betty
      - Gwendoline
        - F.C. Peter of Faskally
        - Juniper

F.C. Timbertown Clansman

- Pons Junior of Wingan
  - Ch. Drinkstone Pons of Wingan (imp.)
    - Ch. Banchory Danilo
      - Dual Ch. Banchory Bolo
        - Scandal of Glynn
        - Caerhowell Nettle
      - Munden Scarcity
        - Ch. Banchory Lucky
        - Banchory Betty
    - Ch. Drinkstone Peg (imp.)
      - Toi of Whitmore
        - Tyg of Whitmore
        - Bute of Trentham
      - Ch. Pride of Somersby
        - Brayton Siddy
        - June of Somersby
  - Orchardton Doris of Wingan (imp.)
    - Ch. Ingleston Ben
      - Duke of Kirkmahoe (imp.)
        - Ch. Withington Banter
        - Kirkmahoe Dina
      - Ingleston Nancy
        - Banchory Roger
        - Brocklehirst Nell
    - Orchardton Dawn (imp.)
      - Ch. Brocklehirst Donner
        - Dual Ch. Banchory Bolo
        - Murrayfield Bet
      - Hardies Choice
        - Dual Ch. Titus of Whitmore
        - Kempston Dinah

- Black and Blue Rain
  - Black and Blue Jett
    - Beechgrove Dick (imp.)
      - Brayton Smut
        - Ch. Brayton Swift
        - Brayton Queen
      - Beechgrove Rose
        - F.C. Peter of Faskally
        - Hammond's Gypsey
    - Beechgrove Gypsey (imp.)
      - Rhininever Rock
        - Coltness Rock, 1910
        - Glenlossie Juno
      - Nithsdale Sal
        - Waterdale Duke
        - Sally
  - War Bride
    - Diver of Liphook (imp.)
      - Cotter of Faircote
        - Beningbrough Tangle
        - Tatters of Faircote
      - Munden Swindle, 1920
        - Ch. Banchory Lucky
        - Mercy of Shipton
    - Ridgeland Black Diamond (imp.)
      - Garrochty Fluff
        - Summer
        - Hammond's Jester
      - Ridgeland Jet
        - Saffrons Bob
        - Exeat Susan

Dual Ch. Little Pierre of Deercreek

Pettistree Dan
— Dual Ch. Banchory Painter
—— Peter The Painter
——— F.C. Ledsham Peter
——— Dinah
—— Glenhead Bess
——— F.C. Ledsham Peter
——— L'Ile Bouncing Girl

Eng. & Am. F.C. Hiwood Mike (imp.)
— F.C. Quest of Wilbury
—— Ch. Ingleston Ben
——— Duke of Kirkmahoe
——— Ingleston Nancy
—— F.C. Muntham Raven
——— Banchory Corbie
——— Beningbrough Tansey
— Cedars Michael
—— F.C. Main
——— The Limit
——— Choice of Kirkmahoe
—— Stourhead Joyce
——— Wincombe Joe
——— Bell

Pettistree Poppet
— Cransford Flapper
—— Peter of Bircham
——— Ch. Banchory Danilo
——— Trilby of Hingham
—— Danbury Faith
——— Hailes Peter
——— Danbury Fudge

F.C. Tar of Arden

Hiwood Risk (imp.)
— Hiwood D'Arcy
—— Ch. Banchory Danilo
——— Dual Ch. Banchory Bolo
——— Munden Scarcity
—— Santino
——— Dual Ch. Titus of Whitmore
——— Kingswalden Sadie
— F.C. Hiwood Chance
—— F.C. Beningbrough Tanco
——— Banchory Corbie
——— Beningbrough Tansey
—— Rockstead Swift
——— Rag Tag
——— June

Peggy of Shipton (imp.)
— Ronald of Candahar
—— Rag Tag
——— F.C. Tag of Whitmore
——— Squib of Belvoir
—— June
——— Sandhoe Jock
——— Sequin
— Gehta
—— Banchory Bluff
——— Dual Ch. Banchory Bolo
——— Brocklehirst Nell
—— Ch. Balberdie
——— Muto
——— Balmuto Pinkie

188

Dual Ch. Cherokee Buck
F.C. Cherokee Medicine Man
F.C. Freehaven Muscles

- D.C. Grangemead Precocious
  - D.C. Shed of Arden
    - Ch. Raffles of Earlsmoor
      - Thatch of Whitmore
        - D.C. Titus of Whitmore
        - Tee of Whitmore
      - Task of Whitmore
        - Toi of Whitmore
        - Teazle of Whitmore
    - F.C. Decoy of Arden
      - Odds On (imp.)
        - The Favourite
        - Jest
      - Peggy of Shipton (imp.)
        - Ronald of Candahar
        - Gehta
  - Huron Lady
    - Ch. Banchory Trump of Wingan (imp.)
      - Blenheim Scamp
        - Balwearie
        - Blenheim Lady
      - Lady Daphne
        - Saffrons Bob
        - Haste
    - Ch. Bancstone Lorna
      - D.C. Bramshaw Bob
        - Ch. Ingleston Ben
        - Bramshaw Brimble
      - Ch. Drinkstone Peg (imp.)
        - Toi of Whitmore
        - Ch. Pride of Somersby

- Grangemead Sharon
  - Eng. & Am. F.C. Hiwood Mike (imp.)
    - Pettistree Dan
      - D.C. Banchory Painter
        - Peter The Painter
        - Glenhead Bess
      - F.C. Quest of Wilbury
        - Ch. Ingleston Ben
        - F.C. Muntham Raven
    - Pettistree Poppet
      - Cedars Michael
        - F.C. Main
        - Stourhead Joyce
      - Cransford Flapper
        - Peter of Bircham
        - Danbury Faith
  - Grangemead Angel
    - F.C. Freehaven Jay
      - F.C. Glenairlie Rover
        - Dalbeattie Tango
        - Lady Matilda
      - Spot of Barrington
        - Duke of We Twa
        - Wendy of Barrington
    - Langbourne Darkie (imp.)
      - Cariboo of Langbourne
        - Ch. Banchory Trueman
        - Stourhead Gilda (interbred)
      - Langbourne Black Bess
        - Iwerne Minster Darkie
        - Manswood Jet

189

Dual Ch. Bracken Sweep

F.C. Timbertown Clansman

Pons Junior of Wingan
- Ch. Drinkstone Pons of Wingan (imp.)

Black and Blue Rain
- Orchardton Doris of Wingan (imp.)
- Black and Blue Jett
- War Bride

Bracken of Timbertown

F.C. Banchory Nightlight (imp.)
- Blackworth Midnight
- Dinah of Wongalee

Connie

Bancstone Peggy of Wingan
- Dual Ch. Bramshaw Bob
- Ch. Drinkstone Peg of Wingan

Banchory Benhmore

Ingleston Nith
- Lochar Mac
- Kinmount Juno

Gay's Vera
- F.C. Beningbrough Tanco
- F.C. Vidi of Adderley

Glenhead Sweep (imp.)

Terence of Lintrathen
- Pete (unreg.)
- Bess (unreg.)

Glenhead Biddy

Glenhead Bess
- F.C. Ledsham Peter
- L'Ile Bouncing Girl

Geoffrey of Northaw
Lochar Kate
Bachelor
Kinmount Pax
Banchory Corbie
Beningbrough Tansey
Vici
Weston Banquet

St. Mary's Donson, 1915
Dalbeattie Rose
Ingleston Don
Heather Belle

Ch. Banchory Danilo
Ch. Drinkstone Peg
Ch. Ingleston Ben
Orchardton Dawn
Beechgrove Dick (imp.)
Beechgrove Gypsey (imp.)
Diver of Liphook (imp.)
Ridgeland Black Diamond (imp.)
Ch. Wilworth Rip
Brookstone Jet
Ch. Beningbrough Tangle
Wendy of Wongalee
Ch. Ingleston Ben
Bramshaw Brimble
Toi of Whitmore
Ch. Pride of Somersby

190

Fort Parrot King

Fort Parrot Queen

Cole of Golden City

Black Spook of Riverside

Duke of Whitmore (Canada)

Susan of Austin

Hurricane's Inky Branta

Shadow II

F.C. Timbertown Clansman

Jet of Kingdale

Ch. Bancstone Judy of Kingdale

Dark Lady

Smithy

Palmer's Honey Girl

Kress Lady Pamela

Nat. F.C. Massie's Sassy Boots,
1956

Blackworth Midnight

F.C. Banchory Nightlight of
Wingan (imp.)

Dinah of Wongalee

Darky of Wingan

Hiwood Risk (imp.)

F.C. Ledgelands Dora

Della of Knocke (imp.)

Penny of Wingan

Blenheim Scamp

Ch. Banchory Trump of Wingan

Lady Daphne

Bancstone Dinah

F.C. Banchory Nightlight of
Wingan (imp.)

Laquer

Cheverells Dina (imp.)

191

F.C. Beau of The Lark (Y)

Ace of Whitmore II
- Ch. Earlsmoor Moor of Arden
  - Ch. Raffles of Earlsmoor
    - Thatch of Whitmore
    - Task of Whitmore
  - F.C. Decoy of Arden
    - Odds On
    - Peggy of Shipton
- Ebony Queen of Austin
  - Kansas Smokey Boy
    - Ace of Whitmore
    - Inspiration of Harwod
  - Miss Suzette
    - Speck of Coatuit
    - Tip of Rodall

Cedar Lake Trish
- Wandy of Minnetonka
  - Smithy
    - Corky
    - Princess Sedean
  - Rea Rita
    - King W
    - Pate De Black
- Queen of Atkins
  - Andy of Cram
    - Ch. Banchory Trump of Wingan
    - Ch. Grand Duchess Victor II
  - Everett's Scooter
    - Tuppy's Paladine
    - Peck of Harwood

192

Pedigree of Nat. F.C. Cork of Oakwood Lane, 1954

- **Nat. F.C. Cork of Oakwood Lane, 1954**
  - Dual Ch. Little Pierre of Deercreek
    - Coastal Charger of Deercreek
      - F.C. Hiwood Mike
        - Pettistree Dan
        - Pettistree Poppet
      - F.C. Tar of Arden
        - Hiwood Risk
        - Peggy of Shipton
    - Marvadel Cinders
      - Ch. Raffles of Earlsmoor
        - Thatch of Whitmore
        - Task of Whitmore
      - Marvadel Topsy
        - Ledgelands Donne
        - Solwyn Duchess (imp.)
  - Anoka Liza Jane of Kingdale
    - Dual Ch. Bracken Sweep
      - Glenhead Sweep (imp.)
        - Banchory Benhmore
        - Glenhead Biddy
      - Bracken of Timbertown
        - F.C. Timbertown Clansman
        - Connie
    - Kingdale's Belle
      - Tar of York
        - F.C. The Spider of Kingswere
        - Queen Kole
      - Jet of Runneymede
        - Trader Horn
        - Bancstone Dinah

Nat. F.C. Spirit Lake Duke, 1957, 1959

F.C. Gun of Arden

Smudge of Prairie Creek Farm

Black Hawk Queen Susan

Toff of Hamyax (imp.)

Detmore Brandy
Tracey Pavane

F.C. Decoy of Arden

Odds On
Peggy of Shipton

Banrigg Banner (imp.)

Ch. Towyriver Don
Venus of Barbon

Black Hawk Cindy Girl

Sambo
Kegonsay Gypsey

Burwash
Detmore Judy
F.C. Beningbrough Tanco
Tracey Pansey
The Favourite
Jest
Ronald of Candahar
Gehta
Ch. Banchory Bolo's Trust
Towyriver Bramble
Towyriver Barney
Gronwen Jet
Gar Bo
Bamrick Lady
Mick of Barrington
Gypsey of Koshkonong

Random Lake Black Ghost

Deercreek's Do It Now

Hullabaloo of Audlon

F. & A.F.C. Marvadel Black Gum

Mint of Barrington
Marvadel Cinders

Symphony at Deercreek

Dual Ch. Shed of Arden
F.C. Tar of Arden

Eng. F. & Am. Dual Ch. Treveilyr Swift

Penlan Don
Treveilyr Starlight

Comay Classy Chassis

Dual Ch. Little Pierre of Deercreek
Wardwyn Warbler

F.C. Glenairlie Rover
Wingan's Daily Double
Ch. Raffles of Earlsmoor
Marvadel Topsy
Ch. Raffles of Earlsmoor
F.C. Decoy of Arden
Odds On
Peggy of Shipton
Ch. Durley Beech
Durley Some Other Time
Jestaphome
Joodaphome
F.C. Hiwood Mike
F.C. Tar of Arden
Ch. Earlsmoor Moor of Arden
Ch. Buddha of Arden

194

F. & A.F.C. Paha Sapa Chief, II

F.C. Freehaven Muscles

Dual Ch. Grangemead Precocious

Dual Ch. Shed of Arden

Ch. Raffles of Earlsmoor (imp.)

Thatch of Whitmore
Task of Whitmore

F.C. Decoy of Arden

Odds On
Peggy of Shipton

Ch. Banchory Trump of Wingan (imp.)

Blenheim Scamp
Lady Daphne

Huron Lady

Ch. Banstone Lorna

Dual Ch. Bramshaw Bob
Ch. Drinkstone Peg of Wingan

Grangemead Sharon

Pettistree Dan

Eng. & Am. F.C. Hiwood Mike

Dual Ch. Banchory Painter
F.C. Quest of Wilbury

Pettistree Poppet

Cedars Michael
Cransford Flapper

Grangemead Angel

F.C. Freehaven Jay

F.C. Glenairlie Rover (imp.)
Spot of Barrington

Langbourne Darkie (imp.)

Cariboo of Langbourne
Langbourne Black Bess

F.C. Deercreek's Be-Wise

F.C. The Spider of Kingswere

Good Hope Smoake

F.C. Hiwood Mike

Pettistree Dan
Pettistree Poppet

Drulochnan Dance of Timbertown (imp.)

Ardoch Sandy
Donside Gwen

Jean of Sandylands

Ch. Jerryslad of Sandylands (imp.)

Ch. Jerry of Sandylands
Mordrem Violet

Jetta of Sandylands

Ch. Jerry of Sandylands
Mordrem Bess

Treasure State Be-Wise

F. & A.F.C. Marvadel Black Gum

Mint of Barrington

F.C. Glenairlie Rover
Wingan's Daily Double

Marvadel Topsy

Ledgelands Donne
Solwyn Duchess (imp.)

Symphony at Deercreek

Dual Ch. Shed of Arden

Ch. Raffles of Earlsmoor
F.C. Decoy of Arden

F.C. Tar of Arden

Hiwood Risk (imp.)
Peggy of Shipton

Dual Ch. Burnham Buff (Y)

Ch. Deercreek's Toddy Talk II
- F.C. Marvadel Black Gum
  - Mint of Barrington
    - F.C. Glenairlie Rover
      - Dalbeattie Tango
      - Lady Matilda
    - Wingan's Daily Double
      - Odds On
      - Orchardton Doris
  - Marvadel Cinders
    - Ch. Raffles of Earlsmoor
      - Thatch of Whitmore
      - Task of Whitmore
    - Marvadel Topsy
      - Ledgelands Donne
      - Solwyn Duchess (imp.)
- F.C. Tar of Arden
  - Hiwood Risk (imp.)
    - Hiwood D'Arcy (imp.)
      - Ch. Banchory Danilo
      - Santina
    - F.C. Hiwood Chance
      - F.C. Beningbrough Tanco
      - Rockstead Swift
  - Peggy of Shipton
    - Ronald of Candahar
      - Rag Tag
      - June
    - Gehta
      - Banchory Bluff
      - Ch. Balbeardie

Taffy of Bur*Mur Farm
- Buff of Navarre
  - Rusty of Navarre
    - Kenilworth Buckshot
      - Kenilworth Jim
      - Ailie of Kenilworth
    - Lochlomond Bonnie
      - Smithy
      - Lochlomond Lassie
  - Northshore Goldie
    - Butch of Barrington
      - Goldacre Dan
      - Patricia R
    - Northshore Trixie
      - Sun of Tarvie
      - Northshore Midge
- Ch. Ginger of Pyreshire
  - Golden Pirate
    - Tipperary Tipp
      - King W
      - Pate De Black
    - Queen Charlotte
      - Smithy
      - Queen Ann
  - Princess Topsy Sue
    - Goldacre Nick
      - Gold Acre Dan
      - Patricia R
    - Black Pepper Lou
      - Nig of Ripley
      - Lady Constance

196

Dual Ch. Grangemead Precocious

Dual Ch. Shed of Arden

Ch. Raffles of Earlsmoor
— Thatch of Whitmore
— — Dual Ch. Titus of Whitmore
— — Tee of Whitmore
— Task of Whitmore
— — Toi of Whitmore
— — Teazle of Whitmore

F.C. Decoy of Arden
— Odds On
— — The Favourite
— — Jest
— Peggy of Shipton (imp.)
— — Ronald of Candahar
— — Gehta

Huron Lady

Ch. Banchory Trump of Wingan (imp.)
— Blenheim Scamp
— — Balwearie
— — Blenheim Lady
— Lady Daphne
— — Saffrons Bob
— — Haste

Ch. Bancstone Lorna
— Dual Ch. Bramshaw Bob
— — Ch. Ingleston Ben
— — Bramshaw Brimble
— Ch. Drinkstone Peg (imp.)
— — Toi of Whitmore
— — Ch. Pride of Somersby

Beautywood's Creole Jane

F.C. Gilmore's Peggy

Montahome Don of Arden

Dual Ch. Shed of Arden
— Ch. Raffles of Earlsmoor
— — Thatch of Whitmore
— — Task of Whitmore
— F.C. Decoy of Arden
— — Odds On
— — Peggy of Shipton

Nell of Barrington
— Bantry Banker
— — Ch. Banchory Trump
— — Polly Prim
— Bantry Baroness
— — F.C. Banchory Nightlight
— — Poppy

Betty of Blake

Ch. Earlsmoor Moor of Arden
— Ch. Raffles of Earlsmoor
— — Thatch of Whitmore
— — Task of Whitmore
— F.C. Decoy of Arden
— — Odds On
— — Peggy of Shipton

Bright of Blake
— F.C. Banchory Varnish of Wingan (imp.)
— — Dual Ch. Banchory Painter
— — Dina of Wongalee
— Cheverell's Dina (imp.)
— — Ch. Ingleston Ben
— — Xmas Nora

197

F. & F.C. Black Brook's Lady Bimba

A.F.C. West Island Comet

Eng. F.C. & Am. Dual Ch. Treveilyr Swift (imp.)

Penlan Don

Ch. Durley Beech
Ch. Worrick of Winscales
Badgery Bridget

Durley Some Other Time
Liddly Thatcher
Liddly Ouzel

Treveilyr Starlight

Jestaphome
F.C. Rockstead Footpad
Sally O'Fon

Joodaphome
Jestaphome
Jennaphome

Black Point Inga's Interest

F.C. Timbertown Clansman

Pons Jr. of Wingan
Ch. Drinkstone Pons of Wingan
Ch. Drinkstone Peg

Black and Blue Rain
Black and Blue Jett
War Bride

Interest of Timbertown

Mint of Barrington
F.C. Glenairlie Rover
Wingan's Daily Double

Maude of Timbertown
F.C. Timbertown Clansman
Bramble of Timbertown

Deercreek's Ebony Sprite

F. & A.F.C. Marvadel Black Gum

Mint of Barrington

F.C. Glenairlie Rover
Dalbeattie Tango
Lady Matilda

Wingan's Daily Double
Odds On
Orchardton Doris of Wingan

Marvadel Cinders

Ch. Raffles of Earlsmoor
Thatch of Whitmore
Task of Whitmore

Marvadel Topsy
Ledgelands Donne
Solwyn Duchess

Stylish Patsy of Deercreek

Dual Ch. Shed of Arden

Ch. Raffles of Earlsmoor
Thatch of Whitmore
Task of Whitmore

F.C. Decoy of Arden
Odds On
Peggy of Shipton

Peggy of Pheasant Lawn

Ch. Banchory Trump of Wingan
Blenheim Scamp
Lady Daphne

Laquer
F.C. Banchory Varnish (imp.)
Cheverells Dina (imp.)

198

Nat. Am. & F.C. Ace's Sheba of Ardyn, 1962

F. & A.F.C. Ardyn's Ace of Merwalfin

Dual Ch. Shed of Arden

Ch. Raffles of Earlsmoor

Thatch of Whitmore

Dual Ch. Titus of Whitmore
Tee of Whitmore

Task of Whitmore

Toi of Whitmore
Teazle of Whitmore

F.C. Decoy of Arden

Odds On

The Favourite
Jest

Peggy of Shipton

Ronald of Candahar
Gehta

Cindy of Merwalfin

Sir Wilfred Grenfell

F.C. Blind of Arden

Odds On
Peggy of Shipton

Bittersweet Ebony

Ebony
Grushenka

Lady Wilfred Grenfell

Timothy of Arden

Fife of Kennoway
Pitch of Arden

Bittersweet Ebony

Ebony
Grushenka

F.C. Rip of Holly Hill

Skip of Timbertown

F.C. Timbertown Clansman

Pons Jr. of Wingan
Black and Blue Rain

Span of Timbertown

Ch. Drinkstone Pons
Wingan Venture

Okanagan Molly

Varnish's Tuff

F.C. Banchory Varnish
Marjay of Wingan

Okanagan Lassie II

Okanagan Rusty
Okanagan Nell

Chanbar Christmas Holly

Dual Ch. Shed of Arden

Ch. Raffles of Earlsmoor

Thatch of Whitmore
Task of Whitmore

F.C. Decoy of Arden

Odds On
Peggy of Shipton

Graysmarsh Christmas

Graysmarsh Middy

F.C. Blind of Arden

Odds On
Peggy of Shipton

Judy of Homeside

Bing of Puget
Bess of Homeside

199

Nat. Ch. Bigstone Hope, 1962

- F.C. Cork of Oakwood Lane
  - Dual Ch. Little Pierre of Deercreek
    - F.C. Hiwood Mike
      - Pettistree Dan
        - Dual Ch. Banchory Painter
        - F.C. Quest of Wilbury
      - Pettistree Poppet
        - Cedars Michael
        - Cransford Flapper
    - F.C. Tar of Arden
      - Hiwood Risk (imp.)
        - Hiwood D'Arcy
        - F.C. Hiwood Chance
      - Peggy of Shipton
        - Ronald of Candahar
        - Gehta
  - Marvadel Cinders
    - Ch. Raffles of Earlsmoor
      - Thatch of Whitmore
        - Dual Ch. Titus of Whitmore
        - Tee of Whitmore
      - Task of Whitmore
        - Toi of Whitmore
        - Teazle of Whitmore
    - Marvadel Topsy
      - Ledgelands Donne
        - Hiwood Risk
        - Della of Knocke (imp.)
      - Solwyn Duchess (imp.)
        - Solwyn Thor
        - Banchory Theime
- Bigstone Rickey
  - F. & A.F.C. Rip's Bingo
    - Just Rip
      - Montahome Don of Arden
        - Dual Ch. Shed of Arden
        - Nell of Barrington
      - Montahome Baby Dinah
        - Banrigg Banner
        - Black Dinah of Barrington
    - Rockett Sal
      - F.C. Yodel of Morexpense
        - F.C. Freehaven Jay
        - Ch. Echo of Arden
      - Duchess of Birchdale
        - Smithy
        - Mac's Black Beauty
  - Little Tops of Bigstone
    - Dual Ch. Little Pierre of Deercreek
      - F.C. Hiwood Mike
        - Pettistree Dan
        - Pettistree Poppet
      - F.C. Tar of Arden
        - Hiwood Risk
        - Peggy of Shipton
    - Tops of Bigstone
      - F.C. Banchory Nightlight (imp.)
        - Peggy of Shipton
        - Blackworth Midnight
      - Scarborough Shenka
        - Dinah of Wongalee
        - Ebony
        - Grushenka

8

Labradors at Shows in America

ALTHOUGH the Labrador in America has always been first and foremost a trial and shooting dog, the nucleus of the first club members was responsible for introducing him to the general American public through the practical and necessary medium of dog shows. For quite a few years they were enthusiastic followers of the bench, and were well aware that this medium, in its place, was of value to the breed.

Unlike his British counterpart, whose astronomical show numbers have always swelled the entries at championship and open shows, and where a still unbroken record was once reached at Crufts for Lady Howe, directly after World War I, with over 900 of the breed, the Labrador in this country is not numerically strong in show attendance. Group wins and best in shows have been awarded sparingly to them, in comparison to the more spectacular gundog varieties. Nonetheless, the few recipients of these honors have been worthy of them, and extra credit is due them for good breed representation. Labradors that have won groups and best in shows from 1958 to 1963 have been: Eng. and Am. Ch. Sam of

Blaircourt, owned by Mrs. G. Lambert; Ch. Gargieson Boy (Ch. Ruler of Blaircourt ex Wendover Bathsheba), owned by Mrs. Margo C. Bryant; Hallbroom Grouse (Brackenbank Tinker ex Pride of Holliday), owned by Everett E. Jackson III; and Ch. Leatty Bickerton Salmon Queen (Dobrudden Buffer ex Bella Mischief), a Yellow bitch, owned by Dr. and Mrs. Clifton Rose. All of these are imports.

In spite of what currently seems to be a general apathy towards bench activities among American trialers, many do appreciate a good-looking, typical dog, and are quick to spot and remember one with style and demeanor in carrying himself; these are two qualities that are rarely demonstrated in an ugly specimen.

America has had a greater number of dual champions than Britain has ever had. It is not easy for a working dog over there to attain a bench championship with the high quality and quantity of bench dogs being shown continually. It is also not easy to attain a field title over there. There are very few trials a year compared to ours; all are limited to twenty-four dogs in a stake, and all are by nomination; if one is not nominated for that year, one may well have to wait another year to get the opportunity again.

Many early American show supporters were converts from other breeds. Among those were the late Prentice Talmage, from Scotties to a partiality for the Yellows; Dr. Milbank, from English Springers and Terriers; the David Wagstaffs, from Chows; and so forth.

Show entries began seriously with the advent of the many Carlisle imports and others of that era. Judges were carefully chosen, and many of them from Canada, such as William Pym, Mrs. Alban Sturdee, Walter Reeves, and John Ritchie, gave of their experience. Alva Rosenberg was one of the first American all-rounders to appreciate the breed and judge it with understanding and authority. He wrote in an article in *Town and Country*, December, 1933: "A round of applause is due the Labrador Retriever Club on the great work it is doing for the breed. It's field trials have been marked with successes and we understand that the bench show sponsored by it drew a most responsive entry. It has been an uphill climb to get them proper recognition at shows, but Mr. Prentice Talmage's Ch. Bentley Dina has already placed in groups so perhaps the goal is in sight."

As was previously stated, the first American bench champion was Boli of Blake, owned by the Hon. Franklin B. Lord, bred in England by Lady Howe. Show critiques were accepted with grace in those days, and here is one by Colin MacFarlane, trainer for Robert Goelet's Glenmere Kennel, on the 1933 Westbury, Long Island Show. (There was an entry of sixteen Labradors for Mr. George Thomas.)

"Boli of Blake must have his points for the title by now; he has a pleasing head and a nice eye but balance and soundness are not his strong points.

"Vigilant of Glenmere, Robert Goelet's American-bred entry is as sound as they make them but he refused to show in Open Class and was pegged back to third. In front of him and behind Boli, was Odds On, Marshall Field's well known field trial dog; Odds On is an upstanding dog with good legs and real catlike feet. He is beginning to show his five years, but of course he has done a lot of hard work. Joan Redmond showed some lovely bitches. [Joan Redmond, later Mrs. Curtis Read. H. W.] Dr. Milbank, one of the most popular men today either at field trials or in the show ring judged Springers at this show, and to my mind made a perfect job. He will be called on often, and will be copied, I know, in his style of judging. It was something new for the ringsiders to see a judge running his dogs across as well as coming and going. These field trial men know what they are looking for."

The year 1934 was a banner one for Labradors at Westminster. The late W. L. McCandlish, then president of the Kennel Club of England, presided as judge with an entry of twenty-seven.

Again, Colin MacFarlane's sprightly pen depicts the scene: "There can be no doubt," he writes, "that the Labrador Retriever has arrived and is in the hands of sportsmen of prominence. Mr. McCandlish judged them, the ringside at the time, being lined by files of shooting owners, of large and heavily stocked game estates. Among these represented were F. P. Lord, Jr., Clarence MacKay, David and Mrs. Wagstaff, M. J. Fitzgerald, Miss Joan Redmond, Roland P. Redmond, J. F. Carlisle, L. Morgan, Harry Hartneet, and Dr. and Mrs. Samuel Milbank.

"Ch. Drinkstone Pons, shown in the Open class [as was the custom then, H. W.] came, saw and conquered for the second year in succession at Westminster, and to my mind, not by the usual nose but by several lengths. Pons is true to type, and I believe were he to return to his native England, would clean up. Among dogs that have been benched for the past few years, he has no rivals. A dual purpose dog is always first with me; therefore, Drinkstone Pons, by his win at the Garden [he placed second in the group at this show, handled by Dave Elliot, first place going to the Irish setter of the day, Ch. Milson O'Boy. H. W.] and a first and fourth at trials, is my choice for top dog for the past year!"

Colin goes on to mention that, "At the East Islip trials I complimented Dr. Milbank on Ch. Raffles's good work and asked him who his scout was on the other side. The Doctor replied, 'Colin, that was one time a Scotsman gave away something for nothing!' I answered him, 'Doctor, Scotsmen seem to be making that a habit, as Dr. Wilson who judged the Spaniel trials at Fisher's Island in 1933—broke and gave that good dog to Mr. Wagstaff!' I could have added that I know Scotsmen on this side who would give either man their best dog! Elias Vail secured a daughter of Nith's Double and a son of Banchory Nightlight, and Mrs. Rowcliffe, well known Spaniel fancier bought the former."

The Labrador Club's first Specialty show was held Thursday, May 18, 1933, in New York City, with an entry of thirty-four for Mrs. Marshall Field.

Exhibitors were the Hon. F. B. Lord, Robert Goelet, William Dick, Kathleen Starr, W. A. Harriman, Wilton Lloyd-Smith, Bentley Kennels of Prentice Talmage, Charles Laurance, Joan Redmond, Henry Root Stern, and others. Dogs and bitches were shown together in puppy, novice and limit classes. The largest class was the novice, with thirteen entered, among them a yellow dog owned by Wadsworth Lewis called Auberry Bruce, by Corona of Boghurst ex Auberry Golden Vanity. The class winner was Kathleen Starr's Huntview Guard (Black and Blue Jett ex War Bride). In the Limit class, won by Boli of Blake, who subsequently won best of breed, one saw three imports, Peggy of Shipton, Hiwood Risk, and Drinkstone Span. Span, by Eng. Dual Ch. Titus of Whitmore ex Drinkstone Gyp, was owned by Wm. M. Decker, and was best of opposite sex at this show. There were five in the field trial class, including Charles Laurance's Meadow Farm Doctor (Dusker ex Garscube Meg), Mrs. Starr's import, Juno Girl (Chino of Purse Caundle ex Lady Juno), F. B. Lord's Banchory Trace (Self Starter ex Jetter),

Mr. Stern's Czar Qu'Appelle (Duke of Harwood ex Qu'Appelle, Imp.), and Mr. Lewis' Auberry Bruce.

The Club's second annual show was held the following year on July 6th, judged by John Ritchie of Canada, with an entry of fifty-six for this well-known Canadian breeder. With such encouraging support, the Specialty has been held annually from that date on, the highest entry having been in 1959 for Judge Jim Cowie, with forty-nine dogs, thirty-five bitches, seventeen specials, for a total of 101 and 161 entries.

A complete list of the Specialties follows:

May 18, 1933
Judge: Mrs. Marshall Field
Best of Breed: Ch. Boli of Blake, Mr. Lord
Best of Opposite Sex: Drinkstone Span, Wm. Decker, Jr.
Field Trial: Czar Qu'Appelle, Henry Root Stern

July 6, 1934
Judge: John Ritchie
Best of Breed: Ch. Drinkstone Pons of Wingan, J. F. Carlisle
Best of Opposite Sex: Polly Prim, M. Fitzgerald
Field Trial: Banchory Trump of Wingan, J. F. Carlisle

September 30, 1935
Judge: Mrs. E. Alban Sturdee
Best of Breed: Bancstone Lorna of Wingan, J. F. Carlisle
Best of Opposite Sex: Ch. Boli of Blake, Mr. Lord
Field Trial: Ch. Boli of Blake, Mr. Lord

June 5, 1936
Judge: Mr. George S. Thomas
Best of Breed: Raffles of Earlsmoor, Dr. Milbank
Best of Opposite Sex: Echo of Arden, Mrs. Morgan Belmont
Field Trial: Raffles of Earlsmoor, Dr. Milbank

June 18, 1937
Judge: J. Gould Remick
Best of Breed: Ch. Banchory Trump of Wingan, J. F. Carlisle
Best of Opposite Sex: Ch. Ledgelands Bridesmaid, Mrs. D. Wagstaff
Field Trial: Grouse of Arden, A. V. Harriman

June 10, 1938
Judge: Mr. H. T. Peters
Best of Breed: Ch. Earlsmoor Moor of Arden, Dr. Milbank
Best of Opposite Sex: Mill Cove Jet, A. Gwynne
Field Trial: Ch. Raffles of Earlsmoor, Dr. Milbank

May 31, 1939
Judge: Mr. Walter Roesler
Best of Breed: Ch. Earlsmoor Moor of Arden, Dr. Milbank
Best of Opposite Sex: Braes of Arden, A. W. Harriman
Field Trial: Ch. Earlsmoor Moor of Arden, Dr. Milbank

May 24, 1940
Judge: Mrs. Walton Ferguson
Best of Breed: Ch. Earlsmoor Moor of Arden, Dr. Samuel Milbank
Best of Opposite Sex: Ch. Gorse of Arden, Mrs. M. Belmont
Field Trial: Ch. The Wench, Mrs. W. Ewing

June 13, 1941
Judge: J. Gould Remick
Best of Breed: Ch. Earlsmoor Moor of Arden, Dr. Milbank
Best of Opposite Sex: Earlsmoor Marlin of Arden, Dr. Milbank
Field Trial: Ch. Earlsmoor Moor of Arden, Dr. Milbank

June 13, 1942
Judge: Mr. Lewis Worden
Best of Breed: Ledgelands Black Swan, Mrs. Wagstaff
Best of Opposite Sex: Udalia's Report, Miss Wagstaff
Field Trial: Not awarded

September 12, 1943
Judge: Mr. G. V. Glebe
Best of Breed: Ch. Earlsmoor Moor of Arden, Dr. Milbank
Best of Opposite Sex: Kilsyth Judy, Gerald M. Livingston
Field Trial: Ch. Earlsmoor Marlin of Arden, Dr. Milbank

September 24, 1944
Judge: Mr. Walter Reeves
Best of Breed: Ch. Michael of Wynward, Mrs. Edmund Poor
Best of Opposite Sex: Ledgelands Titmouse, Mrs. Wagstaff
Field Trial: Ch. Earlsmoor Marlin of Arden, Dr. Milbank

September 30, 1945
Judge: Mr. Walter Roesler
Best of Breed: Wardwyn Whiskers, Mrs. Poor
Best of Opposite Sex: Good Hope Aberdeen, Mrs. John S. Williams
Field Trial: Good Hope Aberdeen, Mrs. John S. Williams

September 12, 1946
Judge: Mr. Alva Rosenberg
Best of Breed: Hugger Mugger, Joan W. Redmond
Best of Opposite Sex: Ch. Wardwyn Welcome, Mrs. Poor
Field Trial: Field Ch. Shadows Ebony Bob, Mr. and Mrs. Howes Burton

June 10, 1947
Judge: Mr. J. Leonard Buck
Best of Breed: Dual Ch. Little Pierre of Deercreek, Mr. and Mrs. P. Bakewell, III
Best of Opposite Sex: Ch. Wardwyn Welcome, Mrs. Poor
Field Trial: Ch. Winsome of Wynward, A. K. Peek

June 11, 1948
Judge: Dr. Samuel Milbank
Best of Breed: Ch. Stowaway at Deercreek, Mr. Gerald Livingston
Best of Opposite Sex: Chidley Spook, Mr. and Mrs. Curtis S. Read
Field Trial: Field Ch. Bengal of Arden, Mrs. James Austin

June 25, 1949
Judge: Mrs. Major Godsol
Best of Breed: Ch. Chidley Spook, Mrs. Curtis Read
Best of Opposite Sex: Chimney Sweep, II, R. Garrett
Field Trial Dogs: Matchmaker for Deercreek, Mr. P. Bakewell, III
Field Trial Bitches: Ch. Miss Dela Winn, Mrs. Harley Butler

May 26, 1950
Judge: Miss Jean Hinkle
Best of Breed: Toots of Dunecht, Mrs. James Austin
Best of Opposite Sex: Miss Dela Winn, Mrs. Harley Butler
Field Trial: Miss Dela Winn, Mrs. Harley Butler

May 20, 1951
Judge: Mr. Walter Roesler
Best of Breed: Hobbimoor's Merganser, T. Horner
Best of Opposite Sex: How-Hi Hunki, Mr. and Mrs. Howes Burton
Field Trial: Wardwyn's Ace of Spades, Mrs. James Austin

May 18, 1952
Judge: Mr. Percy Roberts
Best of Breed: Ch. Chidley Spook, Mrs. Curtis Read
Best of Opposite Sex: Ashur Deacon, Mrs. B. Barty-King
Field Trial: West Island Easter Parade, C. Brokaw

May 17, 1953
Judge: Mr. Walter Reeves
Best of Breed: Port Fortune Smoke Screen, J. G. Hinkle
Best of Opposite Sex: Udalia's Trace, C. L. Andrews, Jr.
Field Trial: Invail's Pennell, C. V. Brokaw, Jr.
Field Trial: Macopin Kate, Mr. and Mrs. H. Burton

May 23, 1954
Judge: Dr. A. A. Mitten
Best of Breed: Chidley Genii, R. Goold and Mrs. Curtis Read
Best of Opposite Sex: Gunner of Landfall, Landfall Kennels
Field Trial: Storm of Landfall, Landfall Kennels

May 28, 1955
Judge: Mr. H. S. Lloyd
Best of Breed: Ch. Gunner of Landfall, Landfall Kennels
Best of Opposite Sex: Chidley Goldfinch, R. Martin and A. Carpenter
Field Trial: Wildfield Mickey Finn, Mrs. Eric Wood

May 26, 1956
Judge: Mrs. Major Godsol
Best of Breed: Whygin Skier of Southdown, Mrs. N. Tuttle
Best of Opposite Sex: Ch. Lockerbie Blackfella, Mrs. James Warwick
Field Trial: Invail's Pogey Bait (liver), Mrs. Rita Haggerty

May 25, 1957
Judge: Mr. Percy Roberts
Best of Breed: Golden Chance of Franklin (yellow), Mrs. G. B. Lambert
Best of Opposite Sex: Ore Hill's Sunday Punch, Allen Buck
Field Trial: Newry's Prince of Darkness, Mrs. Joan Blount

Ch. Lockerbie Blackfella (Ballyduff Treesholme Terryboy ex Ch. Ballyduff Candy), sire of thirteen champions, three in Canada.

Ch. Golden Chance of Franklin (Ch. Troublemaker of Franklin ex Pretty Iris), owned by Mrs. Grace Lambert.

September 28, 1958
Judge: James Wright
Best of Breed: Ch. Golden Chance of Franklin (yellow), Mrs. Lambert
Best of Opposite Sex: Landfall's Vulcan, Landfall Kennels
Field Trial: Newry's Prince of Darkness, Mrs. Blount

May 15, 1959
Judge: James A. Cowie
Best of Breed: Ch. Ore Hill's Sunday Punch, Allen Buck
Best of Opposite Sex: Ch. Golden Chance of Franklin, Mrs. Lambert
Field Trial: Ch. Ore Hill's Sunday Punch, Allen Buck

October 13, 1960
Judge: Mr. Hollis Wilson
Best of Breed: Ch. Dark Star of Franklin, Mr. and Mrs. B. Ziessow
Best of Opposite Sex: Ch. Golden Chance of Franklin, Mrs. Lambert
Field Trial: Ch. Ore Hills Sunday Punch, Allen Buck

October 1, 1961
Judge: Mr. Jerome M. Rich
Best of Breed: Ch. Whygin Campaign Promise, Mrs. Mcarthy
Best of Opposite Sex: Ch. Diant Jupiter (yellow), Mrs. Neil Tuttle
Field Trial: None in competition

June 9, 1962
Judge: Mrs. L. W. Bonney
Best of Breed: Ch. Whygin Gold Bullion (yellow), Mrs. H. Ginnel
Best of Opposite Sex: Ch. Whygin Black Gamin, Mrs. B. Birdshall
Field Trial: None in competition

1963
Judge: Joseph Quirk
Best of Breed: Ch. Sam of Blaircourt, Mrs. Grace Lambert
Best of Opposite Sex: Ch. Inky of Deerhaven, Mrs. Peter Wolcott

1964
Judge: Mrs. Helen Warwick
Best of Breed: Ch. Sam of Blaircourt, Mrs. Grace Lambert
Best of Opposite Sex: Sandylands Tara, James F. Lewis, III

English and American Ch. Towy-river James, painted by Ward Binks and owned by Mrs. S. Hallock Du-Pont.

Ch. Whygin Poppitt (Ch. Rupert Dahomey ex Cedar Hill Whygin), owned by Mrs. Helen Ginnell.

Ch. Diant Jupiter (Ch. Landyke Lancer ex Ch. Diant Juliet) and daughters, Chs. Littlemore Talc and Tirrivee Diana.

Among the kennels of renown that started in the 1930's was Chidley, of Mrs. Read, who began exhibiting and breeding as a very young girl. Much of her early stock was based upon two imports, Diver of Liphook and Ridgeland Black Diamond. Diver of Liphook was a son of Ch. Cotter of Faircote ex Munden Swindle. Her excellent brood bitches carried much of this line, besides those of Ch. Earlsmoor Moor of Arden and Dual Ch. Bramshaw Bob. She was fortunate in securing from Mr. Carlisle Ch. Bancstone Bob of Wingan, one of the litter out of Drinkstone Peg, bred in England by Bramshaw Bob. From this she bred one of her best dogs, Hugger Mugger. Her lovely bitch, Ch. Chidley Spook, by Mugger, had a Canadian dam, by Shine of Tibshelf, a grandson, through his dam, of Sandringham San and Shell. Mugger sired some grand dogs in Mrs. Johnson Smith's Chs. Ashur Cameron and Daphne (a yellow), Chs. Chidley Spook and Chidley Goldfinch (yellow), and Mrs. Steven McClellan's Ch. Wildfield Mickey Finn. The quality of her stock bred true, due to her unwavering adherence to the type so clearly stated in the Standard. It was a definite loss to the furtherance of show stock that her interest turned to another breed, delightful as it is. However, we cannot begrudge the Norwiches, and feel confident that she will continue with Labradors. None of us—and there are many—to whom she gave the first push in the right direction will forget her guidance and help in solving the problems of breeding to an ideal.

The prefix of Squirrel Run, owned by Mrs. S. Hallock DuPont, was one of the most discerning regarding this same quality in the breeding of dogs. Mrs. DuPont's first imports came over in 1935 and were Eng. Ch. Towyriver James and Dinah of Tibshelf. Percy Roberts handled both to their American titles. In her own words, Mrs. DuPont describes some of her dogs:

"As far as Squirrel Run Kennels are concerned, our breeding started with the importation of Barry and Dina. The best brood bitch, as far as quality of offspring, was possibly Hawlmark Caress (Sandringham Stow ex Felicity), with Friends Choice of Sandylands a close runner-up. This last bitch produced only one litter, the result of which I still have. She was by Keewatin Big Ben ex Trixie of Keewatin, both these being by Ch. Poppleton Black Lancer and going back to Hayler's Danilo and Hawlmark Twilight. She was by far the best qualified for show, as fine a bitch as I've

212

Int. Ch. Sam of Blaircourt, bred by Grant Cairns, owned by Grace Lambert; holder of 9 record-setting BIS's.

ever seen, bar none, but as she came during the War, we could not show her. Towyriver James was really a magnificently trained gundog, and was used often on water fowl and upland game. Hawlmark Caress was descended on both sides from Banchory Bolo, and on her dam's side to Barry's father, Ch. Banchory Bolo's Trust. My father, George Simmons imported a pair of Labradors in 1928—Ringwold Ben and Patricia of Hepmangrove and we had pups from them. Mr. DuPont had Labradors before we were married, but they were registered as Whitely Kennels."

Her many excellent dogs, such as Chs. Squirrel Run Jack, Juba, Jove, Raven, and Ares (one of the best I have ever seen, but never shown due to broken fangs), descend straight from her original foundation of Towyriver James.

The prefix of Ledgelands, owned by the late Mr. and Mrs. David Wagstaff, was very prominent in dual purpose breeding and a strong contender at shows. Some of their imports included Solwyn Duchess, St. Mary's Duke, Hiwood Risk, and Delle of Knocke, from whom they bred Field Ch. Ledgelands Dora. Their roster of bench champions was large and high in quality and included Chs. Titmouse, Ray, Gleam, Black Swan, and Bridesmaid. Mrs. Wagstaff knew her dogs well and was a most painstaking breeder; she was also an astute and popular judge at shows. Mr. Wagstaff was one of the earliest field trial judges. Both did immense services for the breed.

In surveying these two kennels, it would not be proper to forget the two people who cared so faithfully over the years for their inmates: Ralf Hellum for Ledgelands, and Harry Cameron for Squirrel Run, a well-known trainer of gundogs in his own right, who took over the dogs when Percy Roberts left to take out his judging license. Over the many years, they both gave devoted and loyal service to their charges, displaying good sportsmanship at all times.

Another kennel has been that of the late Miss Jean Hinkle, a popular show judge and an honorary club member. In spite of her beloved Terriers' coming first in her heart, she was a staunch friend of the Labrador. In her passing, the fancy has lost a true friend and ally.

The late Mrs. James Austin of the Catawba affix, a director of the Labrador Club and vice-president, in 1944, of the National Retriever Field Trial Club, was an importer and owner of many first-class dogs, including Ch. Toots of Dunecht, Ch. Zelstone Duke, Dual Ch. Bengal of Arden, and Ch. St. Jones Blackie. She generously supported the bench when entries and interest were at a low ebb. Many of her dogs worked well in trials, not in the least being Field Ch. Young Mint of Catawba.

It may not be considered the place here to mention Mr. and Mrs. Howes Burton of How-Hi, as they were of course primarily connected with trials, and bred one of the early American field champions in Shadow's Ebony Bob, a product of Dave Elliot; but the late Mr. Burton, as past club president and for many years its secretary-treasurer, was licensed, as is Mrs. Burton, to judge all Retrievers at shows. When time permitted they enjoyed exhibiting as well, and always handled their own dogs as true sporting people. "Howsie" will be remembered with affection and esteem by all who knew him.

As time went on, other kennels came to the fore, such as Mrs. Josephine Mills' Uneva prefix, and although she is still active today, she was best known for her three outstanding Blacks, Chs. Uneva Soot, Coal, and Teal. She is well aware of what constitutes a good Labrador; she has always been interested in Obedience work, and bred and owned Trouper, the first U.D.T. Labrador. Ch. Soot was the first Labrador bench champion with the same Obedience degree.

Wardwyn, owned by Mrs. Edmund Poor, had some lovely dogs, many from the older lines of Arden, in Chs. Jackpot, Lucky Penny, Whiskers, and Welcome, and Windbound, the dam of Field Ch. Ebony Bob.

Alvaleigh is owned by J. H. Lee Fisher, well-known breeder of top Derby dogs, and also breeder of Mrs. Lewis' Field Ch. Di-Mundy's Danny, in conjunction with Mrs. Alva Robinson, who imported Danny's dam, Ch. Zelstone Kate. The kennel contained many good-looking workers, some of which were shown on the bench. Champions included Jet of Melrose and Plenty of Pep. One of the best brood bitches kenneled was Earlsmoor Biscuit, litter sister to Wardwyn Windbound.

West Island is the prefix of Mrs. Junius Morgan, an enthusiastic amateur handler at trials. Mrs. Morgan has always divided her loyalties equally between the field and the shows. Her four home-bred field champions are listed elsewhere, and her many black homebred bench champions bear testimony to her allegiance to the show ring and include Black Beulah, Little Fox, Black Baron, Pons Peter, and Desis, the last-named a grand bitch by Field Ch. The Spider of Kingswere ex Grangemead Vixen.

Kennels, some of which started after the war and into this decade —and many of which breed and show both colors—include Mrs. B. De Garis' Abracadabra; Mrs. B. Barty-King's Aldenholme; Mrs. Harley Butler's Dela Winn; and Dutchmoor, owned by Mr. and Mrs. John Van Bloom. Kennels figuring in trial pedigrees are Mr. and Mrs. F. Ziessow's Franklin, breeder of best in show record holder, Ch. Dark Star of Franklin; Harrowby, of Mrs. Gerard B. Lambert, whose comparatively recent association with the breed is being enhanced by judicious purchases from abroad, including Eng. and Am. Ch. Sam of Blaircourt. Harrowby's added tie with field trial interests, under whose ownership are found four field trial champions, all of which qualified for the 1962 Nationals, should help the fancy towards a more balanced approach of the dual purpose doctrine that seemed to flourish in the early days more positively than today. Landfall, of Rear Adm. and Mrs. Chas. L. Andrews, Jr.; Labcroft, of Mr. Julius Chandler; Lockerbie, of Mr. and Mrs. James Warwick; Longwood of Miss Susan Hard; Littlemore, of Mrs. N. R. Tuttle; Rupert, of Mrs. Carleton Howe; Sprucewood, of Mrs. Anne Simoneau, Walden, of Mr. and Mrs. Kurt Unkelbach; Whygin, of Mrs. Helen Ginnell; Wildfield, of Mrs. S. McClellan; Tudor of Mrs. Squire; Mallow of Mrs. Hennessey.

Winners of The Hiwood Mike Trophy

Trophy lists are boring, but there is one of particular interest connected with the bench because it is of dual purpose character.

The Hiwood Mike Trophy was presented to the Club in 1942 by Mrs. John S. Williams, in memory of Hiwood Mike. It was to be awarded at the discretion of the Field Trial Judges "to the best looking, best working Labrador at the Club's annual trial," with custody for one year, owned permanently by the Club.

It was the American duplication of the British Perpetual Challenge Cup offered by Lady Howe annually, at the conclusion of their Club trials. It was awarded directly on the field after the last series.

Eng. & Am. Ch. Sandylands Tanna (Aust. Ch. Sandylands Tan ex Sandy-lands Shadow), bred by Mrs. Broadley, owned by J. Lewis, III.

Ch. Lockerbie Sandylands Tarquin (Ch. Sandylands Tweed of Blaircourt ex Sandylands Shadow), bred by Mrs. Broadley, owned by Helen Warwick.

The Hiwood Mike Trophy was given for the first time at our twelfth trial, in 1942, with Thomas Merritt, Thomas Marshall, and Mrs. Gilbert Chapman as judges. Mrs. Morgan Belmont's Gorse of Arden, winner of the Open stake, won the trophy.

This tradition of awarding it on trial grounds was discontinued after 1947, and given thenceforth at the club's annual Specialty, for first in field trial classes. One can well understand the impossibility of awarding it any longer at our present-day trials, with our tremendous entries, with just enough daylight allotted to all series, and weary handlers and dogs anxious to call it a day.

Although British trials may have changed imperceptibly over the years in a competitive sense, the basic manner in which they are held is the same. Stakes, limited to twenty-four dogs over a two-day period, enable them to be run at a leisurely pace, compared to ours, and the Howe Trophy is still given each year at the end of the second day. We were fortunate in having seen it in 1959, the last time it was held at Idsworth, Lady Howe's old home. In the darkening shadows, under the trees, the entries stood unobtrusively, each with its handler, while Lady Hill-Wood, Warner Hill, and Mr. Gilliat went over the dogs. In seeing Labradors judged thus, it brought to mind sharply that these were the sort of people who fashioned the Standard, written for working dogs, and devoid of all artificiality and passing trends. In like manner, our Hiwood Mike Trophy, even if attached to shows today, should mean a great deal to us. The American dogs that have won it were grand representatives of their breed, and whether we compete for it, watch it, or judge it, we should not forget its origin and fine purpose.

*1942—Gorse of Arden; breeder W. A. Harriman; owner, Mrs. M. Belmont

1943—Buddha of Arden; breeder, W. A. Harriman; owner, Mrs. Edmund Poor

1944—Kilsyth Bang; breeder and owner, Mr. Gerald Livingston

1945—Buddha of Arden

*1946—Little Pierre of Deercreek; breeder and owner, Mr. Paul P. Bakewell, III

1947—Wardwyn's Jack Pot; breeder and owner, Mrs. Edmund Poor

1948—not awarded, thence incorporated with the Specialty classes

1949—Miss Dela Winn; breeder and owner, Mrs. Harley Butler

1950—Miss Dela Winn

1951—Wardwyn's Ace of Spades; breeder Mrs. Poor; owner, Mrs. Madeleine Austin

1952—West Island Easter Parade; breeder, West Island K's; owner, Mr. Clifford Brokaw, Jr.

1953—Invail's Pennell; breeder and owner, Mr. Brokaw

1954—Storm of Landfall; breeder and owner, Rear Admiral Chas. A. Andrews

1955—Wildfield Mickey Finn; breeder and owner, Mrs. Eric Wood

1956—Alvaleigh's Plenty of Pep; breeder and owner, Mr. J. H. Lee Fisher

1957—Newry's Prince of Darkness; breeder, Mrs. Rita Haggerty; owner, Mrs. Joan Blount

1958—Newry's Prince of Darkness;

1959—Ore Hill's Sunday Punch; breeder and owner, Mr. Allen Buck

1960
1961 } No Competition
1962

* Dual champions

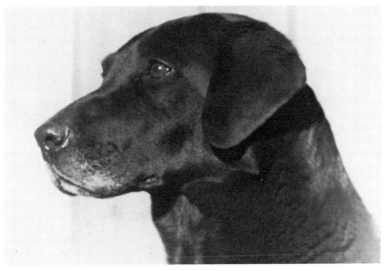

Am. & Can. Ch. Dark Star of Franklin (Ch. Labcroft Mr. Chips ex Am. & Can. Ch. Pitch of Franklin).

9

Grooming for Show

THE Labrador is one of the few breeds which require a minimum effort to be well presented for exhibition, a dream of a dog for overworked handlers. This section, therefore, will be happily brief in grooming details, compared to those of breeds less touched by fortune whose destinies are wrapped up in props and powders, endless tools, treadmills, grooming charts, tranquilizers and confining crates from which the victims rarely emerge except for their brief appearances in the show rings.

A Labrador may at all times have free access to wind and weather, land and water, turf and bramble; he may be in a duck-blind one day and shown with full confidence on the following, providing he is neat and clean and in prime condition.

Prime show condition means general fitness, the right amount of weight over well-developed muscles (usually a few pounds more than a field trial dog on a working schedule would carry), a clear eye and a coat in top bloom. A Labrador ought to be in full coat for top winning, for although it may not be a life and death matter with him, as with the long-coated breeds, coat condition can make or mar his general outline, the shape of his tail, and the overall impression of substance a judge will seek in summing up for his final decision. I do not mean that a dog has to rely completely on his coat for a show of solidity; any judge worth his salt will know just how much is shadow and how much is substance, but it is not fair to ask a judge to assume anything, and if we put before him a dog which has scarcely any coat it places him in a difficulty. The expert leaves his shorn lamb at home and that saves at least some expense and trouble, because the unpleasant truth is that a Labrador without a full coat is like a "holiday without money!"

For coat care (apart from a diet well-balanced in protein, fat, and calcium), the blacks are the simplest to groom before a show. Little bathing is needed or recommended, as too much soap and water not only dries out the natural oils in the skin but brings on a temporary false softness to the outer coat, thus ruining the harsh texture that should be evident. A good brushing with a bristle brush or hound-glove and an occasional rubbing into the hide of some natural oil—or even using one of the good commercial sprays, if one is so inclined—should be sufficient to bring out the natural luster to the surface of a good black coat.

When dealing with Yellows, particularly those bordering on the lighter tones, a bath may be essential if a show is near. This is especially true if the dog is regularly worked and lives outdoors in grassy pens, with hay or straw for bedding. A mild soap and warm water will then have to be used, with a dash of laundry bluing added to the rinse water. There are few highlights to a yellow coat, and no oil need be used on them; in fact, it tends to give them a sticky look and darken the coat to no purpose.

As to manual trimming, let us borrow a canny phrase from one of the worthiest of little dogs—the Norwich Terrier—and say that "tidying" is a more appropriate and sensible term for grooming a Labrador, and leave the details optional and to the good sense of the owner.

I have seen Labradors on trimming tables with masses of hair littering the floor underneath, their backsides shaved, their tails taken down for fear that a stray feather may be the deciding factor between No. 1 and No. 2. So much unnecessary snipping, shaping, and cutting can become a farce.

Accustomed to shearing other varieties of gundogs, many Americans can scarcely contain themselves with the little a Labrador has to offer in the way of coat styling. One might point out facetiously that were a hunting dog's ability to rest entirely upon his whiskers being left on, or a bench dog's career to rely upon their being periodically removed, we should come to a ridiculous pass. Many of us do prefer the clean, sharp outline the whisker trimming can give to a muzzle, but any other demonstrations of scissor or razor effects should be deplored. Much better that a coat with a bit of length be in plain view than shorn under false pretenses. If there were more preoccupation with the pitiful unsoundness so often seen in the rear and front ends of the average exhibit, and less artistry in the camouflaging of coats, it would be a giant step in the right direction for breed improvement.

An important point of grooming that is sometimes overlooked is the appearance of the foot. A truly well-made foot seldom needs attention, but a Labrador foot which lacks the rounded toes, strength and firmness, or suffers higher up from a too-sloping pastern, develops long claw-like nails that require constant paring unless the dog is used consistently on rough ground. Short nails will never make a poorly constructed foot good; but they will certainly enhance the appearance of a good one, and are a prime asset for fastidious but simple grooming.

In summing up, one can truthfully say that it is only courtesy to a judge to exhibit one's animals in immaculate condition. No doubt there are breeds of dogs that have benefited esthetically by modes, fads and fancies of "man's fixings," but not the Labrador. Such maneuvers are not for him; he is best left as Providence designed him. The fewer alterations resorted to, the better for the pleasure of judging and appreciating him.

It was our intent to end this chapter here, feeling that only a superficial summary was needed for the subject. However, a most important point relevant to it was touched upon in my second paragraph. The matter of "prime condition" has been a question in the minds not only of novices witnessing their first few shows, but also of shooting friends who occasionally attend. So many of them ask, "How much show condition is needed for a working dog —to win? How much condition does the inveterate show dog need to lose, to make it at least *look* workmanlike?"

An inspiration presented itself in the form of the following article, written by Mr. Wilson Stephens, Editor of *The Field,* who has kindly permitted me to use it for this chapter.

Double Vision About Retrievers

Nobody will tell me why retrievers are sent into the ring in such a condition that, if worked, they would be useless within minutes. I have asked, in vain, several elder statesmen of the show game. Let us look at the facts, and then consider whether they ought to continue.

All dogs *should* be fit when shown. A retriever *must* be fit when worked because his effectiveness depends on his accurate sampling of the air through his nose, and his accurate reaction to what his senses of smell and taste tell him about the sample.

If the air is being gulped in and panted out again he is sampling too quickly to be accurate. In short he is scenting under a handicap which makes his work first difficult, then impossible. If he is hot and bothered by the exertion of his legs and lungs, his brain will also work less well, so that he loses drive and initiative. As he slows up, he covers less ground, leaving more unhunted.

A retriever works at a canter, not a gallop. But this canter must be tireless, enabling him to take everything in his stride without his mind noticing it. His physique must be so efficient that the business of movement becomes an unconscious incidental to the questing of his nose. It is to assess this efficiency of body that shows are held for gundogs.

If all this seems obvious, as indeed it is, the condition of dogs in retriever classes seems strange.

To take the most popular variety first, the general run of Labradors which I see at shows compare unfavourably for fitness with Boxers and Rhodesian Ridgebacks. These breeds are cited because their coat texture makes possible fair comparison with Labradors. Incidentally both breeds are normally shown in splendid fettle, muscles toned up, skins bright, no surplus flesh, hard as nails. Yet neither is bred or used for any purpose known to me which demands that they break out of a trot from one year's end to another. I know, of course, that they do so; but they need not.

To any Labrador-owner who considers this an odious comparison I say, don't take my word for it. Trust the evidence of your own eyes. Class by class, they come in too fat. Many are gross in jowl and dewlap, flabby, thickly underlined in frame and sloppy in foot. If such a picture tells a story it is one of over-feeding and lack of exercise. It is not confined to Labradors.

Goldens and Flat-Coats, and not just a few of either, turn out in a state which can only be described as corpulent. The tendency is less marked in curlies, though some over-padded specimens appear. It may be more than a coincidence that curlies, less often over-fleshed than the other three varieties, are also less often worked and, by converse, are more of a show breed only. If so, where is the connection?

Once I saw Warner Hill judge a class of Labradors which quivered jelly-like with surplus tissue when he had them moved. Warner Hill knows shooting and hound work as well as the ring. He must have known, too, that the dogs under him would be wheezing wrecks if worked for ten minutes. So I searched his face thinking:

> "If those lips could only speak
> If those eyes could only tell."

. . . some clue to his feeling might be gleaned. But W. H. maintained the facial inscrutability proper to the judiciary, and the chance has not arisen since to consult this fount of wisdom.

So, in the search for truth, I turn to my own experience. I show flatcoats, occasionally. One day I took a bitch into the ring and received, at the behest of a judge long experienced in field trials as well as in shows, V.H.C. (Very highly commended.)

Think not that I complain. If there was error, it was overvaluation. As she was, and as she showed, on that day it was very memorable to me. After going over the bitch, these were the words decent of him to give us a card of any kind; and a damning reflection on those who got nothing. But was it true, what the judge said, as he spake: "Pity she's in working condition."

If it was, for pity's sake why? It happened in September. Shooting had started. Flat-Coats are a working breed. My bitch had already done several days. I ask, in the name of commonsense, what sort of condition should a retriever be in, at that time of year anyway, if it is not working condition? Follow me further.

Lunching with a lady of great repute as a retriever breeder, who also judges both trials and shows, I asked to see one of

224

Dual Ch. Calypso Clipper, bred and owned by Mr. John Van Bloom, acquired his Dual title in 1963 and was National Qualifier for that year.

her winning dogs with which I am well acquainted. My old friend bustled cheerfully from his kennel as tubby as any "bonviveur" among business magnates. My hostess caught the surprise in my eye. "Don't forget he's been shown," she said defensively.

Recently I visited another friend, first and last a shooting man. He shows retrievers, sparingly but successfully, and runs them in trials. So we went to see the hero of the occasion, a dog I had last seen quartering ground with a stride which was near poetry.

The rotund figure in the kennel was scarcely recognisable. "I would not care to insure him against thrombosis if you worked him like that," I remarked with my usual tact.

"That's how they like 'em," replied my friend, drily but with obvious truth.

"How long to get rid of that barrel?" I asked, wondering if that too, too solid flesh would ever melt.

"A bone a day, and nothing else, for a week or so works wonders," came the answer.

In this matter I do not shelter behind the journalistic reservation that comment is directed only at a minority, and that the majority are beyond criticism. The overweight retrievers are far from a minority. If there is any sense in owners of working dogs stuffing them up like Smithfield steers to compete in shows, and then wasting off the flesh again so that they can do their job, I shall be glad to learn what it is.

At present no better explanation exists for this double vision over retrievers than the confused idea that "substance" must be emphasised at all costs, or an obsession with individual points such as stop or depth of brisket which obscures the vital point that what really matters is the whole dog.

If what I have written is supported by general experience, then we have two standards of physical condition for retrievers. This *might* be justified in summer; it *can't* be justified all year round. It is impossible to blame "show kennels" for this strange vogue, or to argue that dogs in this state could work, since those who both show and work their dogs admit frankly that they could not. It is time the fashion changed.

WILSON STEPHENS

10

Labradors in Other Countries

FOLLOWING is a list of Labrador Retriever Clubs* in England and Scotland, and a review of the breed's activities in the Commonwealth:

The Labrador Retriever Club: President, The Lord Rank; Chairman, M. C. V. Gilliat; Hon. Secretary, Mr. Cliff Brown, 19 Dulverton Road, New Eltham, London, S. E. 9.

The Labrador Club of Scotland: Hon. Secretary, Mr. John Manson, Glengour House, Ferryhills, Lower Keithing, Fife.

The Midland Labrador Club: Hon. Secretary, Mrs. H. Taylor, Whatstandwell, Matlock, Derbyshire.

The Northumberland & Durham Labrador Club: Hon. Secretary, Mrs. W. Gillespie, 24 North Road, Ponteland.

The Labrador Club of Ulster, Eire: Hon. Secretary, Mr. T. Lowry, 268 Castlereagh Road, Belfast.

The Yellow Labrador Club: Hon. Secretary, Mrs. V. Wormald, Glenstuart, Arran, Scotland.

* The officers listed are contemporary with the year of publication of the book.

The Three Ridings Labrador Retriever Club: Hon. Secretary, Mrs. Ch. H. Howarth, Aberford, Nr. Leeds, Yorks.

The Labrador Retriever Club of Ireland: Hon. Secretary, Mrs. Eustace Duckett, Castlemore, Tullow, Co. Carlow.

These are not field trial clubs, but individual breed clubs, each holding their own field trials, Open, and Championship shows.

The year 1913 marked the organization of the first Irish Retriever Club, called the Irish Retriever Society, in County Limerick. Since that time others have joined the ranks, including the Irish Labrador Club of Dundalk and the Southern Irish Gundog Club. The Labrador Retriever Club of Ireland was formed in 1945, under the auspices of Mrs. Eustace Duckett, whose Castlemore prefix is well known to many. From an initial membership of thirty, the club has grown to great proportions. This club has a ruling that no dog may be called a field trial champion without having secured a first, second, or third prize in a Graduate, Limit, or Open Class, at a recognized bench show. I believe this is the only club with such a ruling, wherein the boot is on the other foot.

Canada

Over 13,000 Labradors have been registered in the C. K. C. Stud Book since dogs were first registered in Canada.

The first imported registered Labrador was a dog called Canaick (Muto ex Blossom), from Scotland, by G. E. Fauquier in 1921.

The first Labrador imported into Canada from the United States was a dog called Gilnockie Boy (Banchory Jazz ex Derthick's Seal's Bessie), in 1922 from Oregon, by Mr. M. B. Armstrong. Mr. Armstrong also imported Wolferton Sapper, in 1923, from his Majesty, George V.

Pioneer breeders were Mr. Armstrong, S. S. Magoffin, George S. Hope, John Ritchie of Lansdowne prefix, the late Mr. Campbell of Holland Marsh, and others. Mr. Hope, now living in Seebe, Alberta, has been associated with the breed since owning his first Labrador in 1896 in Scotland—a litter sister to Stellshaw Nell, dam to Brayton Sir Richard (1899). Type shows up well in these two old dogs.

There are over twenty-five field trial clubs in Canada, not confined to one Retriever variety, and including Irish Water Spaniels. The National C. R. C. has, since 1950, staged annual championship stakes in various parts of Canada.

Dave Elliot was the first to take retrievers for training to Canada. He went to Saskatchewan in 1935, with some of Mr. Carlisle's dogs.

Contemporary kennels are that of Mr. Chevrier's Avandale; Nascopie of Wm. Copeland, a popular trial judge who has also judged shows abroad; Stephen Greey of Greeymar; R. Blyth of Northolt; D. Haynes of Rosedale; Drs. Angus and Sheila MacLachlin of Highlander; Mr. Frank Jones of Annwyn; and others.

There was a short-lived but choice kennel of Yellows, based on Treesholme lines, owned by the late Mrs. Doherty, whose stock often enhanced American shows in the 1950's. Mr. Blyth has had two excellent dual champions in Ace and Queen of Spades, and was fortunate in his breeding to have had a top producer in Ch. Gypsey Queen in 1951. His lines combine Holland Marsh and Avandale, and have drawn upon Grangemead, Little Pierre, and Shed of Arden stock in the states.

The Drs. MacLachlin, with their Highlander prefix, are truly a fine example of amateur sportsmen indulging in a hobby of raising first-class dogs, which they do as a relaxation from their busy lives as doctors in London Hospital, Ontario. They always use the best possible material, and not only from imported working stock, but have leaned heavily upon Grangemead as a successful combination for dual purpose qualities.

The Rosedale prefix of Sgt. Haynes has had dogs of really good type—and the added hobby of dog sled racing. He first started out with his Labs for the exercise and the enjoyment of it. He then entered a local race, found it was no effort at all, and trained in distances from twelve to twenty-six miles in preparation for the International Race. He won his first race in the Ottawa Sled Dog Club trials in 22 minutes and 50 seconds, setting a new course record. His team consisted of six Labradors; his lead dogs are all bitches. When competing in the International Derby competition, with a thirty-three mile course packed with heavy snow and high winds, he came in seventh in a field of twenty-six team entries, made up, with the exception of one other Labrador team, of the traditional huskies!

Well-bred, good-looking field trial stock also finds its way into prominent kennels over the border, and most Canadians make great efforts to maintain the right type. Three of the best known cur-

Field Ch. Duxback Scooter (Baker's Jerry ex Carnmoney Moira), owned by Mrs. Grace Lambert and bred by J. H. Uhrich of Canada.

Sgt. Hayes and his team. In January, 1962 another five Labrador team won the Western New York Arctic Sled-Dog Championship in competition with the traditional Huskies. Time taken was one hour, fifty-five minutes and thirty seconds. The course was 40 miles. Twenty miles were covered each day.

rent contenders of each color at trials in America, bred in Canada, are Mrs. Lewis's liver, Can. Am. & A.F.C. Ch. Kimbrow's General Ike, Mrs. Lambert's Field Ch. Duxbach Scooter, a Black, which goes back to Sandylands breeding, and Mr. T. Fajen Jr.'s outstanding Yellow, Field Ch. Brandy Spirit of Netley, a grandson of Dual Ch. Staindrop Saighdear, from the Crozier Kennel through Crozier's Silver Lance. Brandy may well be instrumental in furthering the Yellow cause to advantage in this country.

India

Active interest in Labrador field trials started with the Maharajah of Jind and Patiala. The Jind affix was well known in pre-World War II days, and the Maharajah was often a spectator, competitor, and purchaser at British trials. Some of the dogs sent over at that period came from Banchory, Whitmore, and Withington kennels. Two of the most prominent dogs of the time were Toilet of Whitmore and the yellow, Jaffa—the latter owned by Dave Elliot, before he left for the United States. Toilet and Jaffa were the first two British breds qualifying for the dual title in India. Jaffa was sold to the Maharajah.

Anyone who has read Dave's great book on *Training Gundogs to Retrieve* will always remember, in his chapter on "Brandy," the poignant scene at the railway station when he left him for his trip overseas to his Indian home.

There have been nineteen Indian-bred field champions and two Indian-bred duels in the last twenty-five years.

Recently a new club was formed, whose patron is Mme. Indira Gandhi, and whose secretary is a very enthusiastic Mr. Sorab Patell, whose worldwide correspondence with various Retriever people has attracted great interest in the club. Their first championship show was scheduled for December 2nd, 1962.

The following excerpts from Denmark, Australia and Africa were taken from the 1961 Year Book of the Midland Labrador Club.

Australia

Mr. McGeachy writes: "The Labrador Retriever Club of Victoria has won all the Major Trials, and collected the Challenges at the Royal Shows for the past four years. Labrador entries at the major shows in 1961 were, Melbourne 200, Sydney 100, Adelaide

H.H. THE MAHARAJAH OF PATIALA WITH HIS JHIND
FIELD TRIALS WINNERS (BANCHORY DAVID, JAFFA,
AND ADDERLEY TYKE)

75, Labrador Club of Victoria 160, L. K. A. 80, with Aust. Ch. Rookwood Nutcracker best dog at Sydney, and Aust. Ch. Wendover Jonah at the Labrador Club of Victoria and the L. K. A.

"Regarding imported dogs, I am sorry to say that none of them run in the Field or Retrieving Trials, though they and their progeny are doing well on the Bench.

"Our Trials are different from yours. In Field Trials, dogs are run in pairs, and have to find their own game, (fur or feather), flush the game, and retrieve. In Retrieving Trials, the game is killed before the Trial begins, and we have across the water retrieve, the double retrieve, and the walk-up.

"In the New South Wales Retriever Trials, Mr. G. Daniells, with his two dogs, Panther Dell Panther and Panther Dell Cheetah, set off from Melbourne on a Thursday, two days before the Trial with 560 miles to go. His car broke down 92 miles from Melbourne, so he phoned a friend at Albury who picked him and the two dogs up, and they set off again. This car also broke down, 200 miles from Melbourne, so Mr. Daniells and the dogs decided to hitch-hike the rest of the way. He got lifts by car, truck and semi-trailer, and finally arrived at the location in Sydney by taxi, just in time to get vetted. Result—Mr. Daniells won 1st and 2nd."

East Africa

Mrs. M. E. Tolley writes: "As you can imagine, 1961 has been a most difficult year for all Breed Clubs, and it looks at the moment as if 1962 is going to be even worse. The political situation here is chaotic, and as so many European farmers are leaving the country, I spend a very considerable amount of time finding good new homes for the Labradors. Our Breed of course is hardest hit, as it is the farming community who mostly have Labradors for private shooting.

"Our two imported stud dogs, Ch. Whatstandwell Sceptre and Prince of Blaircourt, were flown back to the U. K. in January. Although Sceptre has left a lot of excellent progeny behind him, Prince is only young, and to date has only sired two litters, so we are back to our own local stock. It seems unlikely that anyone will go to the expense of bringing further fresh stock out from the U. K. under present conditions.

"The Club of course is losing members as they go, and we are not getting the number to replace them. However, we endeavour to continue to hold two Field Trials a year, Social Meetings, and support three Championship Shows per annum. 1961 has been a difficult year from the point of view of weather also. First we had severe drought and since October have been flooded out. Our birds don't like either of these conditions, so we have only been able to hold one Field Trial. We had one arranged for this month, but the Lake is so flooded that it is impossible."

South Africa

Mrs. D. Wallace writes: It may be of interest for you to know that, having started from scratch in 1958, the Labrador Retriever Kennel Club now has just on 100 members. The Labrador is growing all the time in popularity out here. Ten years ago the breed was almost unknown. At the end of last year, according to the registrations with the S. A. Kennel Union, they were ninth in popularity, which is not bad going.

"We are very pleased that we shall be having the opportunity in August this year of meeting Mr. and Mrs. Warner Hill, who are coming out to judge at one of our shows."

Denmark

Baron luel-Brockdorff writes: "In 1960 there were just over 80 new registrations of Labradors with the Danish Kennel Club, and in 1961 there have been 106 new registrations. This is, as far as our Club (The Danish Labrador and Retriever Club) is concerned, very satisfactory, and as our membership list grows slowly but surely, we are quite pleased. A good-looking and truly well be-haved Labrador always creates an interest wherever it goes.

"There have been a few importations, but none of them have as yet been shown on the bench or been entered for trials. As yet the standard of the Danish Labrador is not very high, but I feel that our members are very much in earnest in their endeavours to heighten it by sound breeding and good importations. Here British breeders can be of great help with their advice, whenever Danish buyers appear on the market.

"Somehow the Field Trial faction of our Club doesn't seem to do so well as I had hoped. There are very few entries for our one and

234

only yearly Field Trial, but the standard of work is satisfactory. This may have something to do with the type of shooting, which is the normal one here. Most shooting is done over very small farms, where the German pointer is useful for its ability to point, hunt and retrieve, and very few of this type of 'shooter' wants to, or can afford to, keep two dogs. Amongst both keepers and guns at the bigger shoots and covert shooting the Labrador is gaining ground fast, so I very much hope to see the number of entries for Field Trials, and the general interest in this form of sport, grow from now on.

"Maybe this slowness in taking an interest in Trials has been all to the good of the breed, as we have this way had time to establish the standard of looks before the increasing demand for speed at Trials got in the way. The Club has made a point of not allowing any Labrador or Retriever to become champion on the bench without having qualified at Field Trials or working tests. A Field Trial Championship can't be got without at least a second prize on the bench. (Our system of giving prizes is different from yours as Judges can award several firsts, seconds and thirds in each class.) In fact no retriever can compete for a C. C. at any show without a Field Trial award or a Qualifying Certificate."

France

Although France's shooting tastes have been primarily for Pointers, English and Braque, and Setters, English and Gordon, there has also been great interest in Retrievers.

Labradors were seen in France as early as 1896, when they were owned by the Comte Adalbert de Bagneux and the Comte de Clary.

The Comte J. de Bonvouloir was familiar with them at that period and wrote a delightful and charmingly illustrated book on all the Retriever varieties. A sportsman and amateur trainer of over fifty years' experience, he has also owned some excellent Goldens and Chesapeakes.

The French Retriever Club was formed in 1911, and the first club trial was held the same year at the Duc de Talleyrand's Chateau de Valancay. In 1913, breed Standards were taken from the English Kennel Club and were established for Curlies, Flatcoats and Labradors, the Goldens arriving later, around 1930. The

Standard for Chesapeakes was adopted also in the late '30's, and the first two of the breed were sent over by Mrs. Howell of Long Island and R. Beasley of Santa Fe, New Mexico.

French trials are held in early spring or autumn with tests on partridge, duck, and hare. Their trials usually conform to the orthodox British "non-slip" Retriever rules, although occasionally they run them "a la francaise," which stipulates that the dogs be held on leash until after the battue, then sent to collect the game after the shot.

French trials are counterparts of an ordinary shooting day with many normal tests for dog and handler, in and out of boats, handlers generally using the gun, etc., with highest marks going to dogs using their native intelligence and independence in gamefinding. For the French, finished style and manners are important, but they value, above all, nose, marking, steadiness and a tender delivery. I am indebted to Madame Yvonne Simeon-Lavallart, renowned French artist and sculptress, and continental field trial judge of Pointers and Setters, for assistance on French information. She also owns Labradors. When she is in Paris she has them kenneled in her own atelier, among the paint pots and statues, going with them three or four times a day by taxi to the Bois, where she runs and swims them for their exercise. Retrievers in France are kept as gentlemen's shooting dogs, privately owned and bred. So far no commercialism has crept in to mar this peaceful pattern.

11

The Blueprint of the Breed and Contemporary Standards

THE following is a "blueprint" of the Labrador Standard, written by Mr. Richard Anderton, prominent judge and breeder of the Hawlmark Labradors prior to World War II.

"Whether it be true in practise or not, there cannot be the least doubt that the ideal structure for any animal ought to be that which enables it to perform its task with the least effort; and over a period of years nature would contrive to bring that about.

"That such a process is painfully slow, goes without saying, but it would be very sure. In some instances, no doubt it would give us a type of animal rather different from our conception of what is suitable. It must not be overlooked that mortals almost always start with certain preconceived ideas, the bulk of which they have to unlearn before they make any real progress.

"Practically everyone who has engaged in the fascinating study of breeding to type will have had to discard some favorite theory, while others would probably do better if they cast a few ideas aside.

"With Labradors, we do at least find that we have a perfectly sane and sensible breed to commence upon—one that has evolved slowly and without any violent eruptions or drastic short cuts. Improvements that have been made have come about by selection within the breed itself, rather than by frantic outcrosses that would take generations to become stable.

"Whether the ideal that is being sought today in England is still exactly the same in all particulars as that which led to the formation of the Labrador Retriever Club twenty years ago is for others more competent to say, but materially it is the same. There have been no vast changes in type, no wholesale revisions such as we know to have taken place with several other breeds during the past twenty or thirty years.

"Probably the greatest advance will be among dogs of *average* quality rather than outstanding individuals, so that for each good Labrador of two decades ago, there may be twenty of equal merit today. That is the very best kind of progress the widespread benefits of which become increasingly recognized, as little faults are eliminated by careful breeding.

"Let us picture the Labrador, then as a product of gradual evolution, without any freakish exaggerations, or tendencies to magnify the importance of any single feature.

"First, the structure should be that of an active dog of sixty to seventy pounds in weight; neither long nor short of leg, nor of neck or body—*in fact the sort of dog that a child would have great difficulty in describing,* except by color. Naturally the structure should be perfectly sound, the limbs move truly, no bones or tendons dwarfed by over development in other parts. This matter of *soundness* seems elemental, and has nothing to do with *type*, but it is often overlooked.

"The prospective breeder may as well commence with the useful axiom that no typical Labrador is unsound and likewise no unsound Labrador is really typical. It is wise to adopt a very high standard of soundness, and to breed from a specimen that is not thoroughly typical rather than from one that is not sound. Persistent unsoundnesses in the structure are most difficult to eradicate in a strain, and one can readily picture the vexation of a breeder when he finds that not one of a promising litter is sound.

"It is foolish to be tempted to turn a blind eye to that which exists, to think that it can be covered up or perhaps corrected. Such improvement is only for the present. The fault will show itself in each succeeding generation.

"In *general conformation,* the Labrador should be rather stoutly built; not fat but of good substance, and quite obviously a strong dog. Those who lean toward the lightly built and think they are gaining speed have not realised that the correctly built dog of substance can move quite sufficiently fast for any legitimate purpose. A Labrador has got to be strong enough to carry a really heavy hare or bird, to jump with it over obstacles, to swim with it against a strong tide, to plough through mud and bracken, and to repeat these procedures if necessary, the whole day long. He may have to walk miles in heavy going, through thick roots, not at a leisurely walk 'in line,' but in frequent and prolonged stretches at a smart pace, turning, twisting, hunting out a line with head well down and every faculty alert. *The dog that tires after an hour or so is not of the right alloy,* and the ability to produce a short burst of speed at the outset of the day is a very doubtful advantage.

"It has been found that the dog that stands up to such gruelling tests the best, is one which is strongly built and short-coupled, well balanced and of medium size. In other words we are looking for a very compact dog.

"The *back* should therefore be short and very firm; the ribs wide and deep, with very little space between the last rib and the loin.

"Looking directly downwards, from above, the outer lines of the body should be almost parallel. If there is any perceptible *tapering* towards the rear, the hindquarters are *not* sufficiently powerful and the dog will quickly tire.

"Upon the *hindquarters* falls the greater part of the responsibility for thrusting the body forward, and with this in mind, the correct action and shape of *thighs* and *hocks* will become apparent. If the hind limbs are too straight and stiff, so that movement is obtained by just swinging like a pendulum from the point where they hinge to the backbone, the result will be very feeble and obviously unsuited to tangled ground. Powerful hind limbs, correctly used, really give the effect that they are pushing heavy ground away behind them, which is precisely what they *are* doing. Thighs in an adult dog should therefore be very well muscled, the bones strong, hocks low-set and at a definite angle, moving well flexed when seen from the rear.

"The chief duty of the *forelegs* is to carry weight. In trotting, quite two thirds, and at the gallop, a full three quarters of the weight is supported by the forelegs, which must therefore be strong, straight and true, and moreover, correctly placed. The elbows should be neatly tucked under the body, but the legs should not be too close together.

"The *shoulder* is designed to absorb the shock or impact that might otherwise prove a strain on the limbs, and for that reason should *slope well towards the middle of the back*. A straight and upright shoulder will be stiff in comparison.

"The lower ends of the limbs are also provided with shock absorbers in the form of *pads* and *pasterns*. The *feet* should therefore serve in the nature of cushions, not too large, nor thin, nor open. The craze for very small feet is wrong, and loses sight of the use that is made of the forelimbs in swimming. The ability to swim strongly is one of the inherent and very desirable qualities of the breed, and should be preserved with great care. No creature with tiny feet and thin legs can be a bold swimmer. It is chiefly for that reason that narrow chests should be avoided, and we can forgive a little thickening toward the top of the shoulder if it is due to the muscles that have been developed in such good cause.

"The *neck* should be of good length to enable the dog to put his nose well down in hunting, and also that his head can be well held up and readily turned in any direction, such as marking the fall of a bird, in questing and in swimming.

"Short thick necks are a prevalent fault, probably caused by breeding for short backs and tails, *the vertebrae tending to become shorter throughout the whole spine*.

"The *head* too should be moderate in all respects. Undue length of head or muzzle is not sought for, but any tendency to stumpiness should be avoided as that would limit the dog's ability to pick up a large object. The *jaws* therefore, should be moderately long, consistent with their purpose, which is to hold anything firmly but gently.

"The *muzzle* should be fairly square, with good outline, most dogs that are tight-lipped having poor scenting powers.

"The *skull* itself, should be fairly wide, but not coarse, the difference being not easy to define in words. Heads that are wedge-shaped or thick through the cheek bones or behind the ears, are definitely wrong. A *good* head should have a neat stop between the eyes, and perfectly flat cheeks below the ears. Fleshy and lumpy cheeks, so we are told, were very common in the early days of the breed and are associated with hard mouths and a 'rat trap' grip that should have no place with a gundog.

"The *teeth* are seldom mentioned in any Standard but it would seem to be one of the essentials that an animal used for picking up game for human consumption should have a mouth that is sweet and clean and wholesome. Unless the teeth have an even fit, it will not be easy to hold game as safely and as tenderly as is necessary.

"The *ears* should be neat, carried close to the head and rather far back. Large, prominent ears give a 'houndy' expression that is foreign to the breed.

"Wide misconception exists in the matter of eyes, which can be brown, yellow, or black, but a rich hazel color is the favorite choice. A point that is not sufficiently realised is that the *expression* of the eye is more important than its color, and that any hard look is altogether wrong, as are eyes that are placed too closely, giving a mean expression.

"The *coat and the tail* are two of the most important characteristics of the breed and are interrelated, because it is the correct clothing of the tail which gives it that thick, rounded 'otterlike' appearance, that is so distinctive. The importance of a good tail will be understood when it is so invariably associated with a good dense Labrador coat, the texture of which should be fairly harsh on the *surface*. Upon turning back the outer hair, the *undercoat* will be seen to be very dense, completely covering the skin, softer and often lighter in color. This is the feature which is so essential, and none that is deficient or lacking in undercoat can be regarded as a typical Labrador. A coat that is too soft or too long will become 'open,' admitting the wet, while a silky or glossy short coat has very little covering value.

"Those who wish to understand a Labrador can put aside all books of advice and tape measures, but get out with the dog in the open country. There, let it hunt and swim, but always endeavor to control its actions while watching them closely. There is no finer companion for a day in the fields and the woods, either with or without a gun, and no better way to learn about gundogs."

Listed below are the two contemporary Standards of both countries:

American Labrador Retriever Standard

General Appearance: The general appearance of the Labrador should be that of a strongly built, short-coupled, very active dog. He should be fairly wide over the loins, and strong and muscular in the hind quarters. The coat should be close, short, dense and free from feather.

Head: The skull should be wide, giving brain-room; there should be a slight "stop," i.e., the brow should be slightly pronounced, so that the skull is not absolutely in a straight line with the nose. The head should be clean-cut and free from fleshy cheeks. The jaws should be long and powerful and free from snipiness; the nose should be wide and the nostrils well developed. Teeth should be strong and regular, with a level mouth.

The ears should hang moderately close to the head, rather far back, should set somewhat low and not be large and heavy. The eyes should be of a medium size, expressing great intelligence and good temper, and can be brown, yellow or black, but brown or black is preferred.

Neck and Chest: The neck should be medium length and powerful and not throaty. The shoulders should be long and sloping.

The chest must be of good width and depth, the ribs well sprung and the loins wide and strong, stifles well turned, and the hindquarters well developed and of great power.

Legs and Feet: The legs must be straight from the shoulder to ground, and the feet compact with toes well arched, and pads well developed; the hocks should be well bent, and the dog must neither be cow-hocked nor be too wide behind; in fact he must stand and move true all round on legs and feet. Legs should be of medium length, showing good bone and muscle, but not so short as to be out of balance with the rest of the body. In fact, a dog well balanced in all points is preferable to one with outstanding good qualities and defects.

Tail: The tail is a distinctive feature of the breed; it should be very thick towards the base, gradually tapering towards the tip, of medium length, should be free from any feathering, and should be clothed thickly all round with the Labrador's short, thick dense coat, thus giving that particular "rounded" appearance which has been described as the "otter" tail. The tail may be carried gaily but should not curl over the back.

Coat: The coat is another very distinctive feature; it should be short, very dense and without wave, and should give a fairly hard feeling to the hand.

Color: The colors are black, yellow, or chocolate and are evaluated as follows:

(a) *Blacks:* All black, with a small white spot on chest permissible. Eyes to be of medium size, expressing intelligence and good temper, preferably brown or hazel, although black or yellow is permissible.

(b) *Yellows:* Yellows may vary in color from fox-red to light cream with variations in the shading of the coat on ears, the underparts of the dog, or beneath the tail. A small white spot on chest is permissible. Eye coloring and expression should be the same as that of the blacks, with black or dark brown eye rims. The nose should also be black or dark brown, although "fading" to pink in winter weather is not serious. A "Dudley" nose (pink without pigmentation), should be penalized.

(c) *Chocolates:* Shades ranging from light sedge to chocolate. A small white spot on chest is permissible. Eyes to be light brown to clear yellow. Nose and eye rim pigmentation dark brown or liver colored. "Fading" to pink in winter weather not serious. "Dudley" nose should be penalized.

Movement: Movement should be free and effortless. The forelegs should be strong, straight and true, and correctly placed. Watching a dog move towards one, there should be no signs of elbows being out in front, but neatly held to the body, with legs not close together, but moving straight forward without pacing or weaving. Upon viewing the dog from the rear, one should get the impression that the hind legs, which should be well muscled and not cow-hocked, move as nearly parallel as possible, with hocks doing their full share of work and flexing well, thus giving the appearance of power and strength.

Height at shoulders:

Dogs: 22½ inches to 24½ inches.
Bitches: 21½ inches to 23½ inches.

British Labrador Retriever Standard

General Appearance: The general appearance of the Labrador should be that of a strongly-built, short-coupled, very active dog, broad in the skull, broad and deep through the chest and ribs, broad and strong over the loins and hindquarters. The coat close, short with dense undercoat and free from feather. The dog must move neither too wide nor too close in front or behind, he must stand and move true all round on legs and feet.

Head and Skull: The skull should be broad with pronounced stop so that the skull is not in a straight line with the nose. The head should be clean cut without fleshy cheeks. The jaws should be of medium length and powerful and free from snipiness. The nose wide and nostrils well developed.

Mouth: Teeth should be sound and strong. The lower teeth just behind, but touching the upper.

Eyes: The eyes of medium size expressing intelligence and good temper should be brown or hazel.

Ears: Should not be large and heavy and should hang close to the head and set rather far back.

Neck: Should be clean, strong and powerful and set into well placed shoulders.

Forequarters: The shoulders should be long and sloping. The forelegs well boned and straight from the shoulder to the ground when viewed from either the front or side. The dog must move neither too wide nor too close in front.

Body: The chest must be of good width and depth with well-sprung ribs. The back should be short-coupled.

Hindquarters: The loins must be wide and strong, with well-sprung stifles; hindquarters well developed and not sloping to the tail. The hocks should be slightly bent and the dog must neither be cow-hocked nor move too wide or too close behind.

Feet: Should be round and compact with well arched toes and well-developed pads.

Tail: The tail is a distinctive feature of the breed; it should be very thick towards the base gradually tapering towards the tip, of medium length and practically free from any feathering, but clothed thickly all round with the Labrador's thick dense coat, thus giving that peculiar "rounded" appearance which has been described as the "otter" tail. The tail may be carried gaily, but should not curl over the back.

Coat: The coat is another distinctive feature of the breed, it should be short and dense and without wave with a weather-

244

Dual Ch. Bramshaw Bob (Ch. Ingleston Ben ex Bramshaw Brimble), owned by Lorna, Countess Howe.

Dual Ch. Shed of Arden—a perfect example of the Standard. Courtesy of Mr. Paul Bakewell, III.

Ch. Chidley Hocus Pocus (Ch. Zelstone Duke ex Ch. Chidley Spook), bred by Mrs. Curtis Read and owned by Lockerbie Kennels, has a classic female head, a clean neck, and balance of ear, skull, muzzle and eye.

resisting undercoat and should give a fairly hard feeling to hand.

Colour: The colour is generally black, chocolate or yellow—which may vary from fox-red to cream—free from any white markings. A small white spot on the chest is allowed, the coat should be of a whole colour and not of a flecked appearance.

Size: Desired height for dogs, 22–22½ inches; bitches, 21½–22 inches.

Faults: Under or overshot mouth; no undercoat, bad action; feathering; snipiness on the head; large or heavy ears; cow-hocked; tail curled over back.

The British Qualifying Certificate for Bench Champion Gundogs

This Working Certificate was incorporated into the rules of the Kennel Club in 1909, and, until 1958, was required for all gundogs before they could legitimately use the bench title of Champion. Unfortunately, due to pressure in certain areas, it has now been altered so that the certificates are no longer compulsory, *but* the title of Champion without a certificate must be preceded by "Sh. Ch." or "Show Champion." To be a full Champion, a dog must still go for his "qualifier."

"A dog which has won more than two Challenge Certificates at shows may be entered at a Feld Trial Meeting, by permission of the Society, in order to obtain a qualifying certificate, granted at the discretion of the judges at the meeting. The certificate must be signed by at least two judges, indicating that they have seen the dog and are satisfied that he fulfilled the following requirements:

"1. Steadiness is not absolutely necessary. 2. That a dog show that he is not gunshy. 3. For a Pointer or Setter, that he hunts and points. 4. For a Spaniel, that he hunts, faces covert, retrieves tenderly. 5. For a Retriever, that he hunts and retrieves tenderly, and that where there is a test for a Retriever, he will enter water."

The American Working Certificate

This is called the Minimum Working Certificate, according to Article VII of the By-Laws of the Labrador Retriever Club, and under the jurisdiction of the Club only.

"1. The dog is not gunshy.

2. The dog will retrieve a shot bird at approximately 50 yards on land.

3. The dog will retrieve two ducks from water, either as a double, or in immediate succession, in order to prove willingness to re-enter.

4. Steadiness is not required, so a dog may be held on line."

The British Standard was drawn up in 1916 and was amended in only small instances. One of these was to delete, from the original paragraph on *General Appearance,* references it was no longer considered necessary to stress regarding Flat-Coat tendencies that were prevalent earlier. The paragraph *used* to read: ". . . Compared with the Wavy or Flat-Coated Retrievers, he should be wider in the head, wider through the chest and ribs, and wider and stronger over the loins and hindquarters." Another amendment appeared in 1950, changing the color clause, which heretofore had only stated, "The Colour is generally black, free from any white marking, except possibly a small spot on the chest. Other whole colours are permissible." I am grateful to Mr. Gilliat for checking on this for me at the Kennel Club.

When the American Standard was formed from the British, their color clause was identical until 1956, when many in the United States thought that Yellows were being discriminated against at shows, and one prominent judge frankly admitted a feeling of insecurity in putting up Yellows that were not "solid" shades. It is understandable, with the lack of familiarity with Yellows until within the last ten years, that the wording of this clause may have given the impression that although other colors than black were permissible they were not desirable. At the request of the American Labrador Club, Messrs. Stuart Crocker, Lee Fisher, and James Warwick were asked to clarify this passage, and it stands today, perfectly clear and fair, for the hitherto controversial shades.

Labrador type evolved slowly, shedding characteristics as the result of the mingling of other blood with the old St. John's breed. The beauty and unique shape of the Flat-Coat head and its corresponding points had to be discarded to establish the Labrador unconditionally, although in both Standards the importance of the "stop" is still stressed, for the simple reason that even today occasional Labradors are found with not enough stop, giving the impression of a Flat-Coat profile.

Leslie Sprake, in his enlightening book on *The Labrador Retriever,* published in 1933, mentions that there were those who were perfectly satisfied with the status quo, with specimens displaying tendencies towards "heavy shoulders, chumpy necks, a dipped back, and a somewhat short muzzle." He lists three of the views on breeding them that existed at that time:

"1. That the type should remain exactly the same as that of the earliest known specimens of the breed.

2. That the type should be kept as near as possible to the original examples, but that obvious faults must be gradually eliminated.

3. That the early type should be more or less ignored, and the required characteristics be considered only from the point of view of what is handsome (but nobody is able to suggest who is to define the standard of beauty or physical utility)."

Fortunately for the Labrador, the second point of view was followed. A better example cannot be offered than that of Dual. Ch. Bramshaw Bob, an outstanding dog of the period, whose quality in this unretouched photograph speaks for itself.

Generally speaking, it is with those who are breeding primarily for conformation, and whose ultimate ends are directed towards bench shows, that the uncompromising responsibility of preserving breed type and the right temperament lies. Some breeders commendably stress combining their bloodlines with working and show stock, or drawing completely upon working lines with proven good looks. The last-named effort is a preferable and satisfactory challenge to many, in that they feel that they are really breeding the "whole dog," rather than taking the comparatively easy road in using bench stock only. This is sometimes reversed in breeders of pure working lineage, who occasionally dip into sources offered by top bench blood.

There is a universal brotherhood whose belief that a bench breeder should stick to his own last, and a trial breeder to his, has created a division of purpose. Unfortunately, the proof of the pudding has been demonstrated in the over-stressing of shows to such proportions, in some gundog varieties, that they truly are just travesties of their former selves, and look quite out of place in a gundog group.

The working breeder would be a fool not to keep his best potential worker, regardless of fine show points, and his counterpart could not afford to let his best-looking stock come to nothing, but the former ought also not lose pride in the appearance of things. Both interests have in common the preservation of type and working ability. The loss of either quality points the way to degeneration of a breed, and there is no reason to sacrifice either. The Standard, analyzed with clarity and insight, should leave no doubt in anyone's mind that it is not discussing the animal with any "show" intent, but as a working dog of a type distinctive and recognizable from all other varieties.

There are no boundaries, either in kennels or geographically, for good type. There are variations of type, but those which are of the true stamp are always within the framework of the Standard. Dogs may vary in *size* from country to country, according to the demands made upon them and the type of terrain where they are worked, but a typical Labrador should look the same, in coat, tail, and expression, whether it comes from England, France, China, or Timbuktu.

The fundamentals of a typical Labrador are identical in both Standards. There have been countless Labradors bred in America that have embraced the best points indicated in the Standard, and we would come to a ludicrous pass were Standards written for every country in which the Labrador might find itself.

A perfect Standard for any breed has yet to be written, and the shorter and more to the point it is, the better it proves to be. The best way to learn about a dog is to breed it and have a thorough grounding and apprenticeship with breeders who know what they are doing. Twisting a Standard's meaning to suit one's own output is not only the line of least resistance, but brings to the surface one of the most virulent forms of eye trouble—kennel blindness. If people are dissatisfied with the way a breed is going the fault lies with the breeders' inability to fulfill their obligations—it is not because a Standard is obsolete, or old fashioned, or irksome to follow.

Perplexing to novices is the definition of the term "show quality." If, as they reason, their particular dog has the right coat, tail, typical head and expression, is that not sufficient? Does a dog of the right type not automatically qualify for the show ring? There are many dogs that are true representatives of their breed, yet fall short of some points of perfection that the Standard requires in physical structure, balance of line, and effortless movement. The embodiment of all these points at their highest level, plus the indefinable show personality, sum up the ingredients that make top show material; that is the ideal, of course, and only to more or lesser degrees do show dogs measure up to that ideal.

Show Temperament

One must have a bold dog to begin with; he must really be an extrovert. The right show temperament is the gilt on the gingerbread. Manners and training can be instilled, but the showiness must come from the animal itself. He must really enjoy a show, and have that extra bit of style and "brio" (fire) that enhances his good points and makes him the center of attention, apart from skillful handling. Showmanship has nothing to do with brains or "heart"; the show ring is a yardstick to measure what meets the eye.

Some of the brainiest look like flour sacks in the ring, making some people believe that the showier an animal is, the shallower is his mentality. I would not associate this with Labradors. Labradors, on the whole, are jolly, friendly souls, but they get easily bored. "Props" (a term judges use for bits of liver or other paraphernalia bulging out of some exhibitors' pockets) can be useful, but if overdone annoy the judge and become slightly ridiculous.

A European judge, invited to America to pass upon a breed known for consuming great quantities of liver in the ring, stopped his assignment at one point, looked around, and finally remarked, "Ladies and gentlemen, I have been invited over here to *judge* your dogs, not to watch them eat!"

A good showman will not only stand with presence but will gait with presence—head, tail, and eye alert, with an almost self-conscious air of knowing he is being looked at. A top showman can often out-maneuver a better specimen for the honors, and there is no question but that such an animal is a real pleasure to take into the ring.

In analyzing this "showiness," which, upon occasion, through superficial judging, can place an inferior dog over a better specimen, one may illustrate by a concrete example. At some annual Specialty shows, field trial handlers and owners have exhibited dogs of real merit—yet had the feeling that both they and their dogs were inadequate and at a disadvantage, from the standpoint of showmanship, when in competition against bench exhibits.

This is less their fault than that of the presiding judge. Many gundog judges today are neither shooting men nor even gundog owners; they have been psychologically conditioned by their years of bench judging to have all breeds presented to them not only in tip-top show condition, but in correlated show manners. And so what happens? They look elsewhere in the ring for the "showman" that catches the eye, that is handled in the way that is customary and understandable to them. The inept and "naturally" handled dogs (with their insecure owners) shrink within themselves, and oftener than not leave the ring unrewarded.

Although a dog's due is to be placed where he deserves, regardless of show handling, it takes a very good judge indeed—thoroughly familiar with the breed *and* the situation—to sort out the dogs that are excellent specimens but do not "show" their wares. This is not easy, and can be somewhat of an ordeal for a judge, but if he knows his breed, it can be done fairly and well. This is not to imply that skillful handling technique is not a requisite for continued success; but in trying to foster lagging interest in shows in our particular variety of Retriever among understandably disinterested persons, one must, as a judge, be able to compromise in relegating "showmanship" to relatively secondary importance in these instances and beware of putting dogs up for flash and manners alone. In the bench game, there are few training or proving grounds for the uninitiated to learn to handle and make the most of their exhibits, compared to field work, where informal sanctions, picnic trials and other forms of training for the novice are offered for initial experience in this branch of dog work.

12

Showing Labradors

THE first class a dog enters is usually his best, as he is fresh from the bench or his box and eager to get going. Classes at American shows are comparatively small and are quickly gotten through with, so that not so much time elapses that the dog tires of keeping his set-up position or of waiting for final judgment. At British shows, however, where one dog may be entered in two, three, or four classes, with these often containing twenty to thirty other exhibitors, one sees a different picture. The dog has to wait his turn, and, although relaxed, is bound to get logey and bored, and shows it.

One often reads in English critiques of a dog going down in one class and then winning another, perhaps beating a dog further along that had defeated him earlier, because he perked up and showed to better advantage. It is impossible to keep a dog on its toes for a long period. Good handlers learn to relax, too. At a British show I attended, when groups were being judged the next group in order of judging was already lined up inside the ring, waiting on the side, with dogs and handlers wilting under the strain. This is not meant as a criticism of the way the show was put on, but just to point out an instance relating to dog showmanship, wherein even the best of temperaments can suffer in long waits for the moment that should be fresh and scintillating.

Some dogs appear better outdoors, others indoors. Although truly sound ones will move well on any surface, there are some that give a better impression on grass, others on hard ground. Even lighting at indoor shows can make a difference in how a dog looks.

It is difficult to judge a dog's irrevocable soundness in many show rings; the ordinary enclosure is very like a "skipper's walk"—five steps and overboard—and I for one am wary of determining a dog's soundness in such restricted conditions.

One more item on show temperament. It includes a very important point—that of stamina. In our country, which is so large, and with shows and trials continuing the year round, any dog worth campaigning needs that extra stamina, the ability to eat anywhere, any time, and anything; to sleep anywhere, to live in a crate during this period of "one night stands," and not to lose too much condition thereby—and to return home none the worse for wear. Only an animal impervious to constant change can take this sort of life.

Regarding the art of handling, there is little point in going into great lengths here. The subject has been covered more than adequately in books on exhibiting dogs. Far be it from me to discourage amateurs, but they must be in it a long time; and in America they are up against a strong and expert professional contingency, unlike Britain, where almost everyone is in the same boat as owner-handlers, and simple and unaffected ways are employed, with an easy-going, "match show" spirit.

At what age may one show a Labrador puppy for the first time? The American Kennel Club rulings are that a puppy of any breed may be shown when it reaches the age of six months, through the eleventh month. At American Specialty shows, puppy classes are divided into age groups of six to under nine months, and nine and under twelve months. Most Labradors mature very slowly. To show a puppy and hope to win points from a Labrador puppy class which is usually empty at most regular shows, he must not only be very good but very mature. It is a waste of time and money to show good but immature puppies, who more than likely will wind up as point-makers for inferior adults, with age as their obvious asset, when waiting a few months would make all the difference. However, if a puppy is very good, he can and ought to win, over titles and show records, if he warrants it, on the day.

An example of a promising puppy that did not fulfill himself was our Ch. Lockerbie Spanker. I take him as an example because he was the most magnificent puppy of his age I have ever seen. He created a record in being the first Labrador champion at the age of seven months and had a short but bright show fling—with ten points and best of breed on his first weekend, on the first day of his seventh month. He became a champion in four shows, up against first-class imported and domestic company, with entries ranging into the thirties, which is large for us. When he reached fourteen months, his adult coat and his general substance and balance did not keep up with him, and although he lost none of his type or soundness, and is now a very commendable and typical adult, the promise, the bloom, and the effect of balance he gave at seven months vanished; nevertheless, he won deservedly at the time, and I respect the judges that did recognize this, in spite of his age and titled competition.

The heights that such a puppy may reach after eighteen months depend upon his ability to carry through this apparent maturity. I say apparent because, if it is evanescent—very much like the period of perfection at eight weeks—it is apt to disappear at twelve months, giving way to the expected awkwardness of undeveloped youth, but ought to come back again permanently by the time the dog is at least three. Much of this is conjecture, and varies with each individual; certain bloodlines tend to produce early temporary maturers.

The most valuable class at British shows is the Junior, for all dogs over six months and not exceeding eighteen months; this often contains the hottest competition in the show, among those which will become the best within the next year or so. It is much more useful a class for breeders than the younger puppy classes which are still indeterminate. It can be compared in its own field to a strong collection of Derby dogs at trials.

Today the accent is on youth, especially in America, but even in Britain Labradors are shown to their CC's much younger than they were in prewar times. Whether they will be "lasters" is yet to be seen.

The old adage that "a dog should look as good at four as he did at two, as good at six as he did at four, as good at eight as he did at six," and so forth, has bearing upon a laster. One considers a dog to be old when reaching ten. There is nothing more heart-warming and attractive than an older dog that is fit, sound, and lithe in movement, and still able to win regardless of grey hairs. Older dogs have everything over younger contenders, including the wise and sensible look that their years have given them.

Ch. Lockerbie Spanker at seven months (Ballyduff Treesholme Terryboy ex Ch. Ballyduff Candy), bred and owned by Lockerbie Kennels.

13

Breeding Labradors

WHAT is a breeder? The two technical sources for the definition of the term are in Webster's Dictionary: "one who promotes the birth of young—or who manages the breeding of animals." The A.K.C. rules are, "a breeder of a dog is the person who owns the dam of that dog when the dam was bred. . . ."

This is only a nominal answer to the question. A breeder is, in the best sense of the term, one with knowledge and integrity, who feels a responsibility for quality produced. The breeder's justifiable pride in such accomplishments confirms this. Quality and pride seldom enter the calculations of those who breed dogs on an assembly-line basis for profit alone. This is not to say that a living may not be made out of dogs, with quality included, but it should be understood by novices, and sincerely felt, that the successful breeding of livestock does not end with a fat bank account, but rather the reverse.

Few breeders are geneticists; few have degrees in biology, anatomy, or psychology, but the successful ones have gleaned much workable knowledge through hard-earned experience, and the greatest dogs that have ever been bred have come from such practical people, seldom from paper theorists.

Breeding programs are not mathematical but are lessons in experiments that have proven to be good with each individual applying them. Really good breeders know what they are looking for and are able to recognize it in their own animals. For the novice in breeding Retrievers, it is important to choose a path from the beginning and follow it.

The old trotting horse authority, John Wallace, once said, "In breeding, 2 and 2 sometimes makes 4, but often makes 3." Generally speaking, one may count on two rather wide specifications: one is that a breed or a variety of breed, such as in our Retriever family, will reproduce its characteristics according to how long or with what strength these characteristics have been established; the other is that these characteristics can only be increased or diminished according to the wisdom of the breeder. Selection has always been his best tool, and the best breeders are the best cullers.

Inbreeding has been successful only when circumstances are right regarding the quality of the stock to be inbred, and this means *perpetuating* and *intensifying* the top qualities that must already be present. Outcrosses are temporarily successful, but one must always return to the original source of good, going back to whatever side it lies in the family tree. Mating title to title, the usual novice approach, does not always bring the desired results, and much less frequently in Labrador show stock than in working strains.

There is an old term used many years ago by Pointer and Setter breeders—that of "old pie" bitches, meaning that for unexplainable reasons, such bitches have *reliably* produced high-class dogs no matter what they were bred to. To procure such a bitch is rare, but a breeder has it made if he owns one. Most of them are well-bred but not worth a second glance outwardly, and are often by-passed by novices, who understandably are on the lookout for the best to the eye. Providing such a bitch is typical all the way through, and sound, there is no better. However, it is always the average that counts, and no matter how well plans are laid in breeding, the superior specimens are the exceptions.

The choice of a Labrador brood bitch to begin a kennel should be governed first on what you can afford. One can take a complete gamble with a puppy, a reasonable chance with a maiden bitch from top bloodlines, and an even better chance of money well spent with a proven one.

There is no question that a sire consistently getting top quality stems, as a rule, from a strong *dam line* going back many generations. Glenhead, Hiwood, Staindrop, Arden, Grangemead and Bigstone are high examples of this truth. It has also been repeatedly demonstrated that the lowest "female tail line" on the pedigree has great influence on your present stock. In a breeder's nutshell is a quote from one of the many treasured letters I have from Edgar Winter, which is appropriate and sufficient here:

"The bitch should contribute at least 80%, using the best dog available with a splash of the same blood as the bitch. The best-looking Labs over here have been bred from top bitches. Saighdear produced a very good bitch line; a top bred bitch, bred to an average dog will produce better stock every time than an average bitch to a top dog. I have proved this for the past thirty-five years, and I never breed to a bitch with any flaws, meaning, the bitch I breed must have the best line of bitches behind her; she must be a good worker, brainy, tender-mouthed, a natural retriever, excellent nose, good tail action, and plenty of drive. Unless I have those qualities I just don't breed. I've bred the best yellows we've ever had over here and they've all come from black stock. The most valuable dog a breeder can have in a kennel is a top bred bitch. She'll pay the rent all right! I could sell every bitch puppy I have twenty times over, as the people over here know they have the backing of great dams. . . ."

A novice will be lucky if he can start with a bitch of good type, bred from proven stock, and a stud with similar qualifications. The good points of the sire should complement those of the dam, also that it should excel in points that are weak in the dam.

He will be luckier still, if, when he gets his first litter, which will be like "a shot in the dark" to him, he has an altruistic expert at his elbow. Then his luck will run out, because, ten to one, he will not heed the advice offered.

The best age for a Labrador bitch to be bred for the first time is around eighteen months, at least after her second heat. If she is a show bitch some will hesitate, as it will be thought wise to let her wave of successes run its course, rather than jeopardizing her career with an early litter; but much of the time this does not hold true for young Labrador bitches, which often seem to benefit by the extra maturity that nursing a litter gives them.

Breeders who plan to make a close study of their subject are always on the lookout for help in solving inheritance problems. This is particularly the case with our Retrievers because it is the aim of most of us to try and produce animals that combine mental ability with bodily perfection. If we could predict with any certainty that the progeny from certain matings would resemble one parent in appearance and the other in intelligence or working talent, a great advance would be made. It is not as simple as that.

Labrador bitches are normally easy whelpers and solicitous mothers with their young. They like to have their owners with them at the time of parturition, and many of them do not even object to strangers. To be with one's bitch is only a common-sense thing to do, as there is always a chance that a puppy will not arrive in the proper way, or not arrive at all, so that in noting this, one can call the vet in good time instead of too late.

Labrador litters vary in size from the extremes of two to seventeen. The average litter is about nine.

Bitches overly highstrung, that are forced to nurse, show constant aversion to their pups and may even attempt to eat them. They should be discarded as unsatisfactory broods.

When novices attempt to breed their dogs, it is wise to have an experienced person nearby. Virgin bitches can be nuisances, but there is always the time when one wants to prove one's young stud dog, and the virgins are usually the only alternative. Much of the time all goes well, but a knowledgeable hand in attendance is the best solution.

This section on breeding Labradors would not be complete without two articles dealing with the subject on different levels. Both were written by Wilson Stephens, Editor of *The Field*. The first was published in September, 1959, to draw attention to the fact that several breeds in the Working Group had fallen short of temperamental requirements for their duties, so that the Home Office felt compelled to resort to the buying of stock from abroad, to compensate for the lack of some of the homebreds' capacities. With Mr. Stephen's permission, I include it here, as it alludes to the significant question of the dual purpose outlook of gundog breeders and their future. Entitled "The Modern Dog and a Reply to Its Critics," Mr. Stephens, a breeder of Flat-Coats, points out that, "On a broader aspect of dog breeding it seems that we are likewise not alone. Even in some sporting breeds, where ability for work must be a constant aim, and strength and soundness essential, there is ground for anxiety.

"Sporting people require a dog which is good in the whole—intelligent, obedient, adaptable, determined, healthy and physically built to do its job without strain. It is to ensure the two latter characteristics alone that dog shows exist, except in the Obedience Rings. A winner at shows should be the ideal vehicle into which can be incorporated the qualities which made a worker in the field. A show winner cannot be said to be more. *It ought not to be less.*

"The winner of a field trial or other test of working ability does not have to come up to any standard at all. Provided it works well enough to do what is asked of it on the day it can be an apparent weed, as some are. Sometimes a field-trial dog attracts the remark: 'Does it matter what it looks like so long as it works well?' When applied to an individual animal this perhaps closes the matter. But it does not close the matter for the generations ahead. Loss of type means, among other things, an unsuitable vehicle in which to carry the working qualities. Degeneration sets in just as readily as it does when the working qualities are lost.

"So it is unfortunate when a cleavage sets in between the protagonists of work and the protagonists of shows. Let the gundogs be taken as an example. Ideally, no gundog should be shown which is not capable of working with the gun, nor should any gundog appear at a field trial which is not a reasonable example of its type. This degree of synthesis will not always be reached, but only by unity of the two viewpoints can it even be approached. Where two viewpoints exist, both should be fostered.

"Of the many breeds of dog, some have no purpose except to be looked at and to give companionship. The whole group of toy dogs, and most of the non-sporting variety, are mere models of their kind with no function to perform. In the terrier group no official test is implemented in this country, as in some foreign countries, of determining whether a dog which looks like a terrier will in fact behave like one. Many owners, of course, take a pride in their terrier's gameness, but not as a result of official encouragement.

"The hounds, the gundogs and some working breeds in the non-sporting group have something left to preserve other than their appearance. How is this to be done?

"It is welcome news that Mr. Vincent Routledge has joined the committee of Cruft's Show. Mr. Routledge, a coursing man and a shooting man who competes in and judges at field trials, has also trained and worked sheepdogs at trials (a very tough form of competition). There are few men as widely experienced in the man-dog partnership. His appointment should be hailed as a recognition of the need to underline the unity between the shows and competition, and an example to others to close the ranks.

"The need at present is for a multi-purpose outlook and for all concerned to be more realistic in their assessment. It invites trouble to assume that a good-looking dog works well in the field merely because its owner says (or perhaps hopes) so. *It invites other trouble to breed from poor physiques or brittle temperaments merely because these defects did not prevent success in a particular form of competition.*

"It is positively dangerous to confuse, as is possible in the gundog group, a Show Champion with a Champion. It is perhaps more dangerous still for the judges to award a working certificate, which converts the one into the other, without demanding an adequate performance. One wonders indeed whether the 'natural aptitude' directive laid down by the Kennel Club is not opening the door to sloppy thinking on the point. Natural aptitude may be interpreted by a kind-hearted judge as something ridiculously short of the evidence needed to establish working ability. Some certificates are certainly granted on grounds which seem frail, and distasteful as it is to see an honest trier disappointed, one sometimes feels tempted to cheer when judges have the courage to withhold a certificate.

"But the training and handling of dogs from less than half the story. The custodians of the future of all forms of livestock are the breeders. They are the span which joins the past to the future. with the present as the pediment in between. We must see that it does not become an impediment.

"Any steps to give encouragement and to draw attention to breeders whose dogs achieve distinction is therefore much to be welcomed. And in particular we welcome warmly the new trophies which have been awarded to the breeders of the winner of the Retriever Championship and of the Routledge-Ranic Cup. We pro-

262

pose an addition. *The Field* Gundog Trophy will this year be awarded on a trials-plus-show basis."

It must be explained here that during the last few months of 1962, a wide and controversial discussion was going on in the British dog weeklies, *Our Dogs* and *Dog World,* in reference to hereditary diseases confronting breeders and purchasers of purebred stock. This took the form of speeches and lectures by two of the world's foremost veterinarians, Messrs. Brian Singleton and S. F. J. Hodgman. Both are members of the Kennel Club, and Mr. Hodgman has long been on the Show Committee of Crufts. Articles on the same subject have often been offered in American dog magazines such as *The American Kennel Gazette* and *Popular Dogs,* so that novices may be assured that it is a worldwide problem and not related to one country alone.

It is not within the province of a layman's book to dwell upon technical and scientific questions at issue that are by rights in the veterinarian's domain, other than, as a breeder, to acknowledge their findings. Nobody connected with dogs in this modern age of veterinary advancement can, in all good faith, deny or ignore the facts, so that it finally becomes a matter of ethics and the plea of ignorance is no longer valid. Unethical breeders will always be with us, so it is to the unsuspecting purchaser and to the novice contemplating entering the dog game that the following worthy article is directed. Again, Wilson Stephens gives us a lucid picture of the problem as it lies, and what one can do about it:

A Vet's Warranty for Puppies

"Small surprise will have been caused by Mr. S. F. J. Hodgman's allusion at the British Veterinary Association's congress to an apparent increase in hereditary abnormalities in modern dogs. Those who know the useful points of an animal must have come to this conclusion for themselves. But Mr. Hodgman, Director of the Animal Health Trust's Canine Centre, has opportunities for detailed observation, and his views therefore underline with authority the more general impressions of other.

"He quoted a telling list of tendencies, and related them to certain pedigree breeds. Quite fairly, he emphasised that the same abnormalities also occur in mongrels, and perhaps even more frequently. But then their incidence is disguised by the fact that little effort is made to rear unsound mongrel puppies, whereas pedigree puppies, since they represent cash, are too often reared when they should be culled. It is only among pedigree stock that defects are noticed, or important.

"Mr. Hodgman first quoted 'excessively abnormal temperament,' including extreme nervousness, mental deficiency or even complete idiocy. He said this seemed to be increasing in miniature and toy poodles and in cocker spaniels, and decreasing in wire-haired fox terriers. Retinal atrophy, general night blindness, was occurring increasingly in Labradors and in miniature and toy poodles; but had been eliminated from Irish setters by careful breeding.

"Many Alsatians suffered from hip dysplasia; so did some Labradors, golden retrievers, boxers and samoyeds. Crypt-orchidism affected boxers, Alsatians, poodles and several toy breeds. Short-legged breeds were becoming prone to slipped discs particularly dachshunds, Pekingese and cocker spaniels. This trouble was increasingly reported in corgis.

"It must be emphasized that where a breed is mentioned, especially a popular and rapidly expanded one, even a hereditary tendency is unlikely to affect all lines and families in it. Part of the presumptive evidence that an abnormality is inherited lies in its incidence in particular strain. The strain pattern in some breeds is so marked as almost to constitute breeds within breeds. The disparity between the show and working strains in Labrador and golden retrievers, and in springer and cocker spaniels provides the pocket. This could be effected by warning buyers plainly of

"If these are the facts, and few will deny that they have the ring of truth about them, the question arises as to how to stop the trouble. The Congress, confronted with this question, sought the traditional duffer's refuge of submitting a resolution to the Kennel Club declaring that they deplored the present trend.

"Something much more positive than this will have to occur if the rot is to be stopped. The veterinary profession themselves must do something, as opposed to saying something. The Kennel Club, it cannot be too often emphasized, does not breed dogs, nor does it control the selection of parent stock by those who do. Nevertheless, there is something that it can contribute to reinforce the much-needed action by the vets in tackling the problem from the right end.

"The essence of any successful action must be a combined operation between the Club and the profession. Merely lecturing breeders will do no good whatever. Not all are selling unsound stock, but those who do so must be hit where it hurts, which is in the pocket. This could be effected by warning buyers plainly of the risks they run in purchasing a puppy of specified breeds.

"Mr. Hodgman himself put his finger on the root of the trouble when he pointed out that British dogs reached their high repute (which they may now be in danger of losing) in days when breeding was carried out as a hobby by people who could afford to destroy sub-standard puppies. Now in different financial conditions, many breeders have to sell as many puppies as possible in order to cover costs, and others are in business to make money.

"The result is that some damage is done by breeders who know perfectly well what they are doing, and some by buyers who think wishfully. Many a puppy sold cheaply as a pet is in fact bought by somebody who thinks or hopes he has got a show dog or a breeding proposition at a cut price. It is at this stage that the problem can be solved. There is always the possibility of warranty.

"Only a fool buys a horse without a vet's warranty. Many a fool buys a puppy on his own judgment and nobody else's. All dog breeders are not crooks, but most are optimists; and so are those with whom they deal.

"A puppy at the age when most sales take place is so attractive a creature that few can envisage the troubles which it may be developing. As the puppy grows up, a bond of affection is formed with its owners such as exists in no other form of livestock, and which renders the human element blind to its faults.

"Not every hereditary disease can be diagnosed in puppyhood. But general soundness can be, and a proviso to cover the possibility of future hereditary unsoundness could do much to induce proper caution to the minds of both buyer and seller. If the Kennel Club could devise some such model form of warranty and proviso, and if the veterinary profession would operate it when asked to do so, buyers of puppies would be given the possibility of protection of which they would avail themselves in increasing numbers as time passed."

265

Puppies by Zelstone Bluff ex Lana of Glenmorag daughter, bred by Lockerbie Kennels.

14

Selecting a Labrador Puppy

THIS is the chapter in most breed books to which the average novice will rush—how to pick a winner! Many of them will refuse to believe that there is no magic formula to be followed in picking a top Labrador puppy, or any breed of puppy for that matter, until they themselves (if they plan to breed) have gone through the many disappointments and frustrations that accompany an ingenious and scrupulous breeding program. This will include not only setbacks in the goals of type, conformation, and stability of working tendencies, but also the tragic introduction to nature's many hereditary afflictions that are impossible to completely avoid. Novice breeders will have to learn to take the good with the bad.

However, the following may be of use to those who would like to try, but have never bred before or chosen a puppy before; it may also be of use for those who perhaps have chosen before, but from indifferent litters—with little or no guidance from the breeder, who may have been equally as unknowledgeable as they. Whether he is a rank novice or an experienced person, the individual—

Puppies by L'lle Airman, litter brother to Ch. Raffles of Earlsmoor ex Field Ch. Braeroy Roe, bred by Mrs. M. K. Macpherson.

choosing what he fondly hopes to be the "best" at an early age for looks, working ability, and soundness "in wind and limb"—is like the proverbial purchaser of a "pig in a poke." A successful selection depends on an extraordinary amount of good luck from Fortune's fickle wheel.

Whether early choices are "pigs in pokes" or not, or whether the method of "shut eye and grab" is employed, I do not hold with the theory that one has equal chance of securing top ones in such a manner unless a litter be of superlative quality all the way through. Since no such litter has ever existed, we may be assured that ingenious breeders will not shut eyes and grab, but will remember that the best in any type of livestock has always been arrived at by canny culling. For those totally unfamiliar with animals in general, no worse approach could be recommended. Since this assumption implies that one choice is as good as another, and maintains that it is as rewarding in the end as careful selection, one need reply no further than to point out that it may be the reason there are so many inferior dogs around. No qualities of lasting value can be reckoned with at weaning time, nor indeed until even after the eighteenth month, so a hit-or-miss formula ought never be considered.

One must bear in mind, when trying to recognize good physical conformation and essential breed characteristics that separate one breed from another, that in puppies development changes rapidly from week to week, almost from day to day, somewhat like an invisible fever chart, rising and falling from excellence to mediocrity and back again, until a certain period may arrive when one may have a surer inkling of what the dog promises to be at maturity. Here, the person blessed with that rare "inner eye," or instinctive gift for noting quality in any species of livestock, may venture to predict the tipping of the scales. Until then—and that time varies with each animal and can be checked on no calendar—all else is pure gamble, with hopes often dashed, prophecies shattered, rules broken.

Let us also realize that in the life of a human being it takes approximately two decades to achieve an adult skeleton. With a dog, all the growth and development are compressed into twelve months —sometimes less than that for attainment of adult height at withers

—and another eighteen months or so for complete physical flowering. During this accelerated growth stage, different bones in a puppy's frame are growing at different rates of speed, which causes the puppy at various periods to look "at sixes and sevens"—the despair of even a knowing breeder. For that reason above all, sure-fire bench material or those which will stand up well to the rigors of work in the field cannot be infallibly selected at weaning time.

In spite of this, there are no valid reasons for "shutting eyes and grabbing"; there are better ways of choosing a good puppy.

It is of the utmost importance to be assured, first, that a Labrador puppy stems from sound working stock, certainly from a tried and true line of producing dams. Lest some unrighteous wrath from whatever purely bench kennels may exist should fall upon my ears for maintaining that it is necessary to choose from working lines, they of all people should understand, even if they will not admit that this healthy principle is essential—that for whatever purpose one buys a dog, a certain amount of discrimination must be used in trying to acquire a most typical specimen. Whether one plans to work a puppy seriously or just keep him as a handsome companion, the truth remains that if a Retriever, or any other variety of gundog, is considered typical, it should be not only pleasing to the eye, but *given the opportunity,* able to display its most esteemed attribute—its working potential. After all, the true difference between a bench Retriever and a working Retriever is not so much in their conformation, which should be nearly identical, but in the latter's invisible qualities. Can a Retriever, if it does not show the slightest instinctive interest in fetching and carrying, swimming, and hunting on its own, or if it shows a decided aversion to game or covert, be considered completely typical?

The term "working stock" is ambiguous and can mislead the novice. The Labrador Retriever Club of America is the only sporting dog breed club in this country with the ruling that no member of the club shall use the title of "champion" until the dog, having won its fifteen bench points, receives at least a minimum Working Certificate, a description of which is found elsewhere in this book. Since this ruling is upheld by the Labrador Retriever Club alone, and does not come under American Kennel Club legislation, (which if it did, would automatically include all sporting breeds under the same provision) it has been criticised by some people as un-

270

fairly penalizing Club members, because, as it stands, non-members may and do show champions without this minimum proof of working tendencies.

"Working" stock is obviously claimed by those whose chief aim in breeding is to produce sound, useful gundogs, and of course it is a foregone conclusion that field trial kennels have a priority in this specification.

So bench titles, although signposts outwardly pointing in the right direction, may be deceiving to novices and are not to be taken for granted. Everyone is aware of the downfall of many a staunch gundog variety because breeders ignored the cardinal principle of giving their dogs some natural work. One must candidly acknowledge that bench interests on both sides of the Atlantic have extinguished the original natural gifts of many sporting dogs to such a degree that the abyss between show and work is insurmountable. So far it has not become thus with our honest, rugged Labrador. It is to the credit of most Labrador breeders, whose interests lie more in evolving perfection of type, that they realize that "improving" a breed does not end with the stacking up of show wins. Countless among them work their bench dogs here in "fun trials" and sanctions, and abroad in modest stakes and Working Tests and even beyond.

In a real working pedigree, field titles, or names of dogs that have produced field winners and first class workers, are certainly sought for, but if such are not in evidence close up, one should have reliable knowledge through the owner of the litter that the lesser lights have proved their worth. There is no use bursting with pride over a lineage whose only claim to fame is one National Champion hidden away in a corner in the fourth generation.

Having determined that your prospective litter is bred with these objects in mind, another fact worthy of attention is what meets the eye in the form of physical endowment in type, balance, soundness and class. It is just as unrewarding to look at a litter with the highest working credentials that has not an iota of resemblance to the breed described in the Standard, as it is to mull over a brood bred solely for bench pretensions.

One may be better prepared in one's choice if one is able to see at least the sire and the dam, if not a second generation behind.

And of course, if the litter is a repeat mating, seeing grown specimens of previous litters is an added advantage.

In choosing our mythical puppy, let us put it at the average age at which a novice usually makes his precarious choice—eight to ten weeks. In order of their importance to me I would classify the following points to consider:

TEMPERAMENT: disposition, personality, bent.

TYPE: apparent, essential breed characteristics

GENERAL OUTLINE OF CONFORMATION: general outline of frame at a glance

CONDITION: weight, cleanliness, obvious health.

The first two qualities could be interchangeable and vie for first place, for without a proper temperament one can do very little with an animal, and without true type one has absolutely nothing at all on which to build for future value.

TEMPERAMENT: The true Labrador temperament is as important as an otter tail, and more so, for what avails such a tail without the disposition to make it wag? (And I *mean* wag, not held between the legs nor stiff over the back in aggression.) Fear and aggression sometimes have bearing upon one another; they can also be completely separate, but aggression is often the result of insecurity.

In general, one can classify breeds of dogs that over the years have become "man-made" or "man improved" through selection, into their respective groups: Terrier, Working, Sporting (Gundogs), and so forth. Three of the most distinctive types of temperament can be found between Terriers, Working or guard dogs, and the Sporting varieties.

In the latter, to which the Labrador belongs, there are also variations in dispositions among the Retrievers, the Setters, and the Spaniels. There are those who hold to the theory that even coat color can have bearing on temperament.

The ideal Labrador temperament is one of a kindly, outgoing, adaptable nature, anxious to please and non-quarrelsome with man or beast. Labradors do *not* make the most efficient guard dogs. They *will* wander in search of scents, they *will* leave friends and fireside with more equanimity than many breeds, and, to a certain extent, unless kept up, their home is under their hat. No breed should have to borrow qualities from another, and a sound Labrador temperament should evince neither terrier nor working dog characteristics.

It worries many people that in some areas abroad Labradors are starting to be used as attack dogs and are bred for such maneuvers. But breeding against nature is very difficult, and happily ineffectual so far in this instance, as Mr. H. S. Lloyd pointed out through his experience in the last War as head of the Army Dog Department, wherein Labradors made most efficient records as mine detectors but failed consistently when efforts were made to fashion them into attack dogs.

There are plenty of breeds available which by nature offer the very characteristics that have no place in a gundog. If novices in their purchases, or breeders in their stock, instill or condone such alien temperamental tendencies, they are doing the breed a very great disservice. Have any of them taken into account that the Labrador Standard is one of the very few Standards which up to now has never thought it imperative to underline temperamental requirements? Other breeds have their definite "shoulds" and "should nots" in this respect, and they prize and seek for what has always been taken for granted in our variety of Retriever. Let us keep it this way, and cancel out any breeding stock that is not sound in mind as well as in structure.

One need not dwell too long on the description of sound temperament in an eight-week puppy other than to say that a youngster, sound in body and soul, will show a gay, irrepressible nature, brash in play, inquisitive and bold, a veritable tailwagger, impervious to the loss of its litter mates or familiar enclosure when separated, and one which the old bitch will be glad to see the back of. Temperament unfurls a wide spectrum in which degrees of boldness, affection, fear, suspicion, and intelligence are very pronounced. Very young puppies seldom display adult characteristics, such as willingness to work, power of concentration, and the common dog sense that is linked to experience. One must settle at this age for what is happily obvious, and hope that some of the prize ingredients such as brains, memory, and the courage to face all odds will come to the top later.

On the other hand, moderately introverted puppies appeal to some people who make no demands upon them, and there is no reason why they should be completely discarded; more often than not they will gradually, through the affection and patience of their owner, accustom themselves to the situations which cause their fear, but they are also very apt to transfer their timidities to each new thing as it comes along, all their lives. If noise and guns are not among their terrors, they can become adequate gundogs. But for exhibitions, or in most forms of competitive work, and most of all in a field of work where the dog has complete responsibility and independence of action, as in guiding the blind, they are excluded. Show personality is a thing apart, and is touched on elsewhere, but the prerequisite for that also is a bold nature.

To me, one of the simplest and best tests of a sound personality is a puppy's equable acceptance of separation from its litter mates and kennel—if only for a stroll or a run somewhere apart—without a backward glance. It may be a bit tedious, especially if the litter is large, to jot down mentally each one's reactions, but one does not need to repeat it more than a few times to get a fairly good idea of each individual. It is absolutely impossible to judge puppies' natures when they are all together behind a wire fence; they must be gauged separately. It is wise not to put faith in future breeding plans in those that continually will not mix with the others, or which run and hide in the house or corner from the rest of the dogs or even from familiar human beings around it. For unadulterated first-class temperament, an eight-weekster should be able to take in his stride any normal changes in his life.

By normal, I mean the customary affectionate person or family coming to choose him and take him home by car, rail, or plane. This is not to suggest that noises like guns, fireworks, or a blaring television set be resorted to, or that a prospective buyer make himself ridiculous by stamping, whistling and gyrating around in front of an astonished puppy, in order to get the right temperamental reactions; many sound puppies are temporarily frightened by lonely trips and unaccustomed encounters with a strange outside world. They will also howl and whimper when left alone in a room or strange pen at the beginning. However, that whimper should be a call for human companionship, and when it is given him he ought to be overjoyed.

If puppies are not tried out one at a time, a deeply timid one can mask his lack of confidence to a certain extent by relying or leaning on the presence of another dog—a litter mate or his dam; take his prop away and his world can be shattered.

However, these are extremes. Often, observant breeders will notice personality develop while still in the whelping box. As soon as eyes are opened and legs are strong enough to support the mock fights that ensue, one can start looking for the bullies, the friendly, lazy ones, and the ones whose hearts hold fear. According to interesting personality experiments at the Jackson Memorial Laboratory at Bar Harbor, puppies do not usually react until the twentieth day or so in any definite manner to human approach. There are always exceptions of course, and we had one recently— a tiny red bitch which, when just seventeen days old, recognized my voice and soft whistle whenever I entered the room, and ran straight across the box to me. I checked carefully on the calendar to be certain of this; she was the first in this litter of ten to accomplish anything; her eyes opened first, lost their bluish cast first, and she stood and ran first. It goes without saying that she became a bold wee hen.

Well-adjusted puppies do not object to being handled and lifted. An apprehensive one will often hold itself stiffly when held. Young puppies should be lifted with one hand firmly under their buttocks, the other supporting their chest under the forelegs; the primitive way of yanking them up by the loose skin on their necks is their dam's prerogative; she has no other means.

TYPE: Type is symmetry, balance, classicism—the "eye and air" of a well-bred dog. It excludes everything that is irregular, discordant in line, vulgar, and common. Breed characteristics are external manifestations of type in any breed and are its very lifeline. Several breeds have many points in common, but each breed has, as its exclusive monopoly, its own type as set in the Standard.

The three most important breed characteristics of the Labrador are Coat, Tail, and Expression. No matter how good a Labrador may appear to be, it does not truly represent its breed if it does not have these three definite attributes, which are the only ones to distinguish it from other breeds, and it should possess them positively and obviously.

The texture of an orthodox Labrador coat is difficult to describe in print or photograph. It has to be seen, felt and compared. Elsewhere in this book, in Mr. Anderton's superb analysis, there is as good a word picture as possible of a first class coat. To review it briefly, its essentials are that the outer coat be harsh and coarse to the hand, and that the undercoat be as thick as possible, soft and woolly and obviously water resistant, a lighter black in the Blacks and a paler yellow in the Yellows, unless (which is seldom) they are solid color all the way through. A good coat covers the entire body and should be examined by judges with more than a superficial running of the hands over the top of the back, although this is where the harshest hairs lie.

There are coats that are completely free from wave or feather but so sparse in undercoat and so sleek and shining that they cannot be considered correct; then there are the good harsh outer coats with a bit of wave and length, and most of these have the prized undercoat. Exaggerated wave or length are not precisely called for in the Standard either, but from a practical working point of view, lack of undercoat should be penalized above this.

EXPRESSION: Typical expression hinges on the size and placement of the eyes, to a certain extent upon their color, on the size, placement and use of the ears, and the general makeup of skull, muzzle and jaw, on whatever length or shortness of neck the dog is blessed or burdened with. Temperament can also influence expression. In summing up expression, one must avoid the hard, sullen look, or lack-luster eye and cultivate the kindly, amiable, warm look that is typical.

TAIL: A good Labrador tail can be well illustrated in the many pictures of this book; specifically one can turn to that of Ch. Sandylands Tweed of Blaircourt. An otter, of course, would be quite handicapped for the life he leads without the sort of tail he owns, and there have been instances where an absolute chow or ring tail has been a drawback to a Labrador swimming. But tails are tails, and not the most glamorous part of a dog's anatomy, barring a graceful Setter's flag. Except where breed characteristics call for it, a ring tail gives even the rank novice a bad taste—very much as yellow eyes will affect some people. The correct otter tail is short enough not to come below the hock and the best have been as thick as a man's forearm from the base, tapering imperceptibly to a modest point at the end. The best otter tails seem to have the least feather, and a truly fine one should retain at least some of its thick shape even when shedding. Its carriage and set is of consequence, too. The set is regulated by the tail's connection at the base of the spine; a tapering, narrow rump often has a poorly set tail. Tail carriage for exhibition is paid great attention in England. Breeders and judges prefer it not to be above the level of the back when gaiting. The well-known comment in critiques, "a bit too fond of his tail," refers to a higher carriage—usually at hound level —which, though smart, is not admired over there.

It is not a proper tail if it is a saber, overly long and thin and uncomfortably feathered. When working afield, part of a Labrador's style lies in the action and carriage of his tail, which is constantly on the move if he is questing, as he ought—alive and spirited. Spirited workers usually own stylish tails.

GENERAL OUTLINE AND CONFORMATION: Here one looks for balance; the first glance and perfunctory inspection a judge may bestow upon his exhibits when they enter the ring is for this quality. With adults, balance is there or it is forever absent, but with young puppies the best time to discover balance is at eight to ten weeks. Later it will disappear (one hopes only temporarily) to make room for all the odd assortments of imbalance compatible with immaturity. This is the age when a good puppy shows to his best advantage, and the enthusiastic novice will spend most of his time rushing back and forth from a copy of the Standard to the puppy and back again, trying to see how much of it matches and how much of it doesn't. But the Standard is the blueprint of the adult dog, and although some favorable characteristics may show up in youngsters, others will not.

One will discover that a first-class puppy has all the balance of the first-class adult dog. These eight short weeks have always been for me the most propitious for noting this evanescent, fleeting impression of balance, or "miniature maturity," wherein such a puppy, out by itself, stands absolutely true. If this strikes a chord within you, so that you would like to run out and seize him, to hold him in that tiny perfection forever, he has probably a lot to recommend him for the future.

However, because puppies change so rapidly, one is always choosing "on the day," and, had one waited a day before or chosen a day later, the picture might have given a different impression.

The puppy I would choose for myself is one blooming with substance, a strong frame, a short back, a dense coat and a cocky disposition, carrying his head as proudly as his ever-wagging tail.

The largest puppies are not always the best by any means, so if the parents are of good size and well-boned there is no reason why a smaller puppy cannot be chosen; the size of his parents would indicate that the puppy would mature to ample size.

As to sex, that is a personal preference. I have always leaned toward bitches, but many breeders hold to the theory that if a dog puppy is picked the quality of the sire should be above that of the dam, and that in the case of a well-known sire it can often be discovered from his previous offspring whether the dogs or the bitches were the most promising.

The suggestion that the puppy should be short-backed is based on the knowledge that generally backs grow longer and longer as time goes on, and that a short-coupled animal very often has the best otter tail, a quality that ought to be perpetuated, all things being equal (let's not forget the necks).

In going into detail, which is necessary as one examines more closely, I like to see a largish head. Small-headed puppies, although they seem to grow in all other departments, never seem to make up completely in head importance unless it is of sufficient size in puppyhood; on the other hand, an overly large head may indicate coarseness of skull at maturity.

I then look at the eyes, for they, without question, are the key to the character and personality of a dog, and one can recognize whatever lies there, in spite of the "bluish tinge" that may not yet have disappeared. Gradually the dog's permanent eye color will appear, usually at teething time, around twelve weeks, or a bit later. As a rule, the lighter the "blue," the lighter will be the adult eye, but this also varies; eyes lighter than called for have been known to darken to an extent at maturity.

Although the American Standard says "black, brown or yellow," there is a great range, in actual color scale, from the bright facets of topaz through "burnt sugar" or hazel, to a warm soft brown, finishing in an expressionless deep black.

Sharp, shy, or otherwise unstable temperaments have often been coupled by breeders to certain eye *coloring*, and they are adamant in pronouncing that color and a dog's disposition go hand in hand for better or for worse. Yellow eyes have for centuries been associated with mongrels that have never displayed consistently kindly

278

temperaments due to their hodge-podge ancestry. In the early days, when many breeds were being determined and classified, great stress was laid upon the elimination of many objectionable features that might be reminiscent of mongrel traits, and the wide-spread antipathy of fastidious breeders towards yellow eyes has lasted until our time.

Ironically, when the British Yellow Standard was first drawn up, it stated in a "face saving" clause that any color eye "harmonizing with the coat" would be satisfactory—thus very neatly excusing a light eye, which in those days was no doubt very difficult to eradicate. Yellow may match yellow "in a pinch," but it neither harmonizes with nor complements a black coat.

Lest one seem dogmatic, one may say truthfully that eye coloring does not completely dominate expression. We have all seen dark-eyed dogs with disagreeable outlooks, and yellow-eyed dogs which were quite pleasant to meet. In my own opinion, expression lies more in the character of the dog, which is reflected so obviously in his eyes regardless of color; sometimes an older dog's yellow eyes seem to mellow and soften in old age. As Mr. Gilliat pointed out, "there is nothing against a lightish eye provided it does not exhibit ill temper or stupidity, but unfortunately this is seldom the case." He prefers a moderately light eye to a really dark one and also holds the view that dark-eyed dogs do not as a rule have the best of sight. This last observation is made of course on the assumption that some light-eyed dogs seem to display better marking ability.

Eye size and placement also have bearing upon good expression. Those too close or too far apart, too large or too small—some even placed so obliquely as to give a "bullterrier" eye-set (often just missing an entropion underlid)—can indicate whether or not the dog has an agreeable or unpleasant outlook.

Ears in young puppies of certain strains are apt to be too large. Often, if they hang abnormally low in a "houndy" fashion on a narrow, peaked skull, there is little chance of great improvement. Large ears may "take up" to a certain degree if the width of skull promises to be wide enough. Small, neat ears, perfectly placed in puppyhood, sometimes develop into an overly high set (may we politely call "pig ear") when the dog is full grown. Ears also play their part in contributing to a classic head, in the manner in which they are used to display alacrity, mettle, and individual spirit.

In muzzles, I like to see moderate depth and length of jaw, not heavy in flews, and not tight lipped. The American Standard's interpretation of "level mouth" means what the British one says—"teeth sound and strong, the lower teeth just behind but touching the upper." With milk teeth, one occasionally will see a slight overshot condition, but this tends to even out with adult dentition. Cause to worry comes with an undershot set; this defect is devilish to eliminate if ever permitted to settle in a line. When questioning puppy bites, one should observe how the front gums meet when the mouth is held closed and the lips turned back. An incurable under- or over-shot mouth is usually caused by the jaw's being either too long or too short, and carrying the teeth with it.

Good heads will already show chiseling under the eye, with a definite stop, and with little or no hint of Flat-Coat silhouette when viewed from profile. Not all heads, however, at this age are as they should be, and to really be able to judge whether they are or not, one needs experience. Some heads take time to form and "break up" as the puppy goes along in growth.

There is a point of interest that has always been left out of all standards, that of the features of dog versus bitch. Feminine and masculine qualities are quite different, even in young puppies, and center in the head. It is a debatable point as to how seriously judges or breeders consider a bitchy-headed dog or a doggy-headed bitch. To me, the former is most disconcerting, and repellent in a stud dog. All things being equal with the bitch in other respects, a doggy bitch can show certain attractive qualities; but if the dogginess is overdone, she loses the essential feminine image that has to be a part of the makeup of a really good bitch.

With puppies, when the ultimate size of the head cannot be forecast, good size is important for either sex. A bitch's head is lighter and finer than a dog's, but it must in no way be inconsequential and weedy just for the sake of femininity.

Necks are bound to be deceiving at eight weeks, but puppies well on the road to extreme throatiness will already show this condition. One may have a better idea of shoulder placement from fourteen weeks on, but severely upright shoulders can be spotted even now. Leg bone is heavy at eight weeks, the heavier, the more to grow on, as a reserve for the stage the dog will reach at a year, when he may suddenly appear to be "fine" in bone; if there is not enough quality of leg bone when he is under six months old, there is a possibility that he will end up too light in the frame all over. I particularly like to see heavy bone at the hocks. When viewing the forelegs from the inside part of the leg, one should be able to feel its solid substance all the way up to the chest.

It is good to see depth of brisket and barrel ribs now; those that are really deficient in this seldom gain much later on. Puppies with the most substance are not necessarily the fattest or the largest; they are the heaviest to the hand in solidity, when lifted.

Puppies destined to have good toplines don't as a rule have disturbing ones now; when they get on a bit they are apt to develop a "high behind," and it is not always easy to predict the outcome; they may still be "high" long after six months, and come down much later than that. A dip near the withers or a roach back is less likely to ever clear up. All these points vary with individuals.

Hindquarters are most difficult to forecast in eight-weeksters; I have chosen puppies built like brick outhouses behind, only to have them disappoint later on, whereas others of indefinite and undeveloped build came into superb proportion and strength. Cow hocks, straight stifles with no bend at hock, out at the elbows—which means a loose shoulder—feet turning out so that the weight of the body rests on the insides of the pads—these rarely improve. Feet are large, but should be in proportion to the leg bone above them, with strong, rounded toes and no hint of splay or the loose, open look due in many cases to sloping pasterns.

Puppy coats may change imperceptibly as time goes on. A really top coat, like a really top tail, is there at birth and carries right through the first casting, into the adult jacket. If one is undecided about the coat texture in a young puppy, it will be decided for you after the first or second shed. It is usually the overly soft open coats, even with a certain amount of thickness, that bring disappointment.

The puppy with the real and rare otter tail has it from the start, although measuring for length, as one can with adults, is not infallible because of the erratic growth rate of the legs. The tail can be carried very gaily, right over the back in excitement. Such a puppy tail carriage is nothing to worry about; it denotes a happy disposition, and will straighten out and come down to the right level in time.

As an added reflection, the choosing of young puppies by experienced breeders can have its problems too. It is perfectly possible to choose the pick of a litter at this age if you are familiar with the bloodlines such as would be in your own kennel or a related one, but it is naturally more of a task to choose from a type to which you are unaccustomed. For novices choosing from a mixed litter, they will be better off in choosing the *dog*, and curbing their temptation for a preference of color.

CONDITION: As the word implies, condition means the state of health and cleanliness a litter is to be found in. It is revolting to visit kennels with dirty pens, with stale food in left-over pans, puppies reeking from the smell of unchanged bedding and other inexcusable kennel stenches. A puppy that is well cared for has its own wholesome pungent puppy odor. This is also the stage of life for them when fat bodies are wanted—not so much weight as to impede exercise and romping, but fat well distributed over the frame. A puppy, overfed with cheap food, with a worm-infested interior, can be easily spotted by the bloated little body that makes the legs emerge as sticks from four corners. Eyes should be bright and clear and the insides of ears pink and not caked with dust.

When all is said and done, before actually deciding on your puppy, whether you are making your choice from your own first litter or someone else's, size up the quality of the litter *as a whole*. Is your "pick" the choice of a poor litter? If so, it has not half the value of a second or even third choice of a really first-class lot. If such a pick stands out too ostentatiously, the rest of the members may be quite insignificant. As a matter of fact, it is a challenge even for an experienced person (and a compliment to the breeder of the litter)—if choosing poses a real problem with a group of seven or eight so "even" in quality—to arrive at a decision.

Here lies the crux, and, to me, the purpose of breeding: it is to raise the standard of the *average* and not to be content with an occasional flyer, usually a "sport" which does not reproduce itself, but through which a kennel's reputation may coast along for years. The status of a breed lies in the quality of its *average* dogs, not in lone individuals, and in a recreation of a better average in each subsequent litter.

Perfection is a goal and not a reality. In breeding and choosing young puppies, there are bound to be disappointments arising in the future that are not visible at the moment. To abide by an accepted Standard without flights of fancy is the only "secret" that is open to all, and that has always been possessed by those who have contributed anything lasting to the breed. Any divergence from Standard type spells disaster because sooner or later it leads to a heterogeneous muddle, or, as Lady Hill Wood has acutely put it, becomes "ad-lib" breeding.

It takes a much longer time and a much more intimate understanding of a breed to learn to evaluate virtues in type which embrace breed characteristics, quality, and balance, than it takes to become a "spotter of faults." It is the comparative newcomer to a breed, just past the stage of bewilderment, full of little bits of knowledge which are dangerous, who is usually the most glib at fault finding.

Why not? Obvious faults are easy to see; whether they are as important as they are obvious is a matter that cannot be solved except through experience.

Taking a concrete example. At a bench show for instance, you will always hear the "all but a novice" asking loudly why so-and-so with the light eye went up . . . or such-and-such went away so close behind . . . or that other with his tail so gay. . . . He will point to all the other animals in the ring, which are dark of eye, immaculate in movement, and decorous in tail carriage; he will take no account of the fact that the winners, despite the apparent fault in each of their cases, were typical of their breed and structurally beautiful to look at.

Any judge who places a mediocre dog, devoid of type but with no outstanding drawbacks, over one that is typical but with a fault, is not only glorifying mediocrity but diminishing the status of the breed.

Choosing a Puppy as a Gundog

This is not a section on training, but only some useful hints for a novice with his first Retriever, to help him discover and bring out the natural abilities of his puppy. He will learn a lot from his dog.

It is less of a gamble to choose from a litter what will become at least an adequate gundog, if the litter is bred right, than to choose for show potential. A rugged little body, an alert and bold nature, these are essential.

Puppies as young as six weeks will pick up and carry little objects around—bits of leaf or stick or whatever comes their way—or be the leaders among their tumbling litter-mates in keeping whatever article they may be playing with. Some will even retrieve tiny distances quite smartly. But all these tendencies, as encouraging as they are to witness, mean nothing more at this age than that this natural instinct of fetching and carrying is not dormant, and this can be observed in bench bred litters as well as those bred from working stock. Precocious puppies (like children) are like the organ-grinder's monkey, and only a novice will attach any undue significance to demonstrations that ought to be taken for granted.

No novice, we hope, will be so idiotic as to throw a young puppy into the water. Shocks of any kind, whether for water or to the gun, can ruin an otherwise top puppy for life. A dog's faults are usually the mistakes of his master. Expert trainers have often been blamed for not turning out a successful product because of the stupidity of early errors on the part of the novice owner's judgement.

Introduction to game and water is no hardship at all if started early enough; a small feathered dummy or bird and cold water will never deter a good puppy at this age. Twelve-weeksters will swim like veterans, with no floundering or paddling, as would their older brothers who come to it later. Even future good manners in water delivery can be gently instilled now, by wading out yourself and taking the dummy from the returning puppy before he has a chance to land, shake, and drop. Upon taking the dummy you can direct him out again, and you will see that he will swivel around automatically, using his tail, if it be the right shape, as a tiny rudder.

Giving him very short and few retrieves is only logical. Apart from tiring him, the mistake of throwing too far on land (where you yourself will have to thrash around in cover to find the dummy), or too far out in water (where the tide will drift it out of sight), is that it makes an unfinished job for the puppy. Even in play, the last retrieve of the day should be completed. It is difficult enough for older ones to see objects floating at water level, especially when the water is a bit choppy; get down yourself to water level and find out.

Tragic and easily prevented drownings have occurred in swimming pools when the dogs could not climb up the steep sides. Keep your Labs, large and small, away from them. Puppies should be taught to enter water from sloping banks into a pond or lake, and, if beaches are used, it is only common sense not to choose a rough day when breakers are high and tides are strong.

An important point to remember and stick by is that, if your puppy is to be a prized gundog, no one should train him but those who know how to instill the rudimentary disciplines of his going out and coming back with the object thrown. He cannot differentiate between his scrambles over a ball with your child and his daily retrieves with you. Certainly, he ought to share the family life, but his schooling must be kept apart.

Labrador puppies have an innate instinct for bringing gifts to those they love; these can range from a pungent rat to a silver ashtray. Whatever it may be, control your distaste, and accept it with grace and a word of praise. If he is continually nagged and chastised for bringing unwelcome offerings you will be sowing seeds of sorrow, in that instead of laying the foundations for enthusiastic delivery when you want him to get your birds, you will be doing just the opposite by psychologically building up in his mind that the bringing of objects to you is wrong.

Hard-mouth, a term used in gundog circles for those Spaniels or Retrievers which crush and mutilate game when retrieving, is held by some to be inherited. It is a touchy subject, and, like gunshyness, can have its roots in the mistakes of early training. Tugs of war with a puppy, wrestling with him to give up his dummy, all may have bearing upon this unfortunate tendency. Certain temperaments are known to lean towards hard-mouth, either as young puppies, in the manner in which they grab your hand or arm in play, or in instances of well-trained gundogs, who have a very tight hold when delivering and seem reluctant to give up their game to the handler. Real hard-mouth is a special study in itself, and it is better to give the benefit of the doubt to the dog, as game has often been damaged by having fallen into sharp cover, or, when stuck in underbrush, may be injured inadvertently by the dog in trying to extract it. The stigma of hard-mouth given to individual dogs can be unwarranted and completely unfair.

There are countless enjoyable ways of discovering whether your puppy enjoys hunting on his own, and if he has a good nose.

The later Mr. Winter's practice of taking young puppies out in the dark to retrieve on land has long been a favorite pastime with ours. Odd bits of biscuit or a familiar dummy, tossed out into the black night in long grasses or bushes, is more than entrancing for them to collect and ferret out, no less important being the knowledge and recognition gained by the owner of his dog's ability in this direction. Nothing can be more disillusioning than to see a Retriever at a loss as to what to do naturally.

Watching an old-timer is one of the best examples of all. If you have an old, well-trained standby, he or she will teach the puppy more in a short time than is humanly possible. A bitch in this instance is often more patient because of her maternal instincts with young things. Puppy sees—puppy does (and this holds true for older dogs' demonstrations of bad habits, too).

As the puppy grows on, serious training will take the place of play. The following books will be of aid and interest to novices determined to train their own dogs:

Training Your Retriever, James Lamb Free, Coward, McCann.
Training Gundogs to Retrieve, David D. Elliot; H. Holt & Co.
Retrievers, B. B. Riviere; Faber & Faber Ltd.
Gundogs, Training & Field Trials, P.R.A. Moxon; Popular Dogs Publishing Co. Ltd.

These books can be of great value, but one must have adequate time to devote to the animal. Advantageous contacts with various field trial clubs in many vicinities may be gotten through their secretaries, whose names and addresses can be obtained from the American Kennel Club, 221 Park Avenue South, New York 3, N.Y.

The Labrador Retriever Club of America
The National Retriever Field Trial Club
The Wisconsin Amateur Field Trial Club

The novice can bring along his dog completely on his own, as a very useful gundog, and if time is plentiful can venture into field trials; but he must know the difference between gunning work and trial competition, the explanation and training of which are fully covered in these books. Because trial tests in America are all uniform, each dog, as it is called up, receives the identical tests for uniform fairness, so that the retrieving of cripples or runners is not permitted.

For the shooting dog, however, the basic concept of game preser-

286

vation is the collecting of cripples. Dave Elliot puts it in clear terms for the novice in the following paragraph:

"That all important cripple should be the basic target for our Retrievers. There are countless occasions when one can pick up our kill by hand, but not the cripples, that seek a hide-out wherever it can be found.

"We love to brag about our marksmanship, but in the course of one season, the number of cripples down all over the country would, I am sure, shock our wildest dreams. If only two birds were crippled by each gun, it would bring the count to over two million for the season, and we know this to be a most conservative estimate. How many of these are left in the swamps, woods, and fields? I would hazard a guess, and the figures would not give us any reason to brag.

"For the past fifteen years the Retriever trials and training has increased by leaps and bounds. Over 100 licensed trials are held annually, not to mention sanction trials, and the get-to-gether days for training, as a far cry from the two Specialty events in the early thirties. This terrific training of Retrievers, in trial competition and their general use all over the world, has done more to save and conserve game than almost any other single act in conservation. I would guess that every week through the year, a new face joins the ranks of Retriever enthusiasts, wanting to learn about trials, and hoping to own a field trial winner. He will learn everything about teaching his dog to retrieve dead birds, and the dog will mark to the best of his ability; pick-up, delivery, staunchness, and handling to whistle, all will be accomplished with the minimum of trouble. But how much will he have learned about the handling of a cripple? The chances are—nothing! This to me, is the weakest link in our chain, the cripple, which should be the most important part of a dog's work, seems to be the one that receives the least consideration. Why? Because the field trials, our foremost educator, do not practice it.

"There is a fairly sound reason for this. Uniformity of tests at our trials is most important, and as we know, it is difficult to get cripples that would give uniform tests; some may run 100 yards, others perhaps 10 yards. There is no way, so far, of governing this; hence, in view of this condition, it has almost become a forgotten art, which is a dreadful mistake. For this reason, I am trying to awaken interest through this small article.

"There are a number of kennels throughout the country that are fortunate enough to have enough natural bird work, to give their dogs experience with cripples; but there are many that do not do so, or will never attempt to simulate cripples in training, by using a wing-clipped duck as an introduction for their young dogs.

"To illustrate how unimportant some field trial enthusiasts regard this, a conversation took place at a controlled pheasant shoot. The owner of a large and successful kennel of field trial Retrievers was at the shoot, and was asked to send one of his dogs for a cripple. He refused, with the remark that he would not do it, as trial dogs were not permitted to, and he did not want to get his dogs into a bad habit. You can easily imagine the commotion these remarks caused among the other guests, amongst them being some well-known Springer Spaniel owners. Is it not feasible to think, that when a man has been in the Retriever trial game for years, and regards the cripple with so little interest, that those with much less experience, are going to ignore this phase of the Retriever's work completely?

"Although no satisfactory method for using this test has been found for trials, there is no reason why it should not be practiced in training; in fact, it should be given every encouragement. A dog that has not been developed in the tracking down of cripples, either in the swamps or on land, is only 50% efficient. A Retriever with an average nose, will learn in the actual shooting field how to do this, but it takes time, and he is going to lose a few birds before he knows how to handle scent. If you have ever watched an inexperienced dog hit scent, you will know what I mean—he will waste valuable time circling the fall. He believes he has found the game, whenever he hits the scent, and not finding the bird, is a mystery to him; and while he is trying to solve it, the cripple is well on his way—another lost bird—a prey to vermin.

"Why not develop your dog for this all important job in the training field, so that when you do go hunting, he will already know how to handle your cripples. We may never be able to practice it in our trials as they are today, but the ability to find your cripples will never hamper him from winning a field trial, and it will add much to your bag and your pleasure in the field, to say nothing of adding to the conservation of game.

"In my own training I use a wing-clipped duck for a young dog. A duck leaves a strong scent, and does not travel as fast as a pheasant or other upland bird. As a starter, I do not allow the duck to get more than 50 yards start, and I never use a field near water, in case the duck should reach it and defeat the purpose of the training.

"As the young dog gains more experience, I allow the duck more time to get away. This phase of the training is not only important, but most interesting in watching the dog's progress, and studying the manner in which he solves his problems. It is most essential in the early stages of this type of training, that you set the stage, so to speak, in such a way to insure his success—failure at this time can be very discouraging. I cannot stress too strongly this particular phase of training."

If your Labrador is to be a family gundog (an ideal existence), there are points to consider when planning his life with you. Even if he is to be a housedog, there are times when you cannot be with him outdoors, and you have to have sensible arrangements to keep him up. Community living in suburbs demands it, and it is essential when living in open country estates. In the suburbs he will run the substantial risk of being hit by a car, or stolen, or poisoned by a neighborly neighbor whose status symbol of manicured landscaping will come before any love of a dog. In open country he will become a tramp and start running after wild game, apt to be shot at by the trigger-happy red-capped Nimrods that infest the countryside during gunning season; he may also succumb to the fate of being caught in traps designed for raccoons and possums.

Dogs should not be given free rein any more than children; Labradors of either sex are wanderers by nature, and no gundog can be relied upon to stay on an unfenced property for long. He must be confined, but without, if possible, the feeling of kennel confinement imposed by the narrow concrete kennel runs of commercial setups, which are essential and practical in their cases. With a little common sense and planning, a family dog can have a roomy, grassy enclosure, easily erected around one of the doors of the house—be it kitchen, porch, cellar or garage—into which he can be sent from the house. This eliminates the need for the owner to walk the animal or stand around in bad weather. New owners often take the line of least resistance in allowing their dogs the run of the neighborhood; they learn the hard way, as a rule, by having to get another dog.

Tying a dog to a line is cruel. A tied dog will become a barker and a bolter; the moment he is untied he will be over the hill and gone. It also makes him helpless in the event that passing children make him a target for teasing, or a stray dog comes spoiling for a good fight.

Most dog lovers realize that living with dogs and children precludes a bandbox existence. The Hollywood approach to white wall-to-walls and fashionable upholstery has to take a back seat. The carping housewife, perturbed at doggy smells or shedding hair, who sloughs off the education of a puppy onto her young children who are not equal to coping with such responsibilities, had better keep goldfish and be done with it.

There are no breeds of dogs that do not, in Nature's scheme, have a normal period of shedding. Although there are some breeds that, when wet, emit a stronger odor (due to the oil secretion in their skin) than others, the Labrador, with his short, easily groomed coat and propensity for fastidious toilet manners, does less decorating indoors than most.

Color and sex are matters of preference. The ancient prejudice against females, dating back to the days of the Crusades, when Eastern countries considered dogs in general to be "unclean" and worthy only of the life of a street scavenger, has long died out.

Bitches are preferred in many utilitarian walks of life, as they are often more alert and protective, and have more powers of concentration than the male, which is constantly on the lookout for conquests and scents. However, Labrador temperament in either sex is equally loyal and affectionate, so that one need only consider that, if a bitch is chosen, it should be carefully protected during its seasons, or spayed as a convenience.

Whatever choice is made, to those for whom this will be their first Labrador, the best of dogs are those which are with their owners day and night. Shooting seasons are short in America, and if a dog is chosen for that purpose alone, will it be his fate to be put into dry dock until the following season? The fidelity and adaptability of the Labrador is proverbial. No detriment can arise from his living with his family, as opposed to leading a solitary kennel life; rather the reverse, in the stimulation of his intelligence and character.

A trial competitor demands a very different sort of life while he is working; he cannot compare with the gundog's short seasonal work. Is a dog to be treated with consistency, appreciated and esteemed by every member of the family, or purchased as a whim or for snob appeal?

There is an irritating and deplorable theory held by many regarding all gundogs and hounds. It holds that hunting dogs should be kenneled and handled as though semi-wild in order to fire up their hunting instincts. A dog is not a zoo animal. It is beyond the realm of reason how anyone can think he knows anything about dogs if he lets them out of their kennel solely to perform their allotted tasks, returning them just as a horse, after a long day, is turned back into its stable, given its feed bag, and subsequently forgotten."

Learning to retrieve dummies in the water—eight weeks-old puppies by Field Ch. Banchory Nightlight of Wingan with their owner, Mrs. Kathleen Starr Fredericks of Timbertown.

15

Kenneling Labradors

I DO believe in keeping Labradors or other gun-dogs in as natural an environment as possible. I do not mean that their kennels should be open to the elements, but that they should have access to large paddocks of grass, undergrowth, and trees, and not be kept continually in concrete runs. I feel very strongly that Labrador puppies should have contact with "mother earth" in the literal sense of the term, being allowed to play, dig and romp in sod, and have a puppyhood where brambles, bushes and turf play a very great part. Plush, artificial surroundings have no place with gun-dogs, and have built up mental frustrations in later life that were manifested in bad temperaments.

For novices, the Gaines Research Department in New York City puts out many sensible and budget-controlled kennel plans. The day of the old doghouse or barrel with burlap flap over the en-trance are a thing of the past, at least with those who care at all about the welfare of their outside dogs.

The extremes of American climate present more of a problem in summer than they do in winter; however, it is one thing to say that Labradors do best in cold weather (which they do), and quite another to keep a cold and wet kenneled dog.

Labradors do not need any artificial heat, except in the case of young litters, but they should be given consideration in the way they are housed. To us, the ideal arrangement in our part of the country in winter has always been the "house within a house." A small kennel building (an ex-chicken house or tool house will do) containing one or two smaller dog houses, well filled with salt hay, has proven most satisfactory. Salt hay or marsh hay are warm, and are dust-free compared to straw. Cedar shavings give no warmth at all, and get completely soggy in damp weather. The kennel should have plenty of light, from a decent window that can be opened and screened in summer. Hound benches are all right, but even when filled with deep bedding, they cannot prevent the dog's body heat from escaping on top, heat which a small house is able to conserve.

A dark "hole of Calcutta" type of kennel is thoughtless and cruel. The importance of light, and the arrangement whereby dogs can see what human activities are going on outside (companionship with their own kind is not enough) are essentials. Their need has been conclusively proven by Guide Dog kennels, whose primary concern and requisite for their inmates is a sound temperament, and which can point to countless examples of the disastrous effects bad kenneling can have upon dogs of many breed. Labradors as a rule are not fighters, and can be paired together for companionship and warmth without fear of war.

Our torrid summers, with flies and constant temperatures ranging into the 90's, are difficult to overcome. Air-conditioning is used in many western kennels to advantage, but is impossible in most small owners' setups and not ideal or really healthy in the long run.

The deadly effects of heart-worm are stressed here because it is fast becoming the No. 1 disabler and killer of all working sporting dogs in America, stretching from the deep South all the way up into many parts of Canada. There is no prevention and no cure. Treatment is painful, and although there have been some successful operations performed, the dog is never quite the same again. It does not affect humans. The only solution is to try in some manner to screen your kennels, or keep the dogs indoors at night.

Novices with stars in their eyes about owning acres of Labradors had best be aware of the pitfalls of keeping too many. Much has been written on the cruelty of man to his best friend through improper training, neglect in pet shops, pounds, mail-order houses and the like; but no less cruel are kennels bulging at the seams with an overflow of dogs no longer useful, who have to live out the rest of their lives in crates for lack of space and the time to give them companionship. Dogs are meant to be of use at any stage of their lives. It is much more charitable to put them to sleep painlessly than have them eke out their days in a mental torpor.

This has been a book about great and prominent dogs, with the suggestion, if one is inclined to breed them, that one try and find a dog that is most typical of the breed. The Labrador's very adaptability in all walks of life other than shooting points to the fact that there is no written or unwritten law that, in owning one, one is compelled to put him to the work for which he was bred. Some of the greatest dogs have never been heard of publicly. One of them may be yours. A great dog is many things to many people.

Is your favorite a trial winner? A show star? A productive brood bitch or stud? A combination of the three? A Guide or War dog, that may be called upon to give its life in the line of duty? A "meat" dog (the disparaging epithet sometimes given to animals that fall short of the demands of top trial competition, but which nevertheless are the backbone of wildlife conservation on many a memorable gunning day)? A family fireside dog?

Greatness in a dog cannot be measured except by what it means to its owner. There is no best, no greatest, no most important that can be agreed upon; everyone to his own pursuits with the animal he owns. One can reckon on the greatest satisfaction in the companionship of a dog if one realizes, in A. Trapman's words, "That a dog loves a glad heart, and it is well to bring as much cheer as possible into the lives of our canine friends, since God has decreed that they should be so brief."

Labrador puppies and a friendly "giant."

294

16

Terminology Pertaining to Labradors

Apple-cheeked: round, protruding cheeks.

Angulation: referring to the angle of the hock, which in Labradors should be well bent. Opposite of "straight behind," where there is no angle.

Balance: symmetrical proportion; neither too high nor too low on leg, nor too short nor too long in body.

Beefy: over-development in the hindquarters, sometimes too much fat over muscles.

Bloom: prime condition of coat, weight; alert expression.

Brisket: the forepart of the body below the chest; in Labradors, of good breadth and depth.

Cat Foot: Compact, well arched toes. Opposite of "splay" or open foot.

Chiseled: a clean-cut head, especially below the eyes.

Cobby: short-coupled, compact body.

Dew-claws: extra, superfluous claws, on the inside of fore and hind legs. Optional to remove fore-claws, within a few days of whelping, but hind claws should be removed. Hind claws not too prevalent in Labradors.

Down in Pasterns: Weak or faulty pastern joints, letting the front feet down. Opposite of "knuckling over," in which faulty pastern joint may tremble, with a forward movement of the pastern itself, as the dog stands.

Elbows out: in which the elbows are not held close enough to the body.

Feather: in Labradors, may occasionally be seen in hair too long on the underpart of the tail.

Foreface: the front part of the head, before the eyes—the muzzle.

Front: the forepart of the body, as viewed head-on—forelegs, chest, brisket, and shoulders.

A good doer: a dog which relishes his food, puts on weight easily, and stays in condition.

Gay tail: tail carried above the back line. Smart, if not overdone, for a show dog, but definitely not a "questing" tail of a worker.

Hard-mouth: a dog that injures game when delivered, due to a tight grip, so that it is unfit for consumption.

Hare-foot: a long, narrow foot, similar to that of a hare.

Height: vertical measure from withers to the ground.

Loaded shoulders: when the shoulder blades are apparently pushed out by over-development of muscles or too much fat.

Leather: flap of the ear; in Labradors the texture is not as fine as in a hound, nor overly thick.

Level Bite: the upper teeth just meet over the tops of the lower.

Line-breeding: controlled inbreeding. The mating of related dogs of the same breed to a common ancestor; i.e., a dog to his granddam, or a bitch to her grandsire.

Long Cast: too long a body between withers and hips.

Lippy: pendulous or loose lips, expecially at the inner corners.

Non-slip Retriever: a dog that walks at heel, marks the fall, and retrieves the game on command. A non-slip Retriever is not expected to flush or hunt out.

Nose: scenting ability.

Occiput: the peak or top of the skull.

Otter tail: thick at the root, gradually tapering, no feather, but hair parted or divided on underside.

Outcrossing: the breeding of unrelated individuals of the same breed.

Pig-jaw: a term for an "overshot" mouth, where the front teeth of the upper jaw overlap the front teeth of the under jaw when the mouth is held shut.

Pads: the tough, shock-resisting undersides of the foot; the soles.

Racy: high on the leg, light of build, sometimes "tucked up."

Soundness: mental and physical state of health in which everything is functioning normally.

Snipey: a weak, pointed, narrow muzzle.

Spring of rib: the degree of rib roundness; with Labradors, well sprung and not flat or "slab-sided."

Sloping shoulders: the shoulder blade set "obliquely," or well laid back.

Stilted: a choppy gait, in front, from straight shoulders; behind, from straight stifles.

Stifles: the joint in front of the hind leg, joining the thigh and the leg bones.

Straight hocked: lack of angulation at hock.

Thigh: the hind quarter from the hip joint to the stifles.

Throatiness: excess loose skin under the throat.

Tuck-up: small waisted, or shallow bodied.

Weedy: lightly built, lacking bone on entire frame.

Withers: the highest part of the body behind the neck.

WORKING TERM DEFINITIONS

A Blind: In American trials, a planted or hidden bird whose place is unknown to the dog.

Break: Breaking to shot: a dog that will go out and retrieve before being sent or commanded to do so by his handler. The British equivalent is "running in."

Cover: Any sort of underbrush, thicket, hedgerows, high bracken, rootfields, etc., into which the game may have fallen.

Delivery: The manner in which a dog brings the game to the handler. This includes style, speed, and the manner in which the game is held.

Down-wind: When the wind blows the scent of the game *towards* the dog.

Drive: A dog displaying keenness, one who has great impulse and incentive in his work.

A drive: At British trials, the guns are placed standing in a line. The birds are then "driven" towards the guns by beaters (men who walk through the thickets or wood, beating the underbrush with sticks to flush the hidden game. In the old days, Spaniels were used for this purpose). The dogs remain at heel until the game has been shot, when one of the three presiding judges designates the dog he wishes to retrieve a certain fall.

Eye-Wipe: A British term for a dog which makes a successful retrieve over another dog who failed in the same retrieve, thus being considered to have "wiped the eye" of his competitor.

Fall: The spot where the shot game has fallen.

Game: In American trials, only pheasants or ducks are used; at British trials, any wild game that is naturally put up, including wood pigeons and hares.

Gamekeeper: One who is employed and who is responsible for the rearing of game, the maintenance and care of moors, shoots, and estates, the breeding and training of gundogs, and the protection of game and property from poachers.

Marking: The dog's ability to mark or determine the fall of the game at a distance.

Pop or popping: An American term relating to dogs which continually look back at the handler for directions to the fall.

Runner: Another term for a "cripple": game that has been winged or wounded, falling to shot, but still able to run and hide.

Series: Tests in American stakes, following each other, water or land.

Steady or staunch: A dog that sits at heel quietly until commanded to retrieve. Steady to shot and wing means that the dog will not break at the gunshot, or to the game if it is flushed.

Up-wind: The opposite of down-wind.

A Walk-up: Guns, dogs, handlers and judges advance abreast across a field, the game, rising in front, is shot. After a certain number of birds or hares have been shot, the judges stop the advance and then designate the dog they wish to find a particular fallen bird.

297

Excerpts from the Standard Recommendations of the Retriever Advisory Committee

Courtesy of The American Kennel Club and The Labrador Retriever Club of America, Inc.

On May 21st, 1957, the undersigned were appointed to the American Kennel Club's Advisory Committee to draft an explanatory supplement—covering problems arising both in the conduct of a trial and the judging of the work of the dogs. The following year, it was adopted by the Retriever Advisory Committee.

> Dr. George H. Gardner
> Mr. C. A. Griscom, III
> Mr. Andrieus A. Jones
> Mrs. J. Gould Remick
> Mr. Edward R. Spaulding
> Mr. T. W. Merritt, Chairman

The *objectives* of the supplement were twofold: *First,* greater uniformity in the conduct of Retriever trials; and *second,* greater uniformity in judging of performances by Retrievers at these trials. The supplement was divided into *two* sections, (1) TRIAL PROCEDURE and (2) EVALUATION OF DOG WORK.

Because the American Kennel Club offers to the public its Rules and Regulations Applying to Field Trials and will furnish the Supplement upon request, it was felt that for novices Section 2— comprising the Evaluation of Dog Work and explaining the characteristics and assets a dog must possess to be a successful competitor and winner in Natural Abilities and Abilities Acquired Through Training—will be of greater benefit to those owning their first Retriever. Expert knowledge on the conduct, mechanics, and running of trials, can be learned later, by membership in a club and participation in its activities.

Evaluation of Dog Work

Judging can never be precise. It is not an exact science but an art, simply because there are so many shades of grey between black and white. At the risk of oversimplification, it might be stated that the primary purpose of a Retriever is to get the birds to hand as quickly as possible in a pleasing, obedient manner and all faults stem from a deviation of this.

Natural Abilities are of great importance in all stakes, whereas *abilities acquired through training* are of less importance in the Qualifying Stake than those carrying championship points, and are of comparatively minor importance in the Derby Stake.

Section 1, a Basic Principle of the "STANDARD," states:

"The purpose of a Non-Slip Retriever trial is to determine the relative merits of retrievers in the field. Retriever field trials should, therefore, simulate as nearly as possible the conditions met in an ordinary day's shoot.

"Dogs are expected to retrieve any type of game bird under all conditions, and the Judges and the Field Trial Committee have complete control over the mechanics and requirements of each trial. This latitude is permitted in order to allow for the difference in conditions which may arise in trials given in widely separated parts of the United States, which difference well may necessitate different methods of conducting tests."

The final phrase in the first paragraph above: *"the conditions met in an ordinary day's shoot,"* should be interpreted for application to field trials, as *"natural hunting conditions."*

Section 2, the other Basic Principle of the "STANDARD," states:

"The function of a Non-Slip Retriever is to seek and retrieve "fallen" game when ordered to do so. He should sit quietly in line or in the blind, walk at-heel, or assume any station designated by his handler until sent to retrieve. When ordered, a dog should retrieve quickly and briskly without unduly disturbing too much ground, and should deliver tenderly to hand. He should then await further orders.

"Accurate marking is of primary importance. A dog which marks the 'fall' of a bird, uses the wind, follows a strong cripple, and will take directions from his handler, is of great value."

While "natural hunting conditions" are subject to great variations in different parts of the U.S.A., the work expected of the dogs should *not* be subject to similar wide variations. In most instances, there should be little doubt in anyone's mind

299

as to the type of work which constitutes a perfect performance in a given test. However, there is unlimited opportunity for an honest difference-of-opinion on the severity of the penalty to assess for any given infraction or deviation from perfect work.

Therefore, there must always be the possibility of owners and handlers being confused and dismayed because their dog is "dropped" from further competition, or not being included in the placings due to faults which other Judges at other trials had not so severely penalized. However, this should be minimized, for everyone has the right to know which particular faults will be penalized severely, moderately, or only to a minor degree. So, some clarification on these points is needed; hence, there has been included at the conclusion of this supplement a suggested *classification of these various infractions;* they have been divided into three categories, namely: *"Serious Faults"; "Moderate Faults";* and *"Minor Faults."*

Natural Abilities

(1) *Accurate marking, or memory of "falls" is of paramount importance.* However, this does not imply that dogs which excel in marking shall not be severely penalized, or even eliminated, for deficiencies in, or a lack of the other required "abilities." However, in Derby stakes the ability to "mark" is all-important; even in our most exacting stakes, tests are usually so devised that "marked" birds constitute a large percentage of the retrieves by which each dog's performance is judged.

Ability to "mark" does not necessarily imply "pin-pointing the fall." A dog that misses the "fall" on the first cast, but recognizes the depth of the "area of the fall," stays in it, then quickly and systematically "hunts-it-out," has done both a creditable and an intelligent job of marking. Such work should not be appreciably out-scored by the dog that "finds" or "pin-points" on his first cast. However, a dog which consistently, i.e. during an entire stake, marks his birds in a closer area, hence, more accurately than another dog, should be judged accordingly. All things are relative, and, conceivably, such differences in marking alone might be sufficient to determine the final placings in a particular stake.

Even with "marked" birds, a handler may be able to render great assistance to his dog by giving him "a line" in the direction of the "fall"; however, there is nothing he can do, short of handling, to aid the dog in recognizing the "depth of the 'fall.'" Often a dog gives definite indication of "memory," and of his marking ability, at or after delivery of a first bird, by aligning himself toward, or by looking eagerly in the exact direction of an unretrieved "fall"; at times, even leaving at once or leaving on command, but without benefit of a precise line to the "fall" given to him by the handler. There is no invariable method by which the relative merits of such perfect completions can be judged; the dog trained to come to-heel and to be lined by the handler briskly and precisely, and in the same manner for each and every retrieve, including the first, cannot be penalized for his work—not even relatively, in comparison with a more spontaneous type of performance.

What precisely constitutes the *"area of the 'fall,'"* defies accurate definition; yet, at the outset of every test, each Judge must arbitrarily define its hypothetical boundaries for himself, and for each bird in that test, so that he can judge whether dogs have remained within his own concept of the "area of the 'fall,'" as well as how far they have wandered away from "the area" and how much cover they have disturbed unnecessarily. In determining these aritrary and hypothetical boundaries of the "area of the 'fall,'" due consideration should be given to various factors:—(1) the type, the height and the uniformity of the cover, (2) light conditions, (3) direction of the prevailing wind and its intensity, (4) length of the various falls, (5) the speed of individual dogs, (6) whether there is a change in cover (as from stubble to plowed ground, or to ripe alfalfa, or to machine-picked corn, etc.) or whether the "fall" is beyond a hedge, across a road, or over a ditch etc., and, finally, and most important, (7) whether one is establishing the "area of the fall" for a single, or for the first bird a dog goes for, in multiple retrieves, or for the second or the third bird, since each of these should differ from the others.

In general, the "area of the fall" for a single should be relatively small; the area for a first retrieve in a "double" should be smaller than for the second bird, and both of these should be larger in a "triple," and larger still for the third bird in it. Also, "the area" for short retrieves should certainly be smaller than for longer retrieves. Since there are so many conditions and variables to be taken into consideration, it is obvious that each Judge, and for every series, must attempt to define for himself a hypothetical "area of the fall" for each bird, and then judge the dogs accordingly. However, the penalties inflicted should vary in their severity, depending on the distance which individual dogs wander out of the area, the frequency of such wanderings, the number of birds mismarked in a given test, and by the amount of cover disturbed in these meanderings.

Dogs which disturb cover unnecessarily, clearly well out of the area of the "fall," either by not going directly to that area, or by leaving it, even though they eventually find the bird without being handled, should be penalized more severely than those handled quickly and obediently to it.

(2) *Intelligence* is a quality not often tested intentionally, since few tests can be designed for that specific purpose. Nevertheless, on occasions, dogs may have an opportunity to demonstrate an unusual degree of intelligence, or lack of it, through the manner in which certain performances are completed. When those occasions arise, and usually they develop by chance rather than by intent, each dog must be credited or penalized on the basis of the intelligence demonstrated.

(3) *Attention* is displayed, even as a dog comes "on line." His eagerness and general attitude when coming on-line, his alertness in locating the "Guns," in acceding to his handler's commands, and in his zeal for the hunt, are highly desirable traits. Conversely, lack of attention and lack of interest should be penalized.

(4) Most retrievers have a *"good nose,"* and, as a rule, they have numerous opportunities to demonstrate this all-important quality at every trial. Usually it is something in his work which suggests that a dog *lacks a good nose* that attracts the Judges' attention. Such suspicion should be recorded, so that it can be verified or eliminated by his performance in subsequent tests. On the other hand, scenting conditions are so mysterious and are so little understood, although obviously affected by many factors, such as: type of cover, wind, frost, rain, location of "fall," acidity of soil and apparently many other conditions, that extreme caution must be exercised before a dog is charged with a "poor nose," and penalized accordingly.

(5) *Courage,* too, is a trait which cannot be tested at every trial. It may be displayed by a willingness to face, and without hesitation, rough cover, cold or rough water, ice, mud, or other similar conditions which make the going rather tough, *and of doing it repeatedly.* The facilities of trial grounds, or the weather, do not often supply the proper situation for a series specifically designed to test the dogs' courage. Because the facilities or weather necessary to such a test are

often limited, such tests should usually come late in a trial, unless there are reasonable grounds for assumption that all dogs will receive comparable tests. When such tests can be arranged, they are frequently of great value to the Judges in evaluating their relative merits in this highly desirable trait which all retrievers should possess.

(6) *Perseverance* is shown by a dog's determination to stick-at-it and complete the task at hand—i.e. systematically, aggressively and without faltering, to search for and make the "find" of the bird he has been sent to retrieve. A lack of perseverance may become apparent whenever: (1) he returns to the handler, voluntarily, and before finding the bird; (2) he either stops his hunt, or continues it in a slow, lackadaisical, disinterested manner; (3) the dog "pops-up" or looks back to his handler for directions on a "marked fall" and before he has hunted for a considerable time; (4) he "switches birds," and (5) he "blinks" a bird, i.e. fails to pick it up, actually leaves it after making the "find." Most of these are serious faults and should be judged accordingly.

"Switching birds" implies that a dog gives up in his hunt after a search, leaves "the area," and goes for another bird, or when he drops a bird he is retrieving and goes for another; however, except in the latter case, a dog should not be judged as "switching" unless he goes to the "area" of a "fall," hunts, fails to find, and then leaves that area to hunt for another "fall." Furthermore, it should *not be considered* as a lack of perseverance, if, while on the way to one "fall," he sees or winds another bird and retrieves it first; or, if on the way to one "fall," but long before he reaches "the area" of that "fall," he changes his direction (for some reason or other) and goes for another bird.

(7) *Style* is apparent in every movement of a dog and throughout his entire performance at trials, for example: by the *gaiety* of his manner in approaching the line, by his *alertness* on line, by his *eagerness* and *speed* on retrieves, by his *water-entry*, by his *pick-up* of birds, and by his *return* with them. Style makes for a pleasing performance; together with ability to mark, they constitute the most important factors for placings in Derby Stakes.

In all stakes, in respect to "style," a desired performance includes: (a) an alert and obedient attitude, (b) a fast-determined departure, both on land and into the water, (c) an aggressive search for the "fall," (d) a prompt pick-up, and (e) a reasonably fast return. Dogs may be credited for outstanding and brilliant exhibitions of style, or they may be penalized for deficiencies in style—the severity of the penalty ranging from a minor demerit, to elimination from the stake in extreme cases.

(8) Section 31 of the "STANDARD" states:

"A dog should be eliminated for hard-mouth or badly damaging game, but, before doing so, all Judges should inspect the bird and be satisfied that the dog alone was responsible for the damage."

"Hard-mouth" is one of the most severely penalized faults in a retriever; furthermore, once a dog has been charged with this fault, he carries that stigma for life. Therefore, "hard-mouth" should only become the Judges' verdict when there is incontrovertible proof of it. Torn skin or flesh, alone, is *not* sufficient evidence, in almost all cases, to constitute such proof, since damage of that type may be caused in a variety of ways, such as by sharp sticks and stones, etc., in the cover; also dogs can unintentionally damage birds when making retrieves from heavy cover, as well as by their fast, "positive," pick-up. Furthermore, at certain times of the year, birds are particularly susceptible to such damage.

Even the fact that a dog delivers a dead bird, when a live one was the object of his retrieve, does not necessarily constitute proof of "hard-mouth" as the bird could have died from other causes (particularly true with "shackled" young ducks).

On the other hand, crushed bone structure usually can be accepted as trustworthy and sufficient evidence of "hard-mouth." This is the only evidence offering such proof, in the absence of a particularly obvious, flagrant and unjustified violation of tearing of flesh.

Other faults are frequently confused with "hard-mouth," although, in reality, they are entirely separate and distinct from it—even though, in addition, the dog may actually be hard-mouthed. "Freezing," in particular, falls into this category. A hard-mouthed dog may have a gentle delivery and, certainly, a sticky delivery does not imply hard-mouth. "Rolling-a-bird" or "mouthing" it, while making the retrieve, may be erroneously associated with "hard-mouth" in the opinion of some, even though the bird is not damaged thereby. If such "mouthing" is a fault at all, then it is one of only minor importance.

Judges should remember that a dog is either found to have a "hard-mouth" or he is not so found, and, if guilty, he must be eliminated from the stake—other various types of inconclusive evidence should merely be recorded in the Judge's notes, pending the manner in which birds are handled in subsequent series.

While not required, it is a considerate gesture on the part of the Judges to keep separately any bird for which they are eliminating a dog for "hard-mouth," and show it to the handler of the dog at a later time, inconspicuously.

Abilities Acquired Through Training

The other group of attributes to be considered by Judges includes those abilities which dogs acquired through training. The importance of these acquired qualities varies in different stakes, for example: A "reasonable" degree of steadiness and general obedience are the requirements in Derby Stakes. A greater degree of steadiness and some degree of the other qualities are expected in the Qualifying Stake. There should be expectation of full refinement in "acquired attributes" in those stakes carrying championship points.

(1) *Steadiness* to the extent of defining what constitutes a "break," is clearly presented in Section 25 of the "STANDARD." However, a degree of amplification might be helpful: Dogs on-line sometimes make various types of movements when game is in the air (and/or when it is shot). Such movements may be interpreted as efforts by the dogs to improve his view of the "fall," and some occur through sheer excitement. *Some dogs creep forward* from the line, as birds are shot. *If the handler makes no effort* to stop or restrain them, a Judge should not interpret such as a deliberate intent to retrieve, since nothing was done to stop the dog. On the other hand, *if the handler does make an effort* to stop his dog, a Judge should assume that the handler believed the dog intended to retrieve and should deal with such infraction accordingly.

A dog should not be penalized for a command to sit as the first bird is being thrown on a "walk-up." In other tests, a dog should not be penalized for a quiet command to sit as the first bird is being thrown, provided the dog is not in motion and the command is, therefore, not to stop a motion with intent to retrieve.

Except for an occasional change in position in order to better see a "fall," all such movements should be penalized as unsteadiness—the degree of penalty depending on the extent and the frequency of repetition of the offense or offenses. It is proper for Judges, if they so wish, to require that dogs which have jumped or crept forward a predetermined distance (usually a few feet ahead of the

303

handler) be brought back to-heel, before being sent for their birds. The require-ment of steadiness is a very important factor in judging the work of retrievers.

(2) *Control* is closely allied to the dog's response to direction, but it also in-cludes obedience at all times. Control also includes "line-manners," walking tractably "at-heel," assuming and staying in any designated position on-line, as well as remaining quietly on-line beside the handler after delivery of the bird to him. When called, a dog should return promptly to his handler—particularly in those instances where Judges decide that he shall be tested again, at a later time, either because another dog "broke" or due to any one of a variety of other circumstances.

In Derby and Qualifying stakes, dog may be brought to the line, and taken from the line, on-leash, unless the Judges specify otherwise.

Article 24 of the "STANDARD" provides that dogs shall be penalized if they are noisily or continuously restrained by their handlers while "on-line." The degree of the penalty should correspond to the extent and frequency of repetition of the infraction. Although such is not required, it is a considerate gesture by Judges, if they are in agreement, to notify handlers when their methods of re-straint are incurring penalties for their dogs.

(3) *Response to direction* is all-important in handling tests, also whenever a dog must be brought back to the "area of the 'fall,'" when he has mismarked. In such response to direction, a dog should take the *original line* given to him by his handler and *continue* on it until he either makes the "find," or until stopped by the handler and given a new line. He should then continue in this new direction until he "finds," or is given further directions, etc.

Faults, or justifications for penalties, include the following: (a) not taking the line originally given by the handler, (b) not continuing on that line for a con-siderable distance, (c) stopping voluntarily, i.e. "popping-up" and looking back for directions, (d) failure to stop promptly and look to the handler, when sig-nalled, (e) failure to take a new direction, i.e. a new cast, when given, and (f) failure to continue in that new direction for a considerable distance.

The seriousness of the penalty for any or all of the foregoing faults varies with the seriousness of the infraction, whether that infraction was repeated and how often, and whether there was a combination of various infractions. However, before inflicting a severe penalty because of a dog's failure to stop promptly at the whistle, Judges should determine whether the wind, the cover, or the dis-tance seriously interfered with the dog's ability to hear his handler. In general, the performance in the test should be considered in its entirety; an occasional failure to take and hold a direction may be considered a minor fault, if offset by several other very good responses. A considerable penalty should be imposed for repeated, willful disobedience of the handler's orders; and less penalty when, after taking the proper direction, he does not continue on it as far as the handler desired. Stopping voluntarily, to look back for directions, in an isolated instance, may be considered a minor fault, but frequent repetition may convert such "popping-up" into the category of serious faults.

Delivery of the bird should be made to the handler directly, upon return from the retrieve; it should be given up willingly. A dog should not drop the bird before delivering it; and he should not "freeze," or be unwilling to give it up. He should not jump after the bird, once the handler has taken it from him. Penalties for faulty delivery may range from minor for an isolated minor offense, to elimination from the stake either for a severe "freeze" or because of repeated moderate infractions.